# THE CRISIS OF SOCIAL DEMOCRACY IN EUROPE

• • •

## EDITED BY MICHAEL KEATING AND DAVID McCRONE

EDINBURGH
University Press

Edinburgh University Press Ltd
The Tun – Holyrood Road
12 (2f) Jackson's Entry
Edinburgh EH8 8PJ

www.euppublishing.com

First published in hardback by Edinburgh University Press 2013

This paperback edition 2015

Typeset in 10/12.5 Sabon by
Servis Filmsetting Ltd, Stockport, Cheshire,
and printed and bound in Great Britain by
CPI Group (UK) Ltd, Croydon CR0 4YY

A CIP record for this book is available from the British Library

ISBN 978 0 7486 6582 2 (hardback)
ISBN 978 1 4744 0303 0 (paperback)
ISBN 978 0 7486 6583 9 (webready PDF)
ISBN 978 0 7486 6584 6 (epub)

# CONTENTS

# TABLES AND FIGURES

## Tables

## Figures

# ABOUT THE CONTRIBUTORS

**Michael Keating** is Professor of Politics at the University of Aberdeen and the University of Edinburgh.

**David McCrone** is Professor Emeritus of Sociology at the University of Edinburgh.

**Colin Crouch** is Professor Emeritus of the University of Warwick, and external scientific member of the Max Planck Institute for the Study of Societies, Cologne.

**David Heald** is Professor of Accountancy at the University of Aberdeen Business School.

**Desmond Hickie** is Professor Emeritus at the University of Chester.

**Ulrich Hilpert** is Chair of Comparative Government, Friedrich Schiller University Jena.

**Yves Mény** is Emeritus President, European University Institute.

**Susi Meret** is Assistant Professor at the Department of Culture and Global Studies, Aalborg University, Denmark.

**Henry Milner** is senior research fellow at the Chair in Electoral Studies, Department of Political Science, Université de Montréal.

**Martin Rhodes** is Professor of Comparative Political Economy and Associate Dean at the Josef Korbel School of International Studies, University of Denver, Colorado.

**Bo Rothstein** holds the August Röhss Chair in Political Science at the University of Gothenburg.

**Donald Sassoon** is Professor of Comparative European History, Queen Mary, University of London.

**Birte Siim** is Professor in Gender Research in Social Science at Aalborg University, Denmark.

**Sven Steinmo** is a Professor of Political Science at the University of Colorado, Boulder, and Chair in Political Economy and Public Policy at the European University Institute, Florence.

**Milada Anna Vachudova** is Associate Professor of Political Science at the University of North Carolina at Chapel Hill.

**Neil Walker** is Regius Professor of Public Law and the Law of Nature and Nations at the University of Edinburgh.

# PREFACE

This book started from a puzzle. Given the failings of neo-liberalism revealed by the economic crisis starting in 2008, why was social democracy not triumphant? After all, its political success over much of the post-war period was bolstered by a particular representation of the inter-war years and a belief that governments had put the old economics behind them, while some social democrats had given early warnings about the follies being committed from the 1990s. Despite the caricature about social democratic governments being free spenders, they have tended in office to be rather fiscally responsible.[1] Nor was there reason to believe that electors had rejected social democratic ideas about public services, although they may in some cases have become less tolerant of welfare dependants.

There is no simple answer to this puzzle but the contributors to this collection agree that social democracy's problems do not stem from a fundamental flaw in the core idea, nor that social and economic change have rendered it redundant. Social democracy is in good health in some places, while elsewhere it is struggling to find its voice. One problem lies in the realm of ideas, where neo-liberalism has gained the ideological hegemony, to the extent that social democratic parties internalise it and seek to modify it only at the margins. Another is the inability to adapt to a more complex but still socially stratified and unequal society. A third lies in the decline of mass party politics and of the social institutions such as trade unions, which provided the means for social democrats to mobilise.

Our contributors do not present a single vision of social democracy but have been encouraged to interpret it in their own ways. The result is a complex picture, highlighting problems but showing that social democratic thought and practice are by no means dead.

We hesitated over the title of the book, fearing that the word 'crisis' was too dramatic or fatalistic. Yet, used in its original sense, a crisis is a moment of change, which provides opportunities as well as threats but makes the status quo untenable. The economic woes of the decade provide such a moment and a challenge.

We dedicate the book to our friend Stephen Maxwell, intellectual and activist, whose dream of an independent social democratic Scotland was profoundly shaped by his internationalist convictions. Stephen died before we went to press but his contribution to our seminar in Edinburgh, commenting on the draft chapters, as well as our discussions over the years, have left a strong and inspiring influence.

## Note

1. Even the much-criticised dash for growth of the first Mitterrand government in 1981–3 registered smaller fiscal and trade deficits than the contemporaneous Reagan administration, while the Thatcher government in Britain was rescued only by the influx of oil revenues (which were to leave no lasting legacy).

# THE CRISIS OF SOCIAL DEMOCRACY

Michael Keating and David McCrone

## The state of social democracy

On the face of it, social democracy is in crisis. At the time of writing, there are very few left-of-centre parties in power in Western Europe. Norway, Denmark and Belgium have social democrat heads of government but in coalition, while the French Socialists govern thanks to divisions on the right and the electoral system. In Central and Eastern Europe, social democratic parties – whether new parties or former communist parties – have failed to fulfil their early promise.

Why should this be? One might take the view that it is all part of the electoral cycle, and that sooner or later social democratic parties will regain power. After all, they seemed to be doing very well in the late 1990s. Yet this does not account for their current and systematic electoral weakness wherever one looks, and begs the question as to what it was in the cycle itself that banished social democrats from office. A more sanguine view might be that 'we're all social democrats now', that the project has achieved success in building and institutionalising the welfare state; in other words, the demise of social democracy is, paradoxically, a function of its success. Other parties, in these circumstances, feel able to steal the social democrats' clothes. We might take the view that the triumph of capitalism is such that, having ameliorated the worst excesses of capitalism, social democracy rests content, or recognises that it has reached the limit of its achievements. Alternatively we might argue that the social and political values of their respective electorates have moved significantly to the right as regards employment law, nationalisation and social welfare; that the erosion of social democracy reflects the ebbing of leftist values more generally. Various 'Third Way' projects may simply have illustrated the point, since social democracy itself was originally conceived of as the third way between revolutionary Marxism and unbridled capitalism. It may also be that the social support base of social democracy is eroding, so that it is no longer possible to put together the coalitions of interests that underpinned social democratic projects in the various states of Europe in the past. Instead, discontent may merely sustain various forms of populism.

Given that capitalism itself appears to be in crisis, and the hegemony of neo-liberalism may be coming to an end, it seems strange that social democracy should fail to reap the benefit. Whichever of these explanations, if any, account for the failure of social democratic parties to win elections, it seems to us an ideal moment at which to examine social democracy as theory, values and practice. Furthermore, the apparent decline of centre-left parties and movements may be telling us something of major importance about our social and political world.

The collection looks both backwards and forwards. We are interested in knowing where and how far social democracy has retreated, and for what reasons. This encompasses the study of the support base of social democratic parties, labour and other civil society organisations traditionally allied to social democracy, and the shift in values and attitudes among the electorate. We are also interested in where social democracy can go from here in addressing key political and policy dilemmas. How can social democratic parties rebuild their support bases and compete for power? How can social democracy itself be reformulated for the twenty-first century? We recognise that there has never been a single social democratic model and are alert to variations in both support and policy. So in the future, there may be different combinations of support and policy in different countries and at different levels. The chapters are thematic and comparative, although not necessarily systematic, as some themes are better illustrated with some specific cases. For example, the Nordic experience is of wider interest.

### What is social democracy?

Social democracy comes in so many different forms that one might be forgiven for saying that there is no such thing, or at least that there is no core set of beliefs and practices. We would argue that the concept is useful but that it is multidimensional. Rather than one of those rigid social science concepts in which each case must include and exclude the same things, it is perhaps a family-resemblance concept in which the cases are linked in different ways. At its broadest, it is a political philosophy seeking to reconcile market capitalism with social responsibility. This is expressed in some classic texts but also in an endless series of 'Third Way' proposals, from Bernstein's revisionism of the late nineteenth century to the 'new middle' a hundred years later. It is also a political tradition, a set of intuitive ideas about fairness and equality and a moral economy that refuses to accept the automatic primacy of markets or the need for inequality. Social democracy can also be seen as political practice, a way of governing which systematically seeks to include the needs of the deprived and to emphasise the public domain over the private, while being rather pragmatic about how this is to be done. For much of the twentieth century, it was associated with an extensive state sector, both in the economy and in public services, but this is to be seen more as a means rather than an end in itself.

Social democracy can also be defined as a party family, a group of like-minded parties across the world, committed to the same goals and sharing the same ethos, although it is not always easy to identify these parties. In the late nineteenth century, the term social democracy was generally used for Marxist parties and some confusion remained up until the Bolshevik Revolution, which marked the definitive breakaway of the Communist family. Names can still be misleading, as in Portugal where it is the right-of-centre party that bears the label. In France, the term social democrat has long been treated with disdain within the *Parti Socialiste* and its predecessors, despite the fact that they are clearly part of the family. When a section of the right of the British Labour Party broke away in the 1980s they took the name Social Democratic Party before merging into the Liberal Democrats, whose social democratic wing has now been marginalised. When Labour underwent its revisionist incarnation as New Labour, the term social democrat was avoided by the party leaders seeking to distance themselves from their own past, despite the fact that it was the revisionist wing of the party which had previously embraced the term. Their intellectual mentor, Anthony Giddens (1998), however, depicted the Third Way as a new stage in social democratic development. The party family can be identified by membership of the Socialist International and the Party of European Socialists. The Democratic Party in the United States is not a recognisably social democratic party, but it is the home for social democrats, who rub shoulders with people who in Europe would be part of the centre-right.

Social democracy has also been a political and even a social sub-culture, rooted in working-class communities, bound by traditions of solidarity and institutionalised in trade unions, social movements and tenants' associations as well as middle-class and intellectual societies. These provide social boundaries, defining 'us' and differentiating us from others and providing mutual support in industrial and social conflicts. In some European countries, this maps onto left/right distinctions going back to the democratic revolutions or church/state conflicts of the nineteenth century. Elsewhere it is the product of industrial conflict, although in some places agrarian struggles have also sustained the coalition. Once set, such patterns of solidarity and of shared meaning can persist for long periods.

So rather than impose a strict taxonomy of parties, or stipulate core doctrines or practices that need to be present for a party to qualify, we prefer to define social democracy in a broad sense, recognising its different manifestations across time and space. Lest this sound too vague, there are some key ideas that are timeless and serve to delimit the social democratic project. A central one is that of tamed capitalism, an acceptance (against classical Marxism) of the necessity and instrumental value of the market but a belief (against economic liberalism) that it needs to be socially and politically constrained. On the one hand, this is because of the socially degrading effects of unbounded capitalism. On the other, it stems from a belief that socially guided capitalism can actually be more efficient, saving the market from its own contradictions. During the twentieth century, the main means of doing this were limited state ownership, Keynesian macro-economic management, indicative planning and corporatist policy-making whereby the state, labour and capital cooperated in their mutual interest.

A second key idea is that of social solidarity and equality. Social democrats have never sought complete social and economic equality, recognising its utopian character and accepting the need for incentives in the productive economy. They do, however, believe in the use of public power to restrain excessive inequalities. The amount of inequality they are prepared to countenance varies by time and place but the principle does imply upper and lower limits to income and wealth. It is straining the meaning of social democracy to declare, as New Labour people did, that one is immensely relaxed about people being filthy rich or that one does not care what people at the top are earning, only about those at the bottom. Similarly, social democrats are not concerned only with equality of opportunity, or meritocracy, but also favour some equality outcomes. Beyond this, there are multiple ways of conceptualising and measuring inequality and many arguments about how it should be addressed. Given the origins of social democracy in industrial class society, inequality has generally been seen as a class matter, arising from uneven opportunities to benefit from economic production, but this is by no means the only dimension of inequality.

Social democracy in its most elaborate forms has not treated these two questions of economic management and social equality as distinct. Rather, social democrats have argued, against neo-liberals, that inequality is itself economically inefficient and that a socially managed economy can better address issues of poverty and need.

Social democrats have also tended to be social liberals, favouring individual rights and the classic liberal freedoms and preferring liberal to repressive penal policies. They have tended to sympathise with minorities, whether defined by ethnicity, religion or sexual orientation, and to support the rights of women for full participation in economic, social and political life.

In international affairs, social democracy has been associated with a cosmopolitan stance, and with internationalism and cooperation as a means of regulating relations among states. It has stressed the common interests of people across borders and supported the rights of colonised peoples. Yet it has also embraced various forms of nationalism. For all the talk of internationism, social solidarity is strongest within the boundaries of nation-states, which have provided the framework for the welfare settlement. This has produced an ambivalent attitude to European integration. Social democrats in the early years were often suspicious of the European project, an attitude which persisted in Scandinavia and in recent years has come back elsewhere. For these social democrats, 'Europe' is a market-based project threatening national welfare settlements. Where new nationalisms have challenged existing states, social democrats have sometimes divided, as in Scotland where the smaller nation appears to offer better chances for social democratic advance than the larger – British – state.

New issues regularly come onto the agenda to change or modify this social democratic core. The issue of the environment has raised questions about the productivist model in which material accumulation would provide the resources to sustain social services while not restraining personal consumption. Environmentalists are not all on the political left but most of them are, and challenge social democracy in its own ideological and political space. The salience of gender poses questions about the definition of groups and the conceptualisation and measurement of equality as we can no longer take for granted that the natural unit is the (male-headed) household. Another issue is intergenerational equality, which poses a new cleavage not corresponding to traditional occupational class divisions. Multiculturalism confronts social democrats with serious dilemmas. On the one hand, they support diversity and community rights. On the other, they are often rooted in republican conceptions of civic equality which refuse to accept that cultural differences are politically relevant, or in notions of class solidarity across ethnic and cultural boundaries. More generally, the rise of individualism presents new questions to a notion of social democracy bound up in collective values and practices.

Of course, it can be argued that none of these priorities is specific to social democracy. Christian democrats and traditional conservatives believe in managed capitalism and have embraced Keynesianism. Social solidarity and justice can be derived from Catholic social thought or paternalism, so feeding into the parties of the centre-right. Social liberalism is primarily the property of the liberal family. Both internationalism and nationalism are found right across the political spectrum. Moreover, the combination of these elements within social democratic parties can provoke conflicts. There are big differences among social democratic parties on the extent of state intervention in the economy or the balance between economic and social considerations. There is a streak of social authoritarianism in many social democratic parties, especially when they are tempted to follow what they see as the prejudices of their core electorate. Nonetheless, we see in these elements the main strands of social democratic thought and practice, allowing us to identify a distinct tradition, even if it merges into other traditions at the edges.

The multidimensional nature of social democracy has always meant that it is realised as a coalition of forces, whether among parties or within individual parties. There is usually a left/right division, although the issues which mark it can vary. Factionalism and tradition as much as policy issues can define these internal cleavages, which often pitch the upholders of tradition against revisionists of various sorts. Social liberalism, environmentalism or nationalism also divide the social democratic family. Some countries have more cohesive and continuous social democratic parties than others; the Scandinavian countries stand apart here. Social democratic parties have sometimes had a core of support in the industrial working class but this has never provided anything like the whole of its support base. Middle-class support and leadership has nearly always been critical. In some cases, there are organic connections with trade unions, while in others there are not. In Italy, France, Spain and Greece there was a historic competition with Communist parties, while in parts of Northern Europe (Germany, France, Ireland) leftist parties have from time to time sprung up to outflank them. Relations with green parties have varied from cooperative to competitive. Self-understandings of social democracy have also varied, each being rooted in a different ethos and combination of ideas and, having enjoyed more or less electoral success, seeing themselves as governmental or oppositional forces.

### Challenges to social democracy

In recent years, the social democratic synthesis of the twentieth century has come under increasing challenge. The transformation of capitalism and the productive economy have undermined many social democratic ideas and practices. Old class divisions no longer make sense and the idea of a 'working class' is ever more elusive, creating problems for those parties (mainly in Northern Europe) which rested on it. Trade union membership is in decline everywhere, especially in the private sector. The decline of manufacturing industry has created a 'missing middle' in the class spectrum, the skilled working class that provided much of the leadership for trade union and social democratic movements. Working-class communities, in which people could see a unity of interest in the workplace and the city, have been disappearing. The growth of the welfare state, a social democratic achievement, has created divisions between those working in the public and the private sectors, exploited by the political right.

Neo-liberal ideology has spread since the 1970s from universities and think-tanks into the media, government and political parties to the point that the market has become in many places almost the sole criterion for judging policy. This is particularly noticeable in England, where universities, schools, hospitals, local authorities and cultural bodies are all subjected to the logic of market competition. Social democracy has historically represented a compromise with market capitalism but has also insisted on the limits of markets even within the economy and certainly on the need for other criteria for social policy and public services.

The transformation of the state and spatial rescaling in general have posed questions for the social democratic project, rooted as it was in the nation-state, although the term 'globalisation' has perhaps been stretched too much to be very useful and has doubtless been exaggerated greatly in scope. Global free trade regimes limit the capacity of states to protect vulnerable sectors and jobs. Regulation of capital and corporatist bargaining are more difficult in a world where firms can move location, although whether they actually do so is an empirical question. As states, regions and localities compete to attract footloose investment there is a danger of a race to the bottom in the form of reduced taxes (and therefore fewer public services) and lax regulation. In Ireland, the maintenance of a low rate of corporation tax has become a national shibboleth supported even on the left, so that working people have to shoulder the burden of a crisis not of their making. The centrepiece of the European integration project is the single market for goods, services, capital and labour, but without the social counterpart that emerged to manage the disruptive effects of the creation of national markets. There is a project for a social Europe but it lags well behind the project of economic Europe. The dogmatic way in which European competition law has been interpreted by the Commission and the European Court of Justice means that national social regulations risk being undermined.

It is now recognised that the welfare state itself has often created new patterns of winners and losers. Especially where it was designed around the model of the male breadwinner, it does not always address new social needs. It has proved difficult to reform as existing beneficiaries have resisted change. So expensive programmes for older people are maintained at a time when age in itself is a poor indicator of need, at least partly because older people vote more than younger ones. Restrictive labour market regulation gives rise to a secondary or unofficial labour market of people with little social protection while trade unions and social democratic parties risk representing only the labour market insiders. Migration has challenged the boundaries of welfare regimes tied to citizenship and created new divisions among the workforce.

One consequence of all this is the rise of new movements and parties challenging social democracy. Some have been to the left of social democracy but these have remained largely on the fringe. Green parties have made significant advances in some places and have forced social democratic parties to take on their concerns, creating some tension with elements within the social democratic coalition. The most serious threat, however, comes from the populist right, with its simplistic appeals to an imagined community of insiders, threatened by a combination in which foreigners, capitalism, social democracy, multiculturalism, Europe and globalisation can be presented as a single danger. Migration and law and order, rhetorically connected in populist discourse, represent points of particular vulnerability for social democrats. The populist right, meanwhile, has embraced the welfare state, although defining the community so as to exclude incomers.

## The issues

The book addresses the predicament of social democracy in Europe from a number of perspectives. We are interested in where social democracy is, how it can move on from here and what it *should* do to revive itself. Our interests are thus both analytical and normative. The idea is not to provide a manifesto or political programme, but to assess social democracy as a political project and show how its advances can be maintained and continued. The first question concerns the electoral fortunes of social democratic parties, whether they are in decline or whether we are seeing a trendless fluctuation. A related issue is the social basis for social democratic parties and whether it is stable, shifting or in decline. The demise of the old industrial working class need not be fatal if social democratic parties can establish a foothold in expanding social sectors, allying them with its traditional base. After all, social democratic parties have never simply been 'labour' parties despite what that term might imply. There is an important question of strategy here, in the way leaders are able to put together a broad appeal, aggregate different strands of progressive policy and face competition from new political parties and social movements.

We are interested in the social democratic programme, or rather the various programmes being presented by social democratic movements. This is not just a list of policies but rather a strategy linking the economic, social, environmental and cultural spheres, underpinned by a set of distinctive values. Different social democratic movements will have different syntheses which, in different contexts, have varying degrees of success. It is not possible simply to transplant experience from one context to another, but there is much scope for learning what works, how it does so, and why. We are also interested in thinking about the way forward, and how social democratic parties can escape from the various traps in which they currently find themselves.

More specifically, we are interested in the scope for government in regulating and steering the economy. How footloose are multinational firms in practice and can they be anchored more effectively by social democratic regimes and therefore drawn back into social compromise? Is Keynesian economic management (including the real Keynes and not just the vulgar version) unsustainable, or is this just a tale told by anti-Keynesians? Here there is a need to challenge what has become received wisdom. For example, the collapse of Keynesianism is often marked by the failure of the Mitterrand experiment in 1981–3, although France's trade deficit at the time was much less than that in the contemporary UK under Thatcher and both budget and trade deficits were worse under the contemporary Reagan administration in the USA. We suspect that in recent decades there may have been a lot of Keynesianism practised under the rhetorical umbrella of monetarist orthodoxy (in the USA in the late 1980s and the UK after 1992). What new instruments are available to social democrats for economic management?

Social democracy has traditionally been seen as a way of dealing with capitalism but which variety? For example, these can have a long-term or short-term focus; based on share value or firm growth; individualist or cooperative; domestic or transnational; corporatist or neo-liberal. Some appear to be more compatible with social democracy than others. Simply to characterise the 'Anglo-Saxon' variety as the only or indeed the dominant form of capitalism is inaccurate.

Then there is the welfare state. Arguably, welfare states need to be restructured, but this does not necessarily mean retrenchment or loss of universality. On the contrary, reform can make welfare states more redistributive and inclusive and even save money in the process, particularly where better-off groups have been able to use their political power to gain advantage, or where public services have been used for political patronage. Tackling the issue, however, is notoriously difficult for technical as well as political reasons; and short-term losers often need to be compensated, making reform expensive. There has been a widespread move to link welfare states to labour market policies and thus to economic management more generally, but this too is notoriously difficult for parties of both right and left. Traditional social democracy was able to make the claim to be both economically more efficient and socially more just; can this be repeated, or has its historical moment passed? There is also the question of taxation, and how it can be made more progressive and linked with the welfare state as well as economic growth considerations. Anti-tax movements in many countries have prevented a rational debate about taxation and fostered an assumption against progressive taxation even among some people who would benefit from it.

European integration has in many ways provided benign conditions for social democracy, by securing economic growth, containing the nationalism which produced two world wars, and sustaining distinct European forms of capitalism, but, as noted above, it also poses some dangers to the European welfare settlement. In the face of populist right-wing parties preaching a return to national solidarity, linked to xenophobia and ethnic nationalism, social democrats need to rethink their strategy at the European level to ensure that there is a social counterpart to the single market. The eurozone crisis has posed the question of whether economic integration is going to move forward towards greater political union, or regress to national protectionism. Europe may also threaten national social settlements, if the competition element of the project is allowed to dominate over the idea of a more social Europe.

Diminishing economic insecurity, migration and Europe have been linked by the populist right as the basis for a new security discourse aimed at those sectors most under threat, often the core of the social democratic vote. It is therefore important that social democratic parties have an alternative security prospectus that is both effective and convincing.

Social democracy is not just a set of policies or even a programme for government. It is also a political movement. It has been borne by political parties and trade unions, two types of movement which are in decline. It may be argued that parties of all persuasions are in decline, as measured by membership or voting for the traditional parties. This is, however, a greater concern for social democrats, who are interested in using public power to achieve social change, than for neo-liberals whose aim is the depoliticisation of the economy. Similarly, trade unions are not the only collective bodies to be losing members but they are important for social democrats. New social movements have incorporated parts of the social democratic agenda but they are less linked to political power, are often less organised and their members less committed. Social democratic parties have, of course, never relied purely on the organised working class and have always incorporated other progressive interests, but their ability to do so is perhaps reduced by the competition from single-issue groups.

Social democracy has often been associated with a strong and centralised state as the vehicle for social and economic change but it also contains localist traditions, which are being rediscovered in the twenty-first century. Social democratic parties have been successful at the sub-state level in France, Italy, Germany and the United Kingdom, although to some extent this is due to the very fact that they are not in office at the state level. This has given social democrats an opportunity to think of new instruments and strategies of social change and for new alliances with social movements, notably environmental movements and green parties.

The economic crisis that broke in 2008 might have been expected to cast doubts on the model of deregulated finance capitalism that had dominated the Western world in recent decades, and for a short while there did appear to be a return to the powerful state and a form of Keynesianism. It was not long, however, before orthodoxy reimposed itself both within states and in international organisations. This cannot be explained by relative success of deregulated capitalism or by any law of necessity. It must, rather, be put down to the failure of social democrats to offer a plausible alternative. In some cases (notably the United Kingdom) they had relied on an over-expanded finance sector to provide the money for expanded public services. More widely, there has been an intellectual failure to think through the bases of a renewed social democracy for contemporary society. At root, we would argue, the problem is one of ideas and politics, rather than of ineluctable economic necessities.

## The chapters

The first section of the book examines the performance of social democracy in Europe. Donald Sassoon presents a historical overview, showing that crises are a recurrent feature of capitalism which have often been misinterpreted as harbingers of radical change. The Long Depression of the late nineteenth century did not bring down capitalism but did lead to social reforms. The inter-war Depression led social democrats to accept a new compromise with capitalism, leading to the reformist programme of macro-management of the capitalist economy, of welfare regulation, state interventionism, and the Keynesian welfare state of the post-war era. David McCrone and Michael Keating look at the performance of social democratic parties in Western Europe and find a pattern of steady, if uneven, decline. It may be that this is true of all mainstream political parties, but that is scarce consolation for a movement committed to long-term, progressive change.

Milada Vachudova finds that social democracy in Central and Eastern Europe has not enjoyed the success expected of it since the transition to democracy and examines the reasons for this. On the other hand, she expects social democratic parties to do well in the future in the face of the weakness of right-wing and green parties. David Heald examines social democratic policies on public expenditure, disentangling the various purposes and instruments. High public spending is not in itself a sign of social democracy and Heald argues that a defence of public expenditure requires a hard-headed analysis of its economic and social impact.

The following chapters look at 'classical' social democracy, that is, the combination of economic and social policies that underpin the best-known social democratic experiments. The Nordic countries inevitably feature strongly here. Indeed, Bo Rothstein and Sven Steinmo suggest that it is only they who can claim to be truly social democratic. The secret is universalism in social provision, binding citizens into the collectivity, but an increasingly pragmatic attitude to how services are delivered. This is combined with economic flexibility and a willingness to let old industries go under. Henry Milner takes a similar line on the success of the Nordic model, but emphasises cultural factors or 'civic literacy' that have encouraged citizens to accept that collective solutions are in their individual interests. Neither chapter sees the social democratic model as being in terminal decline, although Milner does detect strains and problems. Susi Meret and Birte Siim take a less optimistic view, showing how right-populist and anti-immigration parties have exploited weaknesses in the Nordic model and appropriated defence of the welfare state and even gender equality in order to undermine the social democratic appeal.

Three chapters on political economy follow, linking the management of capitalism, labour market policy and welfare, a nexus central to the social democratic project. Martin Rhodes surveys contrasting models of political economy and social democratic efforts to reform labour markets and welfare states. The paradoxical conclusion is that social democratic parties have lost less electorally in countries where welfare states have been weaker and labour markets less regulated – the liberal welfare state countries. The severest challenges are faced by those social democratic parties that, historically, were builders or co-builders of large, highly decommodifying welfare states, as in the Nordic and continental-conservative countries. In Germany, social democrats have lost votes to the Greens and the Left Party, while in the Nordic countries they have been outflanked by the mainstream conservatives, while losing to the populist right, both of whom have embraced welfarism.

Colin Crouch argues that it is increasingly difficult to maintain the old social democratic synthesis, as the globalisation of the economy, the decline of the organised industrial working class, and the growing dominance of neo-liberal ideas have been shifting the balance of power against those forces on which social democracy depended. 'Third Way' social democracy responded by no longer regarding capitalism and corporate power as problematic and reshaping their programme around them. Such a stance involved overlooking several major problems, however, notably the power of the business corporation, which has reached deeply into public services and is not necessarily to be identified with the free market. Crouch argues that the corporation must be regulated and advocates the 'social investment welfare state' as an alternative formula. He also believes that, given the weakness of political parties, social movements may be a better way to realise social democratic goals, confronting corporate power directly.

Ulrich Hilpert and Desmond Hickie address the difficulties for social democratic economic policy following the demise of national Keynesianism and the challenge of industrial competition from Asia. These difficulties have been compounded by neo-liberal policies in Europe. They argue that a new social democratic settlement can be forged based on labour and employment, focused on high-value industries, education and research. Using high skills and education, labour can play a critical part in delivering economic prosperity and social welfare in modern societies. There is room for social democratic policy, but it needs a flexibility of design that reflects the flexibility shown by high-technology workers, businesses and the modern industries and regionalised economies in which they work.

Yves Mény shows how European integration has come to be defined largely as a market-making mechanism, with social compensation for market losers left to national governments. Their ability to respond is increasingly constrained by single market regulations zealously enforced by the European Court of Justice. Yet the resulting divorce between economy and society is unsustainable in the long run, calling for a political response if the welfare settlement is to be preserved.

Social democracy has often been associated with liberal security policies or penal welfarism. Such approaches are, as Neil Walker shows, more difficult to sustain in the face of populism and a culture of security that tends to reject the economic and communitarian solutions of social democracy on grounds both of pragmatism and of morality. A social democratic security policy needs to address this issue.

For much of the twentieth century, social democracy was associated with a strong and centralised state, able to wield the levers of power for progressive aims. Yet earlier traditions were often local and regional. State transformation and rescaling have removed from the nation-state many of the instruments for social and economic management, while decentralisation has vested significant powers at local and regional levels. Social and economic struggles take place at a variety of spatial scales. Michael Keating looks at how social democracy and social democratic compromises can develop at the sub-state level.

In conclusion, David McCrone and Michael Keating draw together the strands of the various arguments. They argue that social democracy has a future but that it needs to undertake serious rethinking both about policies and about politics. The current crisis of finance capital provides a historic opportunity to do this.

# THE LONG DEPRESSION, THE GREAT CRASH AND SOCIALISM IN WESTERN EUROPE

Donald Sassoon

## Introduction

The Left that is the left today is what was called the social democratic left. In its contemporary guise it is no longer in the kind of anti-capitalist mode which still existed thirty odd years ago when Mitterrand's *Parti Socialiste* faced the 1981 elections promising to begin the long haul out of capitalism, or when the British Labour Party's 1983 manifesto still mentioned socialism as a realistic perspective. This is all the more remarkable since capitalism itself is not doing well. But then the alarm bells as to the future of capitalism have been ringing for a long time. 'Europe today is in the biggest recession since the 1930s, with unemployment over 10 percent.' This is the view of Richard Layard, a distinguished economist, founder of the Centre for Economic Performance at the London School of Economics and a member of the House of Lords. Had the statement been made recently, it would cause no surprise, but it was made in 1989 – and it caused no surprise then (1989: ix). J. Van Duijn (1983: 203) asked whether the 'depression we are suffering' is 'as severe as that which struck the industrial world in the 1930s' and concludes that it is not, but the implication is that it is the worst since then. He was writing in 1983. Finally, Andrew Tylecote (1991) offers as a sub-title to his interesting *The Long Wave in the World Economy*, 'The *current* crisis in historical perspective' (my emphasis). The book was published in 1991. It is not clear what 'the current crisis' was, though there is a hint that it would be an ecological crisis damaging to the developed world; predictions are made about the plight of the South; China remains unmentioned, although more recently Tylecote has remedied this by writing extensively on China (see for example Tylecote 2006).

Announcing crises is part and parcel of the history of debates about capitalism. When socialists were more revolutionary, or at least more socialist than they are today – not a major feat – the prospect of an impending crisis confirmed their view that capitalism was destined to collapse, overwhelmed by its inner contradictions – the occasion for the final showdown, a kind of pleasurable Armageddon. The future of capitalism was always perceived as clouded by anxiety even by its supporters. In reality the exceptional period of capitalism was the period between 1945 and 1973 when no serious crisis plagued the global economy. Yet it was during these blessed *Trente Glorieuses* – we owe the term to Jean Fourastié (1979) – that some of the causes of today's problems originated. This was a period when the narrowing gap between the US economy and those of the rest of the West, above all Japan and Germany, made it difficult to maintain high levels of profit. But profits were also squeezed by the ability of the trade unions to push up real wages, in turn made possible by the amazing economic growth of the previous decade. The strikes of the late 1960s, the largest in European history and particularly pronounced in France and Italy, affected all Western European economies. These were followed, in 1973, by a massive increase in the price of primary products, above all oil when the OPEC cartel led by Iran, Iraq, Kuwait and Saudi Arabia successfully raised oil prices by 70% (Yergin 2008: 587).

The increase in the two central costs of manufacturing, labour and raw materials, contributed to the gradual shift of manufacturing away from the West. This in turn led to a decrease in the power of the trade unions whose remaining strength came to be concentrated in the public sector. Instead of facing capitalists, the unions faced the state as an employer.

This double crisis (high wages and high cost of primary products in the 1970s) should be seen as a crucial part in the long-term restructuring of global industrial capitalism with the centre of manufacturing shifting to the East: first to Japan, then to the four little tigers (Hong Kong, Singapore, Taiwan and South Korea), and finally to China.

The most evident symptom of this restructuring was the collapse of the Bretton Woods system (devaluation of the dollar in 1971) which signalled the beginning of the end of US economic supremacy. The US balance of payments, which showed a healthy surplus of six billion dollars in 1964, turned into deficit ten years later, and has been in deficit ever since – reaching 500 billion in 2010 (U.S. Census Bureau 2012). Since then, there has been a succession of crises, stock market collapses and massive instability. Thus on (Black) Monday, 19 October 1987, stock markets around the world crashed. By the end of that month stock markets in Hong Kong had fallen by 45.5%, by 26.45% in London, and in New York by 22.68%.

Then we had the Japanese crash of 1990, which is particularly significant because until then Japan was seen in the same light as China is seen now: as a possible successor of the USA for the role of economic hegemon. The Nikkei index which had been at 100 in 1949 steadily grew to 5,000 (early 1970s), then 10,000 (1984), and finally 39,000 in 1989. It has been downhill ever since. It is now under 9,000. Like the 1929 crash and many subsequent crises including the recent global downturn, it started as a real estate bubble. By the 1980s the value of land in Tokyo exceeded that of the whole of California (which is larger than the whole of Japan) and the value of all Japanese land was four times that of the USA (Kindleberger 2000: 113–14). Then there was the dot-com bubble of 1995–2000, the Mexican crisis of 1994–5, and the 1997 Asian financial crisis which affected in particular South Korea, Malaysia and Indonesia.

So, as the followers of Karl Marx and John Maynard Keynes never cease to remind us, crises are the normal feature of capitalist development. They may be contained. They may be mitigated by regulatory frameworks. They cannot be eliminated. These crises, like their predecessors, were unforeseen by most economists. It follows that we cannot predict the long-term consequences of the present global downturn or its effects, though it is unlikely to be favourable to the left. No doubt plenty of experts will explain not only why this crisis has occurred but also where it is going. Some will be right, but we do not know who. The signs are that we are set for a fairly long international restructuring. But, as a historian, I leave predictions to others. The art of forecasting, at least in this field, has not improved significantly since the days when we examined the entrails of goats in the hope of perceiving the future.

My task is, of course, simpler. What I propose to do is to examine the effects on the left of the two main global crises which have so far occurred in the history of capitalism: the crisis of 1873–96 and that of 1929. The first was called the Great Depression and was the formative period for social democracy at a time when it was coterminous with 'the left', until the crash of '29 appropriated the title. To avoid confusion I will refer to the 1873–96 crisis as the Long Depression and to the second as the Great Crash.

We also have to remind ourselves that although the word 'globalisation' is fairly recent, it was perfectly clear to observers at the end of the nineteenth century that an interdependent world market was being created. Marx and Engels had famously noted it as early as 1848 in *The Communist Manifesto*, but by the end of the century it was a widely accepted notion. Thus, in 1891, the Reverend William Cunningham, President of the Economic Science and Statistics Section of the British Association, in his address entitled 'Nationalism and Cosmopolitanism in Economics' pointed out:

> We no longer contemplate isolation from the rest of the globe; we only grumble because other people interpose barriers which check free commercial intercourse between all parts of the known world . . . We have given up all idea that the nation should be self-sufficing . . . So far as our economic scheme is concerned, we regard England as part of a greater whole – not as an independent national organism, but as one portion of a cosmopolitan economic organism; we desire to have the freest

communication with all parts of the world, for on this our very life, our national prosperity in all its branches, depends.

Giovanni Dalla Vecchia, an Italian commentator writing in the liberal English periodical *The Contemporary Review* about the bread riots in April 1898 in Southern Italy, attributed their causes not just to taxation, political corruption and the failure to colonise Ethiopia but also to international economic factors such as the rise in the price of bread which was a 'consequence of the Hispano-American war' (1898: 113).

Writing in the 1880s, Charles Booth noted the changes that had come over the population of Clerkenwell in central London. 'Half a century or so ago,' he wrote in his *Life and Labour of the People of London*, the local -industries '. . . watch and clock-making, gold-beating, diamond-cutting, and the manufacture of jewellery were in a flourishing condition, and throughout this district masters and journeymen worked and lived in prosperity . . . [now] . . . Under the stress of cheap foreign production the Clerkenwell trade has steadily declined.' The masters and their artisans have left, their place taken by 'a lower class' (1903: 191).

## The Long Depression 1873–96

What happened during the Long Depression? Prices dropped and growth faltered, though it never turned negative. The depression was global. It left unaffected only areas outside the modern world. There was a realignment of the world economies. The United States replaced Great Britain as the leading industrial power. The proximate causes need not detain us since they are often purely conjunctural: railway over-building, the after-effects of the Franco-Prussian War, the consequences of the American Civil War, a shortage of gold. Such causes are of limited interest, as is the role of the Florida real estate crisis in the crash of '29 or that of the sub-prime crisis in the USA which led to the downturn of 2007–8.

Strictly speaking, as most economic historians have pointed out, the depression of the 1870s and 1880s is a myth. Some, such as S. B. Saul, have argued that since there was no single pattern in that period, 'the sooner the "Great Depression" is banished from the literature, the better' (1969: 55). There was no real depression in the sense of stagnant or negative growth. What did happen was a general fall in prices. This led entrepreneurs and economists to adopt pessimistic scenarios since lower prices would lead to lower profits.

There was real recession (negative growth) only in the years 1907–8 in most industrial countries (Bairoch 1997: 411). During the Long Depression, however, and for most of the two decades that followed, the twelve leading European economies continued to grow. While growth in the fifty years 1820–70 averaged 1.75% a year, it increased to 2.13% a year in 1870–1913,

Table 2.1  Consumer Price Indices 1873–96

|       | Belgium | France | Germany | Italy | UK    | USA   |
|-------|---------|--------|---------|-------|-------|-------|
| 1873  | 115.4   | 98.6   | 89.5    | 99.5  | 119.6 | 121.2 |
| 1896  | 76.9    | 89.4   | 78.7    | 79.6  | 81.4  | 84.2  |
| 1913  | 100     | 100    | 100     | 100   | 100   | 100   |

*Source:* Maddison 1982: 236–7

Table 2.2  Rates of growth of world GDP
(annual average compound growth rates)

|                  | 1820–70 | 1870–1913 | 1913–50 | 1950–73 | 1973–2003 |
|------------------|---------|-----------|---------|---------|-----------|
| UK               | 2.05    | 1.90      | 1.19    | 2.93    | 2.15      |
| Belgium          | 2.24    | 2.02      | 1.03    | 4.08    | 2.07      |
| Germany          | 2.00    | 2.81      | 0.30    | 5.68    | 1.72      |
| France           | 1.43    | 1.63      | 1.15    | 5.05    | 2.20      |
| Italy            | 1.24    | 1.94      | 1.49    | 5.64    | 2.17      |
| Top 12 European* | 1.75    | 2.13      | 1.16    | 4.65    | 2.05      |
| USA              | 4.20    | 3.94      | 2.84    | 3.93    | 2.94      |
| China            | −0.37   | 0.56      | −0.02   | 4.92    | 7.34      |
| Japan            | 0.41    | 2.44      | 2.21    | 9.29    | 2.62      |

* UK, Germany, France, Italy, Norway, Sweden, Denmark, Finland, Switzerland, the
Netherlands, Belgium, Austria
*Source:* Maddison 2007: 380

then down to 1.16% in 1913–50. It shot up to 4.65% during the *Trente Glorieuses* and then down again to 2.05% in 1973–2003 (Maddison 2007: 380).

During the Long Depression, the fall in prices led to several stock exchange panics such as the crash of the Vienna Stock Exchange in May 1873 and that of the Paris Bourse in 1882. In 1887 there was a tariff war between France and Italy. In 1879 Bismarck broke with his liberal allies and bowed to the pressures from landowners (worried by cheap imports of grain from the USA) and adopted protectionism. In 1892 the Third Republic too reverted to protectionism (the Méline tariff). The USA, whose tariff barriers were extremely high throughout the nineteenth century, confirmed its commitment to protectionism with the election of the Republican Benjamin Harrison in 1888. The Tariff Act 1890 (the McKinley Tariff) increased duties to 50%. Admittedly, when the Democrats returned to power they lowered the tariffs, but they remained far higher than anywhere in Western Europe. Great Britain alone remained faithful to the free trade doctrine which had served her well for so long, though there were protectionist pressures. By 1913 protective tariffs in the USA were at 44%, in Japan at 30%, in France at 20%, in Italy 18%, and in Germany

Table 2.3 Social legislation

| Pensions | Unemployment benefits | Industrial accident insurance | | Health insurance | |
|---|---|---|---|---|---|
| Pre-1914 | Pre-1914 | Pre-1900 | 1900–14 | Pre-1900 | 1900–13 |
| Germany | Norway | Germany | Most other | Sweden | Switzerland |
| UK | UK | Switzerland | industrial | Belgium | Norway |
| Italy | Denmark | Austria | countries | Germany | Great Britain |
| Denmark | France | Norway | except | Austria | |
| France | | Finland | Canada | Finland | |
| New Zealand | | Great Britain | (1930), USA | Italy | |
| Sweden | | Italy | (1930) and | Denmark | |
| | | Denmark | Portugal | France | |
| | | France | (1962) | | |

Health insurance was introduced between 1914 and 1945 in New Zealand, the Netherlands, Spain, Australia and Finland. In Canada in 1971; in Portugal in 1984. Not (yet) in the USA.

13% (Bairoch 1993: 40). As for Russia, its economy was virtually closed, with 84% of protective tariffs.

This was part and parcel of a general strengthening of the importance of the state. States spent more: in the USA by 1890 federal spending had reached new heights (one billion dollars). France and Britain expanded their old empires while others (Germany and Italy) tried to join the colonialists' club. States became more authoritarian. In 1878 Bismarck declared wars against the Catholics (*Kulturkampf*, in Prussia only) and against the socialists (virtually banned between 1878 and 1890) and lost both. In Italy Francesco Crispi's governments of the 1890s waged a virtual war against the South with full parliamentary backing (Duggan 2002: 643).

The strengthening of the state did not always lead towards greater authoritarianism. The basis of the modern regulatory welfare state was created in the decades at the turn of the century particularly in states rich enough to produce social reforms: Germany (the pioneers), and also Belgium and Great Britain. Others followed. The spate of legislation was quite impressive and workers worked less (see Table 2.4 overleaf).

In many countries, laws decreed a compulsory day of rest. Factory inspections became customary. A limit was set to the length of the working day. Great Britain introduced free lunches for poor children in school (1906). The social question moved to the centre of the political stage. Pope Leo XIII's encyclical *De Rerum Novarum* (1891) promulgating the 'Rights and Duties of Capital and Labour' shifted the attention of political Catholicism towards the working class. The French social Catholic Albert de Mun, speaking at the University of Louvain on 12 February 1885, declared, 'Let us go to the people . . . let us go to the workers, to know them, to love them. Let us go to them to

Table 2.4 Average weekly hours worked 1870–1913

|  | 1870 | 1890 | 1913 |
|---|---|---|---|
| Belgium | 72.2 | 66.5 | 59.5 |
| France | 66.0 | 66.0 | 62 |
| Germany | 67.6 | 65.1 | 57 |
| Great Britain | 56.9 | 56.3 | 56 |
| Italy | 63.3 | 63.6 | 62.4 |
| Scandinavia | 69.6 | 60.0 | 55.8 |
| Australia | 56.2 | 50.5 | 44.7 |
| USA | 62.0 | 60 | 58.3 |

*Source:* Huberman 2004: 957

find out what makes them suffer and what they want . . . in their isolation they have no other force than violence and are looking for friends who would help them rather than use them' (quoted in Puissant 1988: 93). Even in Russia the tsarist government enacted a body of social legislation setting the terms and rules under which factory owners could hire workers, and directed that wages had to be paid regularly, prohibiting payment in kind (Giffin 1975: 83).

A major factor in such social reforms was the advance of labour, for the vast majority of the social reforms which had taken place in that period consti- tuted the central plank of the Second International (1889) and the programme of the German Social Democracy Party (SPD), the Erfurt Programme of 1891. This amounted to a programme of major reform of the capitalist state: univer- sal adult suffrage, the right of referendum, the election of judges, the separa- tion of church and state, parliamentary control over foreign policy, devolution of power, freedom of association and opinion, repeal of all laws discriminating against women, equal rights, legal aid, the eight-hour day, labour insurance, free medical service, free burial, free education at all levels, including higher education. All of this was to be paid for by graduated income, property taxes and death duties. These were the core demands which in one form or another would constitute the agenda for the regulated capitalism of the twentieth century largely implemented in the second half (Sassoon 2010).

Not only were the vast majority of socialist parties created during the Long Depression, but they also achieved remarkable electoral results in its aftermath (1900–18). As can be seen, some socialist parties did better or even signifi- cantly better before 1918 than in recent elections.

In the period following the Long Depression trade unions became stronger and more active. In 1890 there were only 2.2 million union members among industrial workers in the developed countries. By 1910 there were 15.3 million unionised industrial workers – eight million in Germany and Great Britain alone (Bairoch 1997: 491). Besides, there were also numerous labour con- flicts with clear political aims, such as universal suffrage. The *Parti Ouvrier*

**Table 2.5** Elections pre-1918 and post-2007: socialist, social democratic and labour parties

|  | Universal manhood suffrage | Percentage of workforce engaged in industry c.1910 | Pre-1905 electoral peak | Pre-1918 electoral peak | Most recent elections 2007–11 |
|---|---|---|---|---|---|
| Austria | 1907 | 23.5 | — | 25.4 | 29.2 |
| Belgium | 1893 | 45.1 | 8.5 | 30.3 | 22.9 |
| Denmark | 1901 | 24.0 | 19.3 | 29.6 | 25.5 |
| Finland | 1906 | 11.1 | — | 47.3 | 21.44 |
| France | 1848 | 29.5 | — | 16.8 | 24.73 |
| Germany | 1871 | 39.1 | 19.7 | 34.8 | 23.00 |
| Holland | 1917 | 32.8 | 3.0 | 11.2 | 19.60 |
| Italy | 1919 | 26.8 | 6.8 | 21.3 | 33.17 |
| Norway | 1898 | 26.0 | 0.3 | 32.1 | 35.37 |
| Sweden | 1907 | 24.7 | 3.5 | 36.4 | 30.7 |
| UK | 1918 | 44.6 | 1.3 | 7.0 | 29.0 |

*Source:* Sassoon 2010: 10

*Belge* used the tactics of the mass strike in 1893, 1902 and 1913 to force a reluctant Assembly to concede universal manhood suffrage (Polasky 1982; see also Gildea 1987: 315). It was a general strike and mass demonstrations in 1905 which led to the replacement of the old Finnish Diet by a unicameral assembly (the *Eduskunta*) of 200 members elected by all Finns, men and women – the first case in Europe of authentic universal suffrage (Kirby 1979: 30–1). In Austria, without the November 1905 mass strike for voting rights, the 1907 electoral reforms would have been unlikely (Abendroth 1972: 44). In Sweden the general strike in 1902, the organisation of 'People's Parliaments', the signing of petitions and the threat of a new general strike in 1907 secured universal manhood suffrage (Schiller 1975: 202).

Though the organised socialist parties were too weak to be able to achieve a parliamentary majority and form a government, their programme was influential not only as one would expect among the classes to which they directly appealed, but also on those in power. The sign of power, let us remember, is not just the power one wields directly, but the ability to force one's opponents to adopt elements of one's programme – what Antonio Gramsci called hegemony. The socialist programme of the *fin de siècle*, much of which was implemented in the course of the twentieth century, co-existed with the certainty of a revolutionary explosion, none more so than in the most important socialist party of the time, the SPD. As August Bebel wrote to Engels on 7 December 1885: 'Every night I go to sleep with the thought that the last hour of the bourgeois society will strike soon' (quoted in Lidtke 1966: 233). Engels was more sceptical, as indeed were many in the SPD, but the signs were there, or so Bebel thought: rising unemployment, increased capitalist concentration, decline of handicraft industries, strikes. But there was no economic collapse. What occurred, instead, was a major European war which had, as one of its many consequences, the further consolidation of the American economy, a country without a strong socialist party. It was this economy which would dominate most of the twentieth century.

### The Great Crash of 1929

Well before the Great Crash, European hegemony was on the wane. But it would be a slow decline which would accelerate only in the last thirty years or so.

The crisis of 1929, or the Great Depression, has become the *ur*-crisis, the proto-crisis, the one crisis all other crises are to be compared to. Its length is disputed since it became apparent that by 1937 a new depression was looming in the USA as well as in the UK and France (though not in Germany): while GNP was back to 1929 level, unemployment remained high and was rising again in 1937–8 and GNP started to decline. The sustained recovery started only after 1941 (Temin 1989: 2).The Great Crash did not signal a major restructuring of the world economy; it did not give birth to a new hegemon; it was not accompanied by major technological breakthroughs (such as the railways and steamships in the nineteenth century or computers and IT in the last quarter of the twentieth century).

The Crash was global essentially because the First World War and its consequences had deepened the interconnection among the main European economies and strengthened the ties between Europe, Germany above all, and the US financial system. A significant factor helping to turn a stock exchange crash into a major world recession was the decision by the USA to protect its own farmers (a quarter of the US labour force was then employed in agriculture) with the Smoot-Hawley Tariff Act which was signed into law in 1930 by Herbert Hoover. Protectionist tariffs had been promised before the Crash,

Table 2.6 Shares of world GDP

|  | 1870 | 1913 | 1950 | 1973 | 2007 |
|---|---|---|---|---|---|
| Leading 12 Western European industrial countries* | 30.5 | 30.8 | 24.1 | 22.8 | 16.5 |
| USA | 8.9 | 18.9 | 27.3 | 22.1 | 20.6 |
| Japan | 2.3 | 2.6 | 3 | 7.8 | 6.6 |
| China | 17.1 | 8.8 | 4.6 | 4.6 | 15.1 |

* UK, Germany, France, Italy, Norway, Sweden, Denmark, Finland, Switzerland, the Netherlands, Belgium, Austria
*Source:* Maddison 2007: 381

**Table 2.7**  Industrial production 1930–7 in five European countries

|      | Belgium | France | Germany | Italy | UK  |
|------|---------|--------|---------|-------|-----|
| 1930 | 97      | 123    | 69      | 85    | 74  |
| 1932 | 73      | 91     | 48      | 77    | 69  |
| 1937 | 100     | 100    | 100     | 100   | 100 |

*Source:* Mitchell 1978: 687–94

during the presidential campaign of 1928, when industrial production was booming while agriculture was in a slump, in the hope of attracting rural votes away from the Democrats (Irwin 2011: 7–29). There were vociferous protests from Europe, whose exports to the USA were deemed necessary to pay debts contracted during the war and the 1920s, and to finance imports. It was regarded as monstrous that the richest nation in the world, with a substantial trade surplus, was restricting trade to the detriment of all (Irwin 2011: 163). The subsequent collapse of the gold standard (September 1931) accelerated the massive collapse of world trade and of production.

What effect did the Great Crash have on the left in general and the socialist parties in particular? Electorally there are no visible broad trends (Table 2.8).

Even in the United States the New Deal, often acclaimed as the American equivalent of social democracy, signalled a far greater role for the state than ever before, but that was the case throughout Europe, not just in Stalin's Russia, Mussolini's Italy and Hitler's Germany but also in the remaining democratic countries.

In the UK, when the crisis struck in 1929–31, the Labour Party was in power as a minority government supported by the Liberals. By 1931 it was out of power and a National Coalition, in all but name a Conservative government, ruled the country until 1940, when the war coalition was established. Nevertheless the Labour vote went up to 38.8% in the 1935 election, while in 1931 it had 30.8%. In France the Socialist vote remained static between 1932 and the Popular Front election of 1936, but the Communists went up from 8.3% to 15.26% and made a centre-left government possible, though it did not last long.

In Germany the SPD, out of office for most of the 1920s, was back in power as part of a *Grosse Koalition* in 1928. Like the Labour Party, it was trapped in a situation in which unemployment grew while investment collapsed (Abraham 1985: 7). And, like the Labour Party, the SPD (with Rudolf Hilferding as Finance Minister) approved a severely deflationary package. The fear of a return to the hyperinflation of 1923–4 – what came to be known as *Angst vor der Inflation* – had paralysed them, like the rest of the political establishment (Harsh 1993: 156; see also 163). The employers, forced by economic circumstances to contain wages, had nothing to offer the unions. These, in turn, could not be expected to give in to the employers.

Table 2.8 Elections 1928–40: socialist, social democratic and labour parties

| | Austria | Belgium | Denmark | Finland | France | Germany | Italy | Holland | Norway | Sweden | UK |
|---|---|---|---|---|---|---|---|---|---|---|---|
| 1928 | | | | | 18.0 | 29.8 | | | | 37.0 | |
| 1929 | | 36.0 | 41.8 | 27.4 | | | | | | | 37.1 |
| 1930 | 41.1 | | | 34.2 | | 24.5 | | 23.8 | 31.4 | | |
| 1931 | | | | | | | | | | | 29.3 |
| 1932 | | 37.1 | 42.7 | | 20.5 | 20.3 | | | | 41.7 | |
| 1933 | | | | 37.3 | | 18.3 | | 21.5 | 40.1 | | |
| 1934 | | | | | | | | | | | |
| 1935 | | | 46.1 | | | | | | | | 38.1 |
| 1936 | | 32.1 | | 38.6 | 19.9 | | | | 42.5 | 45.9 | |
| 1937 | | | | | | | | 21.9 | | | |
| 1938 | | | | | | | | | | | |
| 1939 | | 30.2 | 42.9 | 39.8 | | | | | | | |
| 1940 | | | | | | | | | | 53.8 | |

Source: Sassoon 2010: 43

In 1932 the first social democratic government with a clear majority in parliament was elected in Sweden. For the first time the labour movement was in the business of formulating policy. Both the Trade Union Confederation (the *Landorganisationen*, LO) and the social democratic government gave priority to economic growth. In so doing they accepted that the depression which ensued from the 1929 crash did not constitute *the* crisis of capitalism and could not be an occasion for implementing the vast socialisation policies which had been reiterated in various programmes. In any case the party had dropped from its 1932 electoral manifesto all references to socialism and to the socialisation of the means of production. It had become necessary to manage capitalism, and to manage it differently. In 1938 the LO entered into a pact (the so-called Saltsjöbaden agreement) with the employers' association (*Svenska Arbetsgivareföreningen*, SAF) which established collective bargaining and a code of practice for the regulation of industrial relations. The unions accepted the management's right to manage while the SAF recognised the unions' right to represent the workers. The actual content of the agreement was not as important as its symbolic significance (Korpi 1983: 47). The Swedish Social Democrats were able to combat unemployment more effectively than the German SPD or the British Labour Party. In so doing, between 1932 and 1938 they laid the foundation for what would become, after the Second World War, the modern West European conception of social democracy: the compromise between labour and capital, with a welfare state and full employment as its twin pillars (Paterson and Thomas 1986: 2).

Until 1914 it was axiomatic for socialist parties that they should not enter into alliances with so-called bourgeois parties. After 1918 this became the normal way in which socialist parties acceded to political power. The French Socialists found themselves in de facto alliance with the Radicals, the British Labour Party with the Liberals, the Spanish with the Republicans, the Swedish with the Liberal Party (1917) and then with the Agrarian Party (1936), the Norwegians with the Farmers' Party (1935), and the Germans with the Centre Party (among others). In most cases the experience was not happy, largely due to the pressure of facing unforeseen problems (such as a world economic collapse).

Authoritarian and semi-authoritarian governments of the right held sway nearly everywhere else, above all in Eastern and Central Europe, which became almost completely under the sway of dictatorships (Lee 1987: 251–92; and for a wider discussion Blinkhorn 1990). In Bulgaria, a military putsch in 1923 paved the way for the royal dictatorship of King Boris in 1934. In Albania, Ahmed Zogu established his dictatorship in 1924 and turned himself into King Zog in 1928. In Poland, the hero of the war against the Bolsheviks, General Josef Pilsudski, took over in 1926. In Lithuania, Antanas Smetona established a dictatorial regime after 1926 which led to the establishment of a one-party system in 1932. In 1929 King Alexander established an authoritarian regime in Yugoslavia. In Romania, thanks to a royal *coup d'état* in 1938, King Carol II had full powers. In 1934, in Estonia, Konstantin Päts established his dictatorship. In the same year in Latvia, Karlis Ulmanis had staged his *coup d'état*. Throughout the inter-war period up to 1944, Hungary was ruled by the relatively benign dictatorship (by the standards of the time) of Admiral Miklos Horthy. In Greece General Joannis Metaxas became the de facto dictator after 1936. In Finland in 1930, under pressures from the semi-fascist Lapua movement, the government promulgated a series of anti-communist bills banning communist publications, arresting all communist and most socialist members of parliament and making all legal activity by the communists impossible (Hodgson 1967: 140).

These were not countries where there was a particularly strong tradition of socialism (with the exception of Poland), so it would be mistaken to assume that major economic crises necessarily damage the left and favour the right. There remains one important lesson. The original view of social democracy at the end of the nineteenth century was that economic crises would offer the left a decisive chance to take over the state. This did not turn out to be true. The Great Crash (unlike the Long Depression) and the unemployment it caused weakened the trade unions and did not bring about a massive redeployment of forces. The left barely advanced throughout the 1930s. This was not true just of social democracy but also of the international communist movement. By 1940 this was moribund: communists were irrelevant in the Americas, on the run in China, defeated in Spain, and underground or banned almost everywhere in Europe with the notable exception of the French Communist Party (still playing second fiddle to the French Socialists). Communism re-emerged as a force to be reckoned with only after the Second World War.

The most important effect on the consciousness of the European left was the politically catastrophic effects of unemployment, though its effects varied enormously from country to country. In 1932 Belgium had reached 23.5%, the UK 22.5% and Sweden 22.8%, though in none of these instances did unemployment lead to the end of democracy. German unemployment in 1932 was higher (30.1%) but not sufficiently so to provide a monocausal explanation for the rise of Nazism.

The avoidance of unemployment became the left's way of making peace with capitalism. If full employment could be achieved and maintained, then the workers could become fully fledged citizens of the consumer society. Their taxes could be used to fund the welfare state and advanced social reforms. The extraordinary capitalist growth of the three decades following 1945 made all this possible. The pessimistic reading of the Great Crash (that capitalism is unworkable; it leads to poverty, hunger and fascism) gave way to an optimistic one, confirmed by the transformation of socialist parties everywhere in Western Europe into fully functioning governing parties. Almost everywhere in Western Europe socialist, social democratic and labour parties became the main rivals to conservative and Christian democratic parties – except in Italy and France, where the communist parties became electorally stronger than their socialist rivals. The success of post-war social democracy was also the basis for the effective dumping of Marxism, the Marxism of the Second International. Social democrats became deeply wedded to their nation-state. They thought that it would enable them to deploy Keynesian techniques of macro-economic management in order to stabilise the capitalist system, maintain full employment and its fiscal basis and guarantee the expansion of the welfare state. But Keynesianism required policy instruments, a framework and an objective. The policy instruments are fiscal and monetary policies. The framework is the nation-state (so that reflationary policies would not simply lead to greater imports). The objective is full employment. But globalisation has undermined national fiscal and monetary policies. Social democracy, having dumped a parent (Marx) decades ago, finds itself bereft of the other (Keynes). And now, in the midst of a new major crisis, it stands, idealess, as a remnant of the past facing an uncertain future.

# SOCIAL DEMOCRACY IN CRISIS: OUTLINING THE TRENDS IN WESTERN EUROPE

David McCrone and Michael Keating

## Introduction

The current crisis of capitalism should provide a major opportunity for social democracy, yet, at the time of writing, there are very few left-of-centre parties in power in Western Europe. Those in Portugal, Greece and Spain were swept away by the crisis of the Euro. In Scandinavia, the heartland of social democracy, Norway has a centre-left government, in coalition with Socialist Left and the Centre Party, while Denmark has a social democrat-led government, but with a mere quarter of the popular vote. Sweden and Finland have centre-right coalition governments. Broadly speaking, the percentages of the vote obtained by social democratic parties in these historic heartlands are the lowest for decades. Elsewhere in Western Europe, the Labour government in the UK lost power in May 2010, and most social democratic parties are in opposition. In Central and Eastern Europe, as Milada Vachudova discusses, social democracy has not prospered.

In this chapter we review electoral trends, focusing on Western Europe because that is the historic heartland of social democracy.[1] While there is an argument for saying that only the Nordic countries are 'proper' social democracies (see Rothstein and Steinmo in this volume), to us that seems unduly restrictive given that socialist/labour parties have been prominent across Europe since 1945. While it is true that they have not been as hegemonic as in the Nordic countries, they still draw upon diverse social and economic policies which are social democratic. We have grouped the data[2] into three categories: the Nordic countries (Denmark, Finland, Norway, Sweden and Iceland[3]); Northern European countries (the UK, Germany, the Netherlands, Belgium, Ireland, Switzerland and Austria[4]); and Southern Europe (including Italy, Greece, Spain and Portugal). We focus on the period since 1945 because it is a suitable caesura in West European politics post Second World War in which most, if not all, the countries were protagonists.

Social democracy, as we noted in the introduction, is a broad category covering several distinct strands and its expression in the form of political parties is consequently varied. The balance among various elements differs from one place to another and it has to map onto social cleavages including class, religion, language, territory and the urban-rural divides. Party competition may enlarge or reduce the political space for social democratic parties, given the presence of communist/socialist, agrarian, religious, communitarian, territorial and, more recently, environmental parties. In some countries, a mass social democratic party monopolises the centre-left space, whilst in others they have to ally with other progressive forces. Social democratic parties have varied in their willingness to modernise and adapt their policies and strategy to changing social conditions. In the 1950s, 1960s and 1970s, this often meant throwing off residues of Marxism and accepting capitalism. The welfare state remains a strong pillar of support for social democracy but it is not always enough to distinguish it from its rivals. In some countries, the welfare state owes as much, or more, to Christian democracy or (in France) welfare nationalism. Moreover, in some countries social democrats have adapted to what they see as a more individualistic society, embracing consumerism in various forms and playing down equality in an effort to appeal to a growing and changing middle class. Yet even these adaptations have proved insufficient to sustain the levels of support necessary to gain office. Social democrats have been able to build broader left and centre-left coalitions on occasion but these have proven fragile and difficult to sustain.

## The Nordic countries

In Sweden and Norway social democratic parties have hegemonised the left and largely dominated the political spectrum as a whole. From an early stage, they combined industrial working class and trade union support with agrarian interests in countries where there are no major religious or linguistic cleavages. There are territorial cleavages, but social democracy was able to straddle these and there has been no serious Communist presence since the Second World War. There has also been a willingness to adapt to new times: 'Sweden's social democrats have stuck doggedly to the tough-minded pragmatism which has been their trademark as a local brand since the 1930s' (Madeley 2002: 165). In Denmark, social democracy has been less hegemonic and in Finland it has had to compete with a communist presence. Social democracy has also incorporated a strong national, even nationalist, dimension. In the case of Norway, Østerud remarked that 'the politics of secession [from Sweden in 1905] were simultaneously a politics of democratisation. Norwegian nationalism of the late 19th century was therefore basically a programme of the liberal centre-left,

*The crisis of social democracy in Europe*

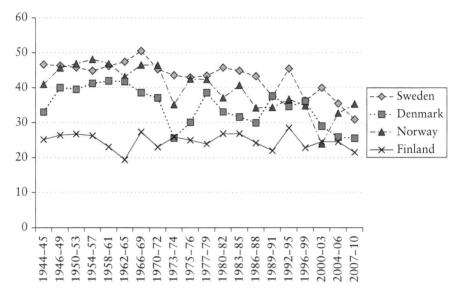

**Figure 3.1** Percentage of vote in national elections, Nordic countries

demanding national independence and democratic reform as two sides of the same coin' (2005: 706). In all the Nordic countries, there has been a rise of right-wing populism playing to nationalism, as well as a significant Green presence.

Broadly speaking, Nordic social democracy is at a low electoral ebb, albeit in better health than in most European countries. Comparing 1946–9 with 2007–10, the mean vote share for the social democrats in the Nordic countries fell from 39.5% to 28.2%. Indeed, with the exception of Iceland, in no country do the social democrats poll more than in the post-war period, even in Finland, where they started from a low base. Forming coalitions with Greens and Leftists seems to us an expression of the problem, not its cause; namely, why have social democrats failed to encompass these new forms of 'progressive' politics?

### Sweden

The Swedish Social Democrats (SAP) have been in government almost continuously since 1945, with five exceptions: in 1976, 1979, 1991, 2006 and 2010. Between 1945 and 1988 their share of the vote did not fall below 43%, even though they lost power in 1976 and 1979. Since 1991, however, they have reached more than 40% on only two occasions, in 1994 (45%) and 2002 (40%), and at the last *Riksdag* election they won only 31%, and 112 seats (out of 349). Having been in government for sixty-five of the previous seventy-eight years, the SAP had never lost two consecutive elections, and 2010 was their worst showing since 1921.

The year 1976 saw the first non-socialist government since 1936, comprising three centre-right parties, the agrarian Centre Party, the conservative Moderate Party and the Liberal People's Party, to give them 180 seats to the SAP's 152. The result was virtually unchanged in 1979, with the centre-right coalition parties having 175 seats to the SAP's 154. In 2006, the SAP tried and failed to form a coalition government with the Left and the Greens, and the centre-right parties formed a government. By 2010, the centre-right alliance won 49% of the vote, and 173 seats in the *Riksdag*, in contrast to the Red-Green bloc, including the SAP, with 44% and 156 seats. The 2010 election saw the emergence of the right-wing 'Sweden Democrats', who won 20 seats.

Arguably the most dominant of the Nordic social democratic parties in electoral terms, the Swedish SAP was only marginally ahead of the conservative Moderate Party in 2010 (112 seats to 107), and its hegemonic days of political dominance seem over.

*Norway*

If the Swedish Social Democratic Party is the lodestar of Nordic social democracy, then Norway's Labour Party is not far behind. Labour's victory in 1945 represented the first majority for any party since 1915. Labour got 50% or more in 1949, 1953 and 1957, a better share of the vote than its Swedish counterpart. This was not to happen again until 2010–11, but only because the Swedish party had lost even more support. It is a measure of the relative decline in the fortunes of the social democrats in both countries that their share of the vote had fallen from just under half to around one-third in sixty-five years.

Labour had an absolute majority in the *Storting* until the 1960s. Thereafter, it led minority governments, either on its own, or in coalition with non-socialist parties, and even Conservatives. By the 1969 election, the coalition of right-wing parties won more seats than Labour (76 to 74). Nevertheless, 'Norway of the 1960s was the robust embodiment of social democratic order. What we have seen during the last two decades is the swift dissolution of this order' (Østerud 2005: 718).

By 1997, Labour had lost power (with 65 seats and 35% of the vote), and a centrist coalition government was formed by the Christian People's Party, Conservative Party, Centre Party and the Social Liberals. At the turn of the century the Labour leader became Prime Minister, but in 2001 his party won only 24% of the vote and 43 seats. The centre-right coalition of Conservatives, Christian People's Party and Liberals was supported on a 'confidence and supply' basis by the rising right-wing Progress Party. The growth in electoral volatility since the mid-1980s means that 'politics became harder to predict, which is broadly speaking a common trend for all Nordic political systems' (Kestilä and Söderlund 2007: 555).

The year 2005 saw a victory for the newly formed Red-Green coalition, which along with the Centre Party took 87 seats, producing the first majority government in twenty years. Labour, however, could only manage 33% (and 61 seats), while the right-wing Progress Party became the largest opposition party with 38 seats. Four years later, the Red-Green coalition held on to power, even though the opposition received more votes. Both Conservatives and Progress parties increased their number of seats (to 30 and 41 respectively). The latest Norwegian election seems to confirm the view that the Norwegian Labour Party has simply become *primus inter pares*.

### Denmark

If we can characterise Swedish and Norwegian social democratic parties as leaders in their respective countries, with 40%-plus of the popular vote in the period 1945 to the 1970s, then their Danish equivalents do significantly less well. The Danish social democrats got around 40% until the late 1960s, which enabled them to form governments albeit with a minority of seats. The Social Democratic Party were in government from 1964 to 1973, but at the 'landslide election' of 1973, when five new parties won seats and half of existing MPs were replaced, the SDP lost one-third of its seats, ending up with 46, on 26% of the vote. Their main challengers, *Venstre*, the Liberal party, formed the smallest government minority in Danish history, with just 22 seats, but were supported by the rightist bloc of the Progress Party, Conservative People's Party, Social Liberals, Centre Democrats and the Christian People's Party.

Regaining power in 1975, the SDP was in government for nearly a decade before being defeated by a coalition of *Venstre*, Conservative People's Party, Centre Democrats and the Christian People's Party, who together won three more seats than the 'red' bloc. This coalition remained in power until 1994. That year the SDP, who won 35% of the vote and 62 seats, led a coalition with the Social Liberals and the Centre Democrats. The election of 1998 was tight between the two blocs, but the SDP-led government continued, although the election saw the emergence of the right-wing Danish People's Party.

The 2001 election was notable for the fact that the SDP was not the biggest party. Rather, *Venstre* formed a government with the Conservative People's Party, with tacit support from the Danish People's Party. This coalition won the following two elections, in 2005 and 2007, only losing power in 2011 to a coalition of Social Democrats (with 44 seats), Social Liberals (17), Socialist People's Party (16) and an emergent Red-Green Alliance (12), giving an overall 89 MPs to the blue bloc's 86. Forming a government with only 25% of the vote (and second to *Venstre*'s 47 seats, on 27%) is now taken as a mark of relative success for the Danish Social Democrats. As Kosiara-Pedersen observed, 'although the election was a victory in terms of the red bloc forming the government, the Social Democrats sank to a historically low level of electoral support for the third election in a row. The payoff between office and votes is not unusual for the Social Democrats, who see themselves as the principal bearer of government office; this is unquestionably their primary goal' (2012: 420).

### Finland

Finland has a much weaker social democratic party (SDP) than the other Nordic countries. Its best performance in parliamentary elections was 28% (and 63 seats) in 1995 when it became part of the so-called rainbow coalition with Conservatives (44), Swedish People's Party (11), Left Alliance (22) and Greens (9). Its poorest performance was 19% in 1962 (38 seats) as well as in 2011 (42 seats). Of the nineteen parliamentary elections since 1945, the SDP has been the biggest party on twelve occasions.

Coalition governments are the norm in Finland, historically under a strong presidency, notably that of Urho Kekkonen between 1956 and 1981. Until the late 1980s, the dominant coalition post-war was between the SDP and the Centre Party (previously the Agrarian Alliance), known as the 'red earth' coalition. Indeed, the Centre Party ('earth') is the striking exception to the decline of former agrarian parties in Western Europe (in 2011 it won 35 seats on 16% of the vote). Finland experienced frequent changes of government coalitions until the 1983 elections, since when governments have tended to go the full four-year term, with the exception of the 2003 coalition between the Centre Party, the Social Democrats and the Swedish People's Party.

While the Social Democrats have been in (coalition) government more often than not, their best electoral showing since 1945 was in 1995, following the election of a centre-right government four years earlier, the first since 1964. The SDP continued to lead the five-party coalition after the 1999 election but lost 12 seats. Four years later, the Centre Party and the SDP formed a short-lived coalition (with the Swedish People's Party), and was replaced by a Centre Party government. In 2007, the National Coalition Party, a party of the centre-right, was the major victor and the 'left' (both SDP and Left Alliance) had their worst result in a hundred years (for the SDP, the worst since 1962). The latest election in 2011 was notable for the rise of the anti-EU and anti-immigration True Finns party, which won 39 seats (34 more than previously). Nevertheless, the ruling coalition was made up of six other parties: the National Coalition Party (44 seats), the Social Democrats (42), the Left Alliance (14), the Green League (10), the Swedish People's Party (9) and the Christian Democrats (6). Together, they accounted for 62% of MPs, reflecting the Finnish liking for 'oversized coalitions'.

## Iceland

Iceland is the unusual Nordic case. As Haradarson and Kristinsson point out, 'one of the distinguishing features of the Icelandic party system in the 20th century compared to many other Northern European countries is the absence of a large social democratic party' (Nohlen and Stöver 2010: 948). The Social Democratic Party (SDP) was founded as the political wing of the trade union movement but split in 1938, such that the Left Socialists (Communists) have been relatively strong in the post-war period. The apparent rise in support for the Left is due to the formation of the Social Democratic Alliance (SDA) in 1999 out of the SDP, the People's Alliance (formerly the Left Socialists) and the Women's Alliance. The economic crisis of 2009 onwards has weakened the conservative Independence Party, and strengthened both the SDA and the Left-Greens.

## Northern Europe

In order to make voting trends in the eight Northern European countries more visually comprehensible, these have been graphed separately such that Germany, Great Britain[5] and Austria are on one graph on the grounds that the social democratic party has no serious 'communist' competitors. The vote shares for the Netherlands, Belgium, France, Switzerland and Ireland are on a separate graph. It is hard to make a case for a resurgent social democracy in electoral terms in Northern Europe outside the Nordic countries. In 1947–9 the mean share of the vote was 31.2%, and by 2008–11 it had fallen to just under 25%, a decline of 6.5 percentage points. Starting from a lower base than the Nordics, the gradient of decline was less steep, but nonetheless considerable.

## Germany

Germany has a social democratic tradition strongly linked to the unionised industrial working class, although its reach has sometimes been limited by religious and territorial cleavages; it is historically weak in Bavaria. For much of the post-war period the SPD was hegemonic on the West German left but it has faced challenges from the Greens and then the Left Party (*Die Linke*) formed from former East German Communists and Western leftists. The SPD was one of the first European social democratic parties to adopt the theme of 'modernisation' and abandoned its residual Marxism at the Bad Godesberg conference of 1958. In the early 2000s, under Gerhard Schröder, the SPD at least briefly embraced the 'Third Way' (as *die Neue Mitte*) and introduced labour market and welfare reforms from which previous Christian Democrat-dominated governments had shrunk. The electoral rewards have not been obvious.

If we compare Germany pre- and post-reunification in 1990 with the social democratic heartlands of Sweden and Norway, the performance of the SPD

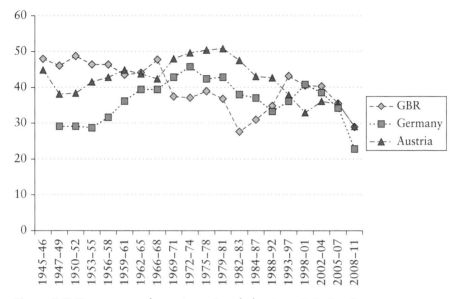

**Figure 3.2** Percentage of vote in national elections, Britain, Germany and Austria

in vote share is on a par with that of the Norwegian Labour Party, with the exception of the period down to the late 1960s. And yet at only six elections out of seventeen has the SPD been able to form a government (excluding the unusual circumstances of a grand coalition with the CDU in 1966 and 2005).

Between 1945 and 1969, when social democratic parties in Sweden and Norway were getting almost half of the popular vote, the German SPD was getting between 29% (in the first federal election in 1949) and 39% (in 1965). The breakthrough came in 1969 with 43%, and the election of the Willy Brandt government in coalition with the Free Democrats (FDP). Between 1969 and 1980, the SPD under Brandt then Helmut Schmidt (1974–87) got 43% and 46% of the vote, and in 1972 the SPD was the largest political faction in the *Bundestag* for the first time since the 1930s (with 230 seats out of 496), although it required a coalition with the Free Democrats to form a government. After the FDP quit the coalition in 1982 to join with CDU/CSU under Helmut Kohl, the SPD lost power in the subsequent 1983 election, when its vote share fell to 38% (losing 25 seats). Under a succession of leaders, the SPD slumped back to just over 30%. Despite its pre-war record in the former eastern Germany, the SPD failed there in the first post-reunification election in 1990, with 33% in the new Germany as a whole, its lowest vote share since 1957. It was not until 1998 that it returned to power (with 41% of the vote), in coalition with the Greens, who won 43 seats. The SPD-Green coalition lasted through the 2002 election, but by 2005 the left and right blocs were evenly matched. Another grand coalition between SPD and CDU was formed, with Angela Merkel as Chancellor. By 2009, the SPD slumped to under 30% of the vote, losing 76 seats, and the CDU/CSU/FDP coalition had an outright majority of seats in the *Bundestag*.

While share of the vote for the SPD in post-war Germany, both pre- and post-reunification, is highly respectable compared with other Northern European democracies, the party always needed a coalition partner, and the FDP allied itself more often with the right than the left (except 1969–82). Only with the emergence of the Greens in the 1980s did a coalition partner emerge for the SPD, since they had ruled out one with the post-communist PDS/*Die Linke* after 1990. Unity on the centre-right has helped to keep the SPD out of power.

### Great Britain

British social democracy has been almost monopolised by a single party, with strong roots in the industrial trade unions and the working class. It has faced few challengers to its left, and right-wing populism has been a minor presence. There is a sporadic challenge from the political centre in the form of the Liberals/Liberal Democrats. The religious cleavage is important only locally, but the territorial cleavage has undermined it in its heartlands in Scotland and, to a lesser extent, Wales. Green challenges have been rather small scale and unthreatening. From the 1950s until the 1980s, there was a series of internal battles, always pitching the Labour 'left' against the 'right', with the former insisting on the 'socialist' label and the latter more happy as 'social democrats'. The latter pushed for removal of Clause IV (public ownership of the means of production) from the party's constitution and for a 'Bad Godesberg' moment. They also produced one of the most important intellectual statements about British social democracy in Anthony Crosland's *The Future of Socialism* (1956), but this was not officially accepted by the party. There was no serious split until a section of the Labour right defected in 1981 to form the Social Democratic Party,[6] presenting a new challenge from the centre. Apart from this, the majoritarian electoral system has helped the party maintain unity and internal discipline. Labour has periodically reviewed its policy portfolio, with moves to the right or left, and at the end of the 1990s it reinvented itself as New Labour. This represented a systematic rejection of its own past, including, apparently, the social democratic as well as the leftist elements, leaving Labour as a kind of social liberal party. Yet even this reinvention, intended to accommodate the new middle classes, did not prevent a steady erosion of support. Croslandite social democrats like Roy Hattersley have argued for the reinstatement of social democracy based on the values of liberty, rights, social justice and equality on the grounds that 'the arguments in favour of social democracy have never been more compelling – or more obvious' (Hattersley and Hickson 2011: 6).

The Labour Party was in power in the immediate post-war period (until 1951), and is credited with introducing the British welfare state, begun by a previous Liberal government, and reinforced by the Second World War. The party was out of power between 1951 and 1964, unlike many European social democratic parties, but successive Conservative governments left much of its welfarist legacy intact until the Thatcherite revolution of 1979.

Labour's share was as good as that for many of its European counterparts (an average of 46% between 1950 and 1970). Its best result, 48.8%, was in 1951, when ironically it lost power because the electoral system gave the Conservatives more seats. Labour's share of the vote fell after 1970, and reached its nadir in 1983 with 28%. It recovered only to 43% in 1997 and successive victories in 2001 and 2005 were achieved on a vote share substantially lower than that attained during its defeats of the 1950s. By 2010 the party was down to just 29% of the vote. The territorial cleavage within the United Kingdom is reflected in the fact that at the 2010 election Labour took 42% of the vote in Scotland, and 36.2% in Wales, but only 28.1% in England (the party does not stand in Northern Ireland).

## Austria

Austrian politics seem remarkably stable, with two main parties. The Socialist Party of Austria (SPÖ) and the centre-right Austrian People's Party (ÖVP) alternated power and were even in grand coalition. This reflected the essentially 'corporatist' form of governance, and consociational democracy. Between them, the two main parties took around 90% of the vote, but after the 1990s this dropped to around two-thirds, largely as a result of the rise of the far right Freedom Party of Austria (FPÖ). The FPÖ doubled its vote share from 5% in 1983, to 10% in 1986, and to 22% in 1995. In the 1999 election it took 27%, with 52 seats, the same number and proportion as the ÖVP. Jorge Haider broke away from the ÖVP in 2005, and was in competition as the far right Association for Austria's Future (BZÖ). In the 2008 election, the far right parties won 29% of the vote, and 55 seats (out of 183). The two historic parties could manage only 55% between them.

There were 'grand coalitions' between the two main parties, the SPÖ and ÖVP, notably in the 1980s and 1990s, until 1999 when the ÖVP and FPÖ formed a coalition (each had 52 seats), which drew sanctions for a time from the EU. By 2002, the ÖVP had its best result (42% and 79 seats) since 1983, but still governed with the far right.

The Greens broke through the 4% barrier which entitled them to seats in 1986, as did the centrist Liberal Forum in 1994 (with 6% and 11 seats), and while the Greens maintained a respectable share of the vote (10% and 20 seats) in 2008, the Liberal Forum fell back below the threshold. The election that year was caused by the ÖVP withdrawing from the grand coalition with the social democrats, and both parties had their worst results in history (26% and 51 seats for ÖVP, and 29% and 57 seats for SPÖ). There is every reason

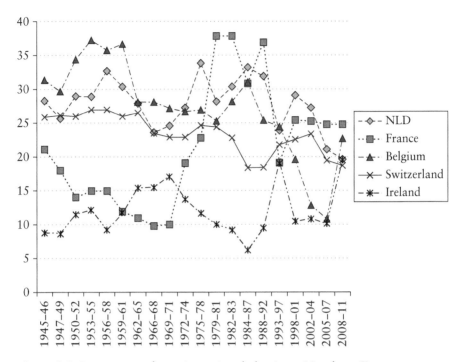

**Figure 3.3** Percentage of vote in national elections, Northern Europe

to think that the Austrian far right will continue to prosper. While older voters tend to be the backbone of the two major parties, by 2008 the Greens were losing their position among young people who were attracted to the far right (around one-third of young people voted for the FPÖ). The FPÖ also does well among the Austrian working class, both skilled (34% to 32%) and unskilled (34% to 21%) (Pelinka 2008).

The voting trends for the five other Northern European countries can be seen in Figure 3.3.

### The Netherlands

Dutch politics were dominated for much of the twentieth century by *verzuiling*, or the social, political and cultural 'pillarisation', reflecting the four pillars of Dutch society: Catholic, Protestant, Liberal and Socialist. Parties representing each 'pillar' were never strong enough in themselves to form a government, especially as proportional representation was introduced as early as 1918. Coalition politics were inevitable. The social democrats became part of the government in the late 1930s, but were required by the electoral system to trade with their partners, notably the KVP. From 1946 to 1958, the so-called Roman-Red coalition of (Catholic) KVP and social democrats ruled the country. The social democrats had to make compromises in order to stay in coalition, and in any case the PvdA was insufficiently large to lead successive governments.

Despite being the biggest party in 1952 and 1956, and again in 1971, 1972 and 1977, the PvdA was out of power until 1994, when, as the largest party, it formed the 'Purple' coalition with the Progressive Liberals (D66) and Conservative Liberals (VVD), thus keeping the Christian Democrats out of government for the first time since 1918. In 2002, the PvdA managed only 15% of the vote and lost office, to be replaced by a right-wing coalition. After the 2006 election a Christian-social coalition of CDA and Christian Union together with the PvdA was formed. The 2010 election was triggered by the resignation of the social democrats, whose attempts to form another Purple coalition failed, and a right-wing coalition formed the government.

In the last decade, one of the three traditional parties has come fourth, and an extreme party of the right (such as Pim Fortuyn's List, or the Party for Freedom) or the left (the Socialist Party won 25 seats in 2006 but 10 fewer in 2010) has taken their place. The Green Left won 11 seats on 7% in 1998, 10 in 2002, 8 in 2003, 7 in 2006, and 10 in 2010. The social democrats received their highest share of the vote (33%) in 1956 and 1986, and managed 34% in 1977, falling back to 20% in 2010. It is fair to say that 'welfare democracy' in the Netherlands was more influenced by confessional politics than secular socialism.

### Belgium

If the Netherlands is complicated because of its confessional politics, then Belgium is even more so. Historically it was marked by a division into Catholic and Lay sub-cultures and electoral blocs. Later this gave way to a regional-linguistic division between Flanders and Wallonia. Belgian politics in the post-war period are easier to comprehend, with three main blocs: the Christian Democrats (with Flemish and Walloon variants), the Socialists, and the Liberals, historically closer to the Socialists, being anti-clericalist until 1961, and again with regional variants. In the immediate post-war election, the Communists, largely because of their war record, picked up 23 seats, and 12% of the vote, but thereafter they were insignificant. The Christian Democrats were the biggest party, and formed a government until a socialist-liberal coalition won in 1954. In that year the socialists won 37% of the vote, their best ever showing, but still less than their Christian Democrat rivals (41%). In 1961, the two parties formed a coalition government until 1965, during which time language laws were passed.

In 1971, the socialists in Flanders and Wallonia formed separate parties, and with the exception of 1974, when together they formed the largest fraction in the Chamber of Representatives with 59 seats out of 212, they are treated as different parties, winning a similar share of the vote in each region (the

French-speaking socialists include Brussels and its environs). Belgian politics are also complicated by the emergence of the *Vlaams Blok/Vlaams Belang*, especially in the early 1990s, on issues of immigration, and greater autonomy/ independence for Flanders. The other emergent political force is the Greens: ECOLO in French-speaking areas, and Agalev (later 'Groen!') in Flemish-speaking ones.

In 1999, a 'purple' coalition was formed out of blue-red parties, notably the Flemish Liberals, the francophone liberals, the two socialist parties, and the two green parties. This coalition fell in 2003, and the greens in particular lost seats. Coalition-forming in the new century became increasingly complex and murky, culminating in 2010 when it took 541 days to form a government headed by a Walloon socialist.

Somewhat like the Netherlands, welfare democracy in Belgium is not the preserve of a straightforwardly 'socialist' party, but the outcome of Christian democracy coupled with liberalism, and reflecting a relatively weak socialist party or parties. In regional elections, the Socialists have lagged in Flanders but kept their lead in Wallonia. Even putting the votes for both socialist parties in Flanders and Wallonia together rarely comes to more than 25%, and given the linguistic/regional fissures which structure Belgian politics, one cannot take this for granted as a bloc.

## France

The French left has historically drawn less on traditions of industrial trade unionism than on older cleavages centred on the legacy of the Revolution, including the division between the Catholic and Lay poles. It has tended to be extremely fractious and only victorious when a candidate has been able to unify its various strands, as in the victory of François Hollande in the 2012 presidential elections. Social democracy has a weak tradition, with even the successive parties that incarnate it (and belong to the Socialist International) rejecting the term and often sticking with obsolete rhetoric about a rupture with capital. For much of the post-war period, there was a significant Communist presence, with the social democratic element only overtaking them in the 1970s after François Mitterrand had united the diverse elements of the moderate left in the *Parti Socialiste*. Since then, splits and divisions have been frequent. Since the 1980s, France has had a significant populist right presence in the form of the National Front, which has progressively extended its reach into the working class in the industrial north and in former socialist strongholds in the south.

French politics are deeply coloured by the war legacy, and the relationships between parliament and presidency. The 'three party alliance' of socialists (SFIO), communists (PCF) and Christian Democrats (MRP) lasted until the 1946 election. When the communist ministers were dismissed from the government it was replaced by a 'third force coalition' comprising the socialists, the Peasants' Party, the MRP and the rally of republican lefts.

The fundamental shift in French politics under de Gaulle's Fifth Republic was designed to remove the instability of French parliamentarism by strengthening the role of the president, abolishing proportional representation in favour of a two-ballot system for parliamentary elections, and reinforcing the government in relation to parliament. This initially gave a built-in advantage to the right and hurt the Communist Party, but put a premium on unity of the left as a condition for success. This could only be done under social democratic leadership, and this was not secured until the 1970s with the foundation of the *Parti Socialiste*.

The breakthrough for the socialists came with Mitterrand's common programme of the left in 1973, when the combined left won 46% of the second round vote. The result was even closer in 1978, when the right-left blocs were virtually identical in share of the vote. In 1981, after Mitterrand's election as president, the left bloc took 57% of the second round votes. The Communists were allotted four seats in government even though it was their worst performance since 1936. By then, the socialists were dominant, with 49% of the second round vote. The victory was not consolidated, however, and the left has never won two consecutive elections, Mitterrand having to 'cohabit' with a conservative government in the final years of both mandates. The tables were turned in 1997, when Lionel Jospin forged the 'plural left' bloc which won a parliamentary majority cohabiting with Jacques Chirac as president. Jospin's humiliation in the 2002 presidential elections, when he was eliminated in the first round by the National Front's Jean-Marie Le Pen, broke the alliance and the left lost again in 2007. The victory of François Hollande in the presidential elections in April 2012 (by 51.6% to incumbent president Nicolas Sarkozy's 48.4%) was followed by victory for the Socialists in National Assembly elections in June, when they gained a parliamentary majority for the first time in ten years.

## Ireland

In Ireland, Labour is historically weak. While the Irish Labour Party received its largest share of the vote in the 2011 election (19%), this is a sign of historic weakness rather than new strength. Politics in Ireland have been dominated since the founding of the state in 1921 by Fianna Fáil and Fine Gael, both centre to centre-right parties. Of the two, Fianna Fáil has been in power for around sixty of the past eighty years, and is akin to a European Christian Democrat party. Fine Gael is more economically 'conservative', but has never governed without the Labour Party, its smaller coalition partner. Such a coalition has been in government in 1948, 1954, 1973, 1981 and 2011. Labour has been in coalition with Fianna Fáil once, in 1992. Labour's worst showing occurred in 1987 (6.4% and only 12 seats in the *Dáil*), and its best in 2011, with 19.4% and 37 seats, when it ousted Fianna Fáil as Ireland's second party.

### Switzerland

And then there is Swiss clockwork predictability: the Social Democratic Party takes a steady 20–25% of the vote in national elections since 1947. Since the 1960s, the Swiss social democrats have had two seats in the governing Federal Council along with the other main parties, the Christian Democrats (CVP) and the Radicals (FDP), and one for the Swiss People's Party, despite, or perhaps because of, the emergence of smaller parties of the right, left and centre from the 1970s.

### Southern Europe

We deal first with the three Southern European states, Spain, Portugal and Greece, which have one feature in common: all suffered from some form of military dictatorship which indelibly marked subsequent democratic politics.

### Spain, Portugal and Greece

These three countries share similar party structures, with the left historically divided between socialists and communists, and the right mobilising smaller fragments of conservative opinion. Broadly speaking, the politics of these countries coalesce into centre-right and centre-left blocs in which the 'socialist' party is the dominant player on the left. Social democracy in these late-industrialising countries does not rest upon a unionised working class, with union density

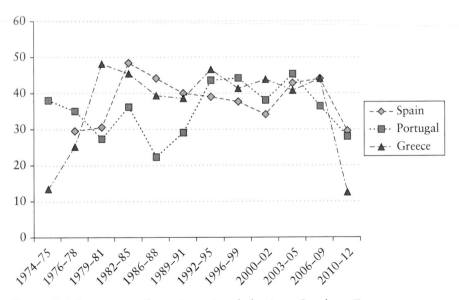

**Figure 3.4** Percentage of vote in national elections, Southern Europe

traditionally low. The role of social democracy has been one of social and economic modernisation, including marketisation of structures inherited from authoritarian regimes. Social democrats have also benefited from a suspicion of the right as not entirely democratic, although by the start of the twenty-first century a democratic right had emerged as a serious contender. There is a religious cleavage as dominant churches have resisted social liberalism and secularisation, and this has tended to play in favour of the left, especially in Spain. Territorial cleavages are important only in Spain, where they have strengthened the socialist presence in the south (especially Andalucia) and weakened it in Catalonia and the Basque Country. The social democratic party (PSOE, *Partido Socialista Obrero Español*) went through a modernising moment at the end of the 1970s under Felipe Gonzalez, who insisted on the abandonment of Marxist baggage and positioned the party in the European social democratic mainstream. After the death of Franco, PSOE emerged as the dominant leftist party in 1977, outpolling the Communist Party by three to one. It eventually formed its first government in 1982 with 48% of the vote and continued in power under Gonzalez until 1996. There followed two periods of centre-right government before the socialists took power again in 2004, and again in 2008. In 2011, PSOE suffered its worst electoral defeat since democracy was restored, with only 29% of the vote (slightly less than it received in 1977).

Portugal followed a similar pattern. The socialist party won the first democratic election in 1975 under Mario Soares, before losing power to a centre-right Democratic Alliance in 1979, and again in 1980. The dominant centre-right party is called the Social Democrats, a historical accident resulting from naming conventions during the post-dictatorship era. In 1983, there was a 'central bloc' coalition between the socialists and social democrats, but the latter won subsequent elections until 1995, when a minority socialist government was formed. This happened again in 1999. In 2002, the gap between the socialists and the social democrats was at its smallest level, and a centre-right coalition was formed. The socialists regained power in 2005, were the biggest party in 2009, but suffered a heavy defeat in 2011, with 28%, to the social democrats in the context of the economic crisis.

There is a similar story for Greece, where the centre-left PASOK was formed out of smaller parties in the mid-1970s after Greece became a Parliamentary Republic in 1975. PASOK won 25% of the vote in 1977, the government being formed by the centre-right New Democracy party. PASOK and New Democracy alternated power for much of the next thirty years, with PASOK forming a government in 1981, 1985, and from 1993 to 2004, and again in 2009, before resigning in the wake of the economic crisis. New Democracy formed governments in 1977, 1989 (including one with PASOK), and between 2004 and 2009.

As the graph indicates, the socialists got around 35% to 45% of the vote in national elections, but in each case the economic crisis led to the fall of the

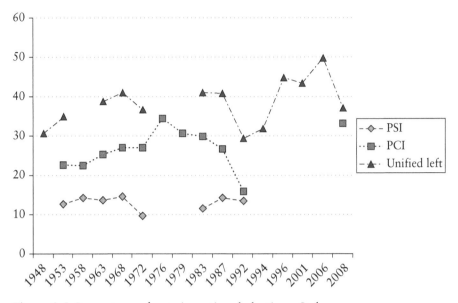

**Figure 3.5** Percentage of vote in national elections, Italy

centre-left government and its replacement by the centre-right in the case of Spain and Portugal, and a 'technocratic' one in the case of Greece. Two national elections were held there in 2012 (in May and June) and proved to be disastrous for PASOK, whose share of the vote fell to 13% and 12% respectively, and who on each occasion took third place behind the radical leftist Syriza party.

## *Italy*

In Italy, the industrial proletariat has been concentrated in the north, while the left has had to reach voters in the south by taking up other challenges, including land reform. The territorial cleavage has been constant and, since the 1980s, increasingly politicised by the *Lega Nord*, which, combining rightist populism with regionalism, has eaten into the constituency of the left.

The electoral trends for the 'left' in Italy can be seen in Figure 3.5.

The socialists (PSI) and communists (PCI) had a common list in 1948, reflecting the cleavage between 'white' (Christian Democrats were the largest faction) and 'red' parties. From then until the 1990s, the left was dominated by the Communist Party, with the Socialist Party (the Italian member of the Socialist International) either reduced to junior partners or playing coalition politics with the centre-right Christian Democrats. The first *centro-sinistra* government was formed in 1963 and, in various guises, the Socialist Party stayed in office for most of the time until 1993, but they were soon sucked into the patronage politics of the *partitocrazia*. There was a brief moment in the 1980s when the subsequently disgraced Bettino Craxi took the prime ministership for what was by Italian standards an extended period, projected a strong image of *decisionismo* and tried to imitate Mitterrand in overtaking the Communist Party, but it was not to be.

The collapse of the 'First Republic' in 1993 as a result of financial scandals (notably, *Tangentopoli*) destroyed both the Socialist Party and the Christian Democrat Party and opened the way to the successive governments of Silvio Berlusconi, who, campaigning as an 'outsider' and new force, was able to restore much of the venality of the old regime as well as their immunity to legal restraint. The left proved largely unable to respond to this mixture of populism, 'videocracy' and money. Centre-left governments were formed under Romano Prodi in 1996 and 2006 which, like their counterparts in Spain, were as much about modernisation and marketisation as about social democracy. The former Communists, together with the progressive wing of the Christian Democrats and other centre-left forces, did manage to coalesce in the Democratic Party (*Partito Democratico* (PD)) in 2007. Yet this force, which covered a large part of the old political spectrum, has been unable to mobilise even the electorate of its old constituent parts. It has been profoundly ambivalent ideologically, unable to accept the label 'social democratic' and lacking a clear identity. It has also left out of the fold substantial sectors of the left, including the rump Communists (*Rifondazione Comunista*) as well as the Greens. Electorally, the left has often done better at local and regional level, when it has presented candidates from 'new politics' backgrounds, who have come up in primary elections without the endorsement of the party establishment.

## Conclusion

The purpose of this chapter has been to survey the changing fortunes of the European social democratic parties. In every case we find a falling share of the popular vote, and few with social democratic governments, even in coalition. The success or otherwise of social democratic parties, however, is not simply measured by share of the vote, but is an outcome of the electoral system (majoritarian democracy or proportional representation) as well as the culture of coalition politics. The German and British social democrats, for example, took a high share of the vote but were, as often as not in the post-war period, out of office because the centre-right parties did better. On the other hand, multi-party coalition politics in the Netherlands and Belgium often gave social democrats a presence in government. Much also depended on competition for votes on the left, notably in Italy and Finland, where communist and post-communist parties competed with social democrats. More generally, the success of political parties, much like football teams, depends on who their opponents are. On the one hand, their historic opponents, the Christian Democrats, are also in electoral trouble, overtaken by neo-liberal and/or parties of the racist right (Duncan 2006). Social democratic parties now find themselves competing with bourgeois, agrarian, liberal and far-right political parties, as well as other 'progressive' forces such as green and leftist parties, allowing the formation of 'progressive' coalitions on the centre-left. Especially where proportional representation operates, one can see the plurality of parties, which in turn produces complex coalitions, while at the sub-state level social democratic parties remain electorally successful.

One might take the sanguine view that social democratic parties are simply at a low point in the electoral cycle, and that sooner or later, as in the 2012 French presidential election, they will bounce back. On the other hand, whatever the grounds for optimism, the financial crisis of post-2008 has not ushered in a new era of social democracy, but the 'strange non-death' of the neo-liberal order (Crouch 2011). In that regard, the post-war history of social democracy does not carry too many positive and straightforward lessons for parties of the left. We have seen in this chapter how relatively unsuccessful electorally social democratic parties have been in Western Europe, at least in their traditional form. There is a strong case for saying that classic social democracy has its own crisis, of politics and ideology, and that is what we are exploring elsewhere in this book.

## Notes

1. This is confined to European parties which belong to the Socialist International. A recent book, *What's Left of the Left* (Cronin et al. 2011), includes the United States as a case in question. Although the Democratic Party might well contain people who think of themselves as 'social democrats', it is not a social democratic party in the West European sense of that term.

2. Because elections occur in different years, they are grouped together in two- or three-year blocks.

3. Possibly because of its small population size (320,000) and the fact that the social democratic party has been far less electorally successful in Iceland, it is not usually included in the Nordic category. We have done so here because of its historical, political and linguistic roots with Scandinavia, and we also include Finland in this group.

4. Switzerland and Austria have been placed in the 'Northern Europe' group because arguably they have sociologically more in common with north than south.

5. We use the term 'Great Britain' rather than 'the United Kingdom' because we are excluding Northern Ireland, with its own party political system, from this analysis.

6. The *soi-disant* Social Democratic Party formed an electoral alliance in 1983 and 1987 with the Liberal Party as the SDP-Liberal Alliance, and finally merged with the Liberals in 1988 as the 'Liberal Democrats'. A small group did not merge and continued to call itself the SDP, surviving until the early 1990s, when it ceased to contest elections.

# THE POSITIONS AND FORTUNES OF SOCIAL DEMOCRATIC PARTIES IN EAST CENTRAL EUROPE

Milada Anna Vachudova

## Introduction

Social democratic parties were active before the onset of communism through-out East Central Europe, some building on the legacy of the Austrian social democrats. After the fall of communism, it was economically right and centre-right movements and parties, many of them rooted in the anti-communist opposition, that won elections in Poland, Hungary and Czechoslovakia, and laid the foundations for liberal democracy and a market economy. Soon after that, however, social democratic parties won elections – in 1993 in Poland, in 1994 in Hungary and in 1998 in the Czech Republic. Their success was based on two broad appeals. The first was economic. Without questioning the transition to a market economy, social democratic parties promised reforms beneficial to the lower and middle classes while using state programmes to cushion the impact of unemployment and inflation. These promises mat-tered, even while in some cases social democratic parties were more vigorous in implementing market-friendly reforms than their 'right-wing' opponents. The second appeal was social and national. Social democratic parties stood for more liberal social values, such as limiting the influence of the Church in Poland, ratcheting down state-sponsored nationalism in Hungary, and embracing the EU in the Czech Republic. Broadly speaking, they attracted 'conservative' left and communist voters – and brought them to accept the market and the West, sometimes promoting tolerance along the way. The picture was quite different, however, in Romania and Bulgaria, where parties using the social democratic label implemented partial economic reforms that enriched the elite and impoverished everyone else, while peddling nationalism to consolidate support, especially among rural voters.

Social democratic parties of all kinds performed poorly in the late 2000s and early 2010s in East Central Europe. For several years there were no social democratic parties in office in the six East Central European states discussed here: Poland, Hungary, the Czech Republic, Slovakia, Bulgaria and Romania. What accounts for the region-wide decline in social democratic support? This chapter considers several complementary hypotheses for this decline. First, this may be simply the swing of the pendulum from left to right, since earlier in the 2000s left-wing parties were in power in most states. Second, social democratic parties were in most states implicated in large-scale corruption that may have severely undermined their popularity. Along with other established parties, social democratic parties may be under threat as voters search for new and 'clean' parties. Third, the economic crisis may have further undermined the appeal of social democratic parties popularly associated with higher levels of spending and lower competitiveness. Fourth, social democratic voters may be attracted to right-wing parties that espouse xenophobic and nationalist views. Meanwhile, centre-right parties may have embraced many popular aspects of the social democratic agenda while promising lower taxes and lower levels of welfare dependency.

### The East Central European case

One interesting question is whether the apparent decline of social democracy in East Central Europe is part and parcel of a broader European trend, or whether it is driven at least partially by factors unique to the post-communist space. What is striking is that it has affected all three types of social democratic parties in the region: those that emerged from communist parties but reformed themselves promptly after (and even before) 1989; those that emerged from communist parties and embraced Western liberal democracy only slowly; and those that have no direct communist lineage.

The rest of this chapter is organised in six parts. The first explores the variation in the positions that social democratic parties in East Central Europe have taken on key economic and socio-cultural issues – and how, as a group, they are distinct from social democratic parties in Western Europe. The second part discusses the different types of social democratic parties in East Central Europe. The third and fourth parts explore, in turn, the 'swing-of-the-pendulum' and the 'discredited-by-corruption' hypotheses for the drop-off in electoral support for social democratic parties in the late 2000s. The fifth and sixth parts consider whether the economic crisis and the appeal of nationalism have also sapped their support – and whether they may now help them win it back.

### Chapel Hill Expert Survey on positions of political parties

What does it mean to be a social democratic party in post-communist Europe? I use the Chapel Hill Expert Survey (CHES) dataset on the positions of national political parties that depicts the structure of political competition in the EU's post-communist candidate states, and sheds some light on how political parties bundle different issues.[1] The dataset provides the position of each party on European integration, as well as its position on two dimensions of political competition: the left/right economic dimension, and the *gal/tan* cultural dimension. 'Gal' stands for green/alternative/libertarian. *Gal* positions are socially liberal, such as support for multiculturalism and for LGBT and women's rights. 'Tan' stands for traditional/authoritarian/nationalist. *Tan* positions are socially conservative, such as promoting a homogenous and patriarchal image of the nation, scapegoating ethnic minorities and emphasising law and order. In the East, this label has tended to underplay the authoritarianism and nationalism of some *tan* parties.

The CHES dataset is built using expert surveys. A team of researchers asks academics and analysts specialising in political parties or European integration to evaluate how party leaders defined the positions of their political parties on European integration, and on three ideological dimensions for European political parties. The time point of reference is either 2002 or 2006, and the analysis is confined to parties with two per cent or more of the vote in the national election of the most proximate prior year.

Figures 4.1 and 4.2 illustrate the axes of competition in the East and the West in 2006. The main axis of domestic party competition in the East is at a ninety-degree angle to that in the West (Evans and Whitefield 1993). This was even more pronounced in the 2002 data. Since then, some parties in the East have shifted away from the left and *tan* quadrant. Parties that combine left and *tan* positions are almost absent from the West. The presence of these parties in the East is a strong legacy of communist party rule, which combined extreme left-wing economic ideology with strong authoritarianism and nationalism. Since 1989, this 'communist magnet' has held parties in the left-*tan* quadrant. Meanwhile, the 'EU magnet' has helped pull parties into the right-*gal* quadrant, since joining the EU required governments to implement free-market reforms and to safeguard the rights and freedoms of all of their citizens, including ethnic and other minorities (Vachudova and Hooghe 2009).

We can see in Figure 4.2 that support for European integration in the East is correlated with party positions that are economically right and socially *gal* (meaning socially liberal). This is less striking than in the 2002 dataset: more pro-European parties now also sit in the left and *gal* quadrant. Opposition to the EU is concentrated in the economically left and socially *tan* quadrant – and hard left and hard *tan* positions are never combined with support for European integration. This is consistent with earlier research that finds that pro-Europeanism in the East is concentrated among parties with right and *gal* positions, and anti-Europeanism among left and *tan* parties (Kopecký and Mudde 2002; Rohrschneider and Whitefield 2005; Taggart and Szczerbiak 2004). This is distinct from the West, where pro-European attitudes are associated with left and

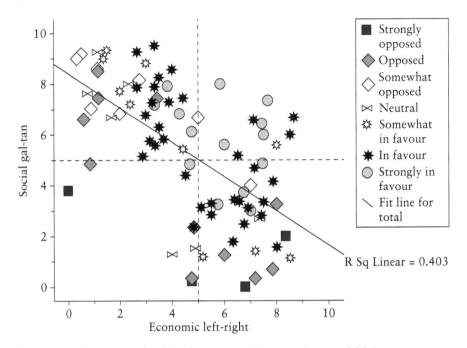

**Figure 4.1** Positions of political parties in Western Europe 2006


*gal* party positions and anti-European attitudes with right and *tan* positions
(Marks et al. 2006).

What does this mean for social democratic parties in the East? We can see
in both the 2002 and the 2006 data that these parties have a greater diversity
of positions than in the West. On the *gal-tan* axis, they fall into three distinct
groups: strongly *gal* (Poland and Hungary), weakly *gal* (the Czech Republic
and Slovakia), and weakly *tan* (Romania and Bulgaria). Figures 4.3 to 4.8
depict party positions for each country in 2006. There is less variation on
European integration: five of the six social democratic parties are 'in favour' or
'strongly in favour' of European integration. Slovakia's is only 'somewhat in
favour'. There is also less variation on the left-right axis: five out of six social
democratic parties are left. Hungary's is mildly right.

We will return to these positions throughout the chapter to understand the
sources of electoral support for the different parties and weigh their prospects
for survival. It is worth observing here that the social democratic parties using
mildly nationalist appeals seem stronger in the early 2010s than those taking
a strong *gal* position.

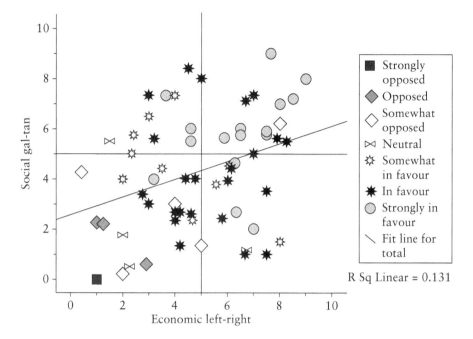

**Figure 4.2** Positions of political parties in post-communist Europe 2006

### Three types of social democratic parties in East Central Europe

Another way of categorising the social democratic parties in these six states is according to (1) their relationship with the communist party that ruled until 1989/1990; and (2) their behaviour during the early years of the democratic transition. Interestingly, this produces the same three groups of states as categorising them according to their position on the socially liberal/conservative *gal-tan* axis, especially if we take into account their likely coalition partners.

#### 1. Early reforming communist successor parties

**Poland:**        Democratic Left Alliance (SLD): main successor party
                   Polish Social Democracy (SDPL): splinter party formed in
                   2004
**Hungary:**       Hungarian Socialist Party (MSzP)

Poland and Hungary's social democratic parties take positions similar to those in the West on the socially liberal/conservative *gal-tan* axis. Poland's SLD is strongly *gal*, as expected, and only weakly left. It is substantially less left on economic matters than one of its two main right-wing competitors, the Law

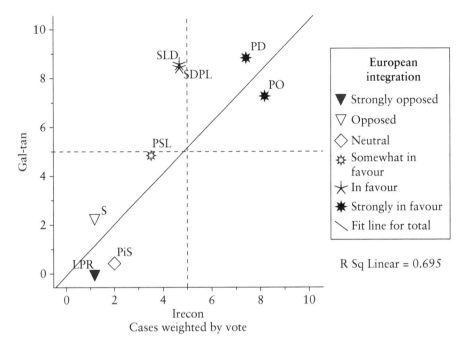

**Figure 4.3** Party positions in Poland in 2006

and Justice Party (PIS). Hungary's MSzP is consistently in the right and *gal* quadrant, having embraced market liberalism more than all of its opponents in Hungary's 'right'. Its *gal* score is lower than Poland's, but it has repeatedly ruled in coalition with a very *gal* party, the SzBSz.

### 2. Historic or new social democratic parties

**Czech Republic:**   Czech Social Democratic Party (CSSD)
**Slovakia:**   Direction (Smer)

The Czech Republic and Slovakia's social democratic parties can be found in the same left and *gal* quadrant as their Western counterparts, but they are only weakly *gal*. Slovakia's party ruled from 2006 to 2010 in a coalition with two small parties, one of which was from the extreme right and takes hard *tan* positions. This earned Slovakia's social democratic party a suspension from the Party of European Socialists.

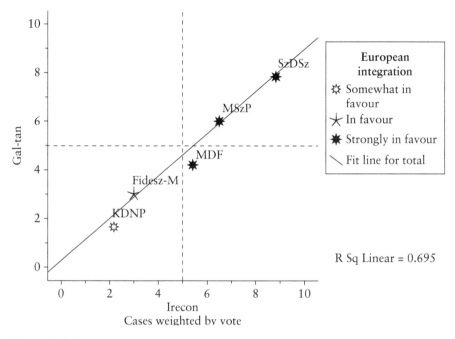

**Figure 4.4** Party positions in Hungary in 2006

### *3. Late reforming communist successor parties*

**Bulgaria:**     Bulgarian Socialist Party (KzB or BSP)
**Romania:**     Social Democratic Party (PSD)

Bulgaria and Romania's social democratic parties are consistently in the left and *tan* quadrant. Both have moved away from the hard left and hard *tan* positions that they held in the early 1990s. However, according to our party experts in 2006, they were still taking authoritarian and nationalist positions, unlike their social democratic counterparts in the East and West.

The distinction between the two types of communist successor parties deserves some elaboration. In Poland and Hungary, the former communist parties faced well-organised competition from parties originating from a strong opposition to communism. They lost the first free elections and engaged in a comprehensive reform of their party agendas, embracing market liberal economics and EU membership. In Bulgaria and Romania, the former communist parties faced a weak and divided opposition, and were able to win the first free elections. They changed their name and shed their communist ideology, but they embraced a mixture of partial economic reform, ethnic nationalism and state capture. Partial reform rewarded well-positioned elites, but

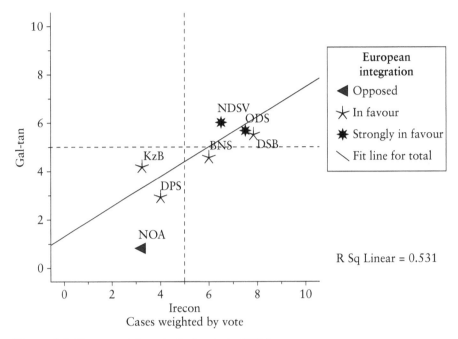

**Figure 4.5** Party positions in Bulgaria in 2006

impoverished the population and prolonged the misery of the economic transition (see Hellman 1998; Ganev 2007; Vachudova 2005). After spending some time in the opposition and preparing their countries for EU membership, these parties did shift their agendas, moving away from nationalism, implementing EU-related state reforms and adopting more market-friendly policies. In recent years, however, it has become clear that they are fighting to keep the practices and spoils of state capture. Their party positions are also quite far from the norm of other social democratic parties, as we saw above.

It may be fair to ask whether there are genuine social democratic parties in the East that seek to implement social democratic ideology in order to bring economic prosperity, social equality and solidarity to their societies. Whatever their recent troubles, the Polish and Hungarian communist successor parties deserve credit for eschewing nationalism and supporting socially liberal policies from the moment of transition. The Polish and Hungarian communist parties helped negotiate the end of communism in their countries and, leading by demonstration, across the region, they set the standard for communist party reform. After losing the first democratic elections, they transformed themselves into social democratic parties and won the second free elections – in Poland in 1993 and in Hungary in 1994 (see Grzymała-Busse 1998 and 2002; Orenstein 1998; Ishiyama 1997; and Bozóki and Ishiyama 2002). The

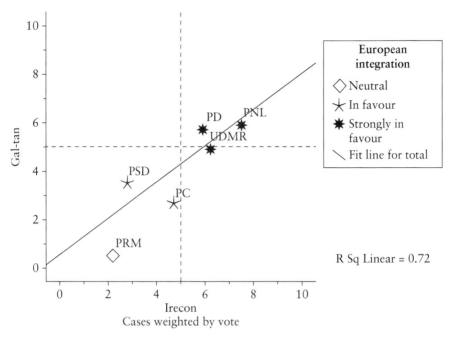

**Figure 4.6** Party positions in Romania in 2006

economic insecurity and hardship of the transition created a strong demand by voters for a political left. The communist successor parties in Poland and Hungary reinforced the liberal democratic equation by providing a moderate, non-nationalist left wing as an alternative for voters weary of economic reform (Vachudova 2005). Unlike the communist successor parties in Romania and Bulgaria, they have successfully reinvented themselves and had few incentives to resort to illiberal methods in order to prevent future political upheavals. The Polish and Hungarian socialist parties did not promise to reverse economic reform; they only promised to restructure the welfare state, shoring up social safety nets for those disaffected by reform (Cook and Orenstein 1999). Once in office, they paid attention to continuing market reforms and impressing international institutions and investors with their constancy as economic liberals. Indeed, in Hungary it was the communist successor party, its hand forced by economic crisis, that implemented sweeping economic liberalisation and fiscal austerity after its election in 1994.

I now turn to some hypotheses to explain the recent electoral misfortunes of social democratic parties in the six ECE states.

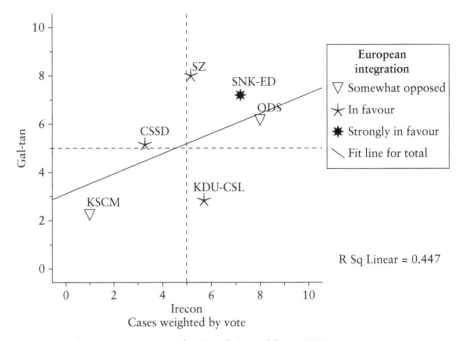

**Figure 4.7** Party positions in the Czech Republic in 2006

### Voting against incumbents?

Since the fall of communism, left-wing and right-wing parties have succeeded one another in power with striking regularity in the East. It is unusual for ruling parties or coalitions to be re-elected. The re-election of a left coalition in Hungary in 2006 and of centre-right coalitions in Slovakia in 2002 and in Poland in 2011 are exceptional. Andrew Roberts calls the inclination of post-communist voters to punish incumbents for whatever has gone wrong on their watch 'hyperaccountability'. Incumbents are held accountable for economic performance, particularly for unemployment. However, economic performance is not reflected in vote gains or losses, but in large or small losses. In other words, the incumbents tend to lose office either way (Roberts 2008).

It is therefore quite possible that the main explanation for social democratic disfavour during the current period is that the pendulum has temporarily swung to the other side. The empirical evidence for this simple explanation is mixed: as of 2012, social democratic parties have been out of office for only one term in Hungary and Bulgaria. In Slovakia, after one term out, they won the elections in 2012 with an outright majority in parliament. In the Czech Republic, Poland and Romania the social democratic parties have not helped form the government for two or three election cycles, but social democratic

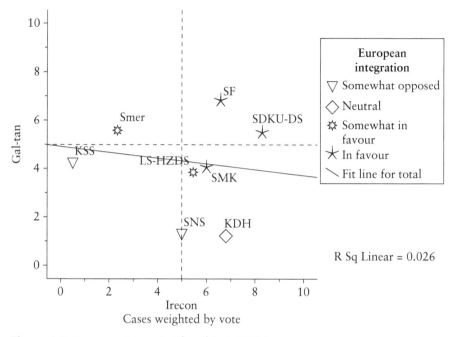

**Figure 4.8** Party positions in Slovakia in 2006

parties currently enjoy substantial popular support in the Czech Republic and Romania, making their participation in the next government likely.

Current levels of popular support for the social democratic parties vary substantially. The Czech Social Democratic Party (CSSD) lost the June 2010 elections with 22% of the vote. But it fared very well in local contests and won an overall majority in the Senate in the October 2010 elections. The Slovak Smer party lost its re-election bid in June 2010, but not because it received fewer votes. In fact, Smer received more votes than in the 2006 elections, climbing from 29% to 35% of the vote. However, support collapsed for Smer's two small coalition partners, the hard *tan* Slovak National Party (SNP) and the Movement for a Democratic Slovakia (HZDS), both of which were widely considered a disaster in government. After the centre-right government elected in 2010 fell due to a coalition dispute over the EU stabilisation fund, early elections in 2012 returned Smer to power with an outright majority.

The Polish and Hungarian social democratic parties, in contrast, are truly down and out. Poland's Democratic Left Alliance (SLD) came to power in 2001 with 41% of the vote, but polled only 11% in 2005. It joined a left/ centre-right electoral alliance that polled only 13% of the vote in 2007 and 8% in 2011. Its dramatic drop in popularity after 2001 was caused by corruption scandals, leadership splits and incompetence, creating 'the image of a corrupt party intent only on guaranteeing benefits for its members and devoid of any leftist orientation' (Materska-Sosnowska 2010: 218).

The Hungarian Socialist Party has met a similar fate. After it won re-election in 2006, its popularity plummeted when the then prime minister Ferenc Gyurcsany was caught on tape saying 'I almost died when for a year and a half we had to pretend we were governing. Instead, we lied morning, evening and night.' This declaration was accompanied by severe economic problems as the global financial crisis hit Hungary hard. The strongly *tan* (but economically left) right-wing party Fidesz won the 2010 elections and secured two-thirds of the seats in parliament. The MSzP polled only 19%. According to the website <www.politics.hu>, in February 2011 the MSzP received only about 11% support in a public opinion poll of all eligible voters, while Fidesz received 37%. In May 2012 the support for MSzP was about the same at 12%, while Fidesz had dropped to 16%: support for Fidesz had plummeted, but this did not boost the MSzP's popularity; some 54% of voters polled were undecided (Balogh 2012).

The Bulgarian Socialist Party (BSP) is also deeply out of favour. It was the dominant member of a strong coalition government that took office in 2005 after its electoral coalition, 'the Coalition for Bulgaria' (or KzB), polled 31%. However, the BSP-led government became deeply unpopular due to expanding corruption and the freezing of EU funds due to mismanagement and theft (Spendzharova and Vachudova 2012). The KzB polled just 18% in 2009 (receiving only 36 seats in the 240-seat parliament), losing spectacularly to a new anti-corruption party called GERB.

The Romanian Social Democratic Party (PSD) was similarly sidelined in the 2004 elections after four years in office marked by high levels of corruption and mismanagement. Traian Basescu from the Liberal Democrat Party (PDL) won the presidency in 2004 on a vehement anti-corruption platform. His party helped form the various coalition governments that have ruled since the 2004 and 2008 elections. The PSD, for its part, worked with other parties to impeach Basescu for his anti-corruption efforts: the impeachment sailed through parliament in 2007 but failed in a referendum (see Spendzharova and Vachudova 2012). The PSD, however, surged ahead in opinion polls in 2012 and looks well positioned to govern again soon. Voters are tired of the austerity programme that has won Romania support from the IMF during the economic crisis. While endemic corruption by the PSD is well known, voters may believe that other Romanian parties are similarly if not equally corrupt.

### Voting against the crooks?

The recent electoral defeats of social democratic parties strongly suggest that corruption scandals have helped determine their fate. They are not alone in this: all ruling parties in the six ECE states have probably been embroiled in at least one corruption scandal over the last twenty years of democratic politics.[2] The collapse of communism created spectacular opportunities for corruption by creating a vacuum that necessitated rewriting the rules of the economy and the state. Those in power in the early years could write those rules to benefit themselves in many ways, including privatisation, asset stripping and siphoning state funds (Hellman 1998). Even when adequate legislation was in place, actors could rely on political connections, dysfunctional state institutions and corrupt judiciaries to perpetuate corrupt practices and prevent prosecution. The states that experienced all-out capture by corrupt networks after 1989, such as Bulgaria and Romania, are the ones that continue to have the greatest problems with endemic, high-level corruption today (Spendzharova and Vachudova 2012).

It is difficult to measure whether social democratic parties are more corrupt than other parties in post-communist party systems. There are certainly strong theoretical reasons to expect at least some link between communist successor parties and rent-seeking connected to the economic transition. Elites in these parties were well positioned to take control of important segments of the economy through corrupt privatisation and other preferential practices after 1989. This was especially true if the communists turned social democrats were able to win the first elections and preside over the first years of reform in a context of weak political competition. Communist successor parties also had more dense party organisation, including regional and local members who could be well placed to influence local economic decisions and to demand pay-offs from the central government. And, of course, the habits of appropriating resources at will from the state and the economy may be hard to break.

Poland and Hungary are mixed cases for the corruption hypothesis: the popularity of the Polish and Hungarian social democratic parties plummeted during their time in office due to a variety of scandals and the appearance of incompetent government. This does not mean that they are necessarily more corrupt than their competitors, which might be impossible to measure. In the 2005 elections in Poland and the 2010 elections in Hungary that ousted the social democratic parties from government, the *tan* and left PIS party in Poland and the *tan* and left Fidesz party in Hungary both campaigned and won based on election manifestos dominated by vociferous anti-corruption platforms. Both parties campaigned on finally ridding the country of the corrupt communist forces. Whether these parties' corruption scandals were really linked to the communist past, however, is a difficult question that would require field research to answer. What is striking is that both PIS and Fidesz are solidly left on the economic left-right scale. In other words, these parties campaigned on less corrupt government – and not on less government involvement in the economy.

Bulgaria and Romania are easier cases to consider in reference to the corruption hypothesis. Unlike Poland and Hungary, they present clear cases of the continuation of state capture by networks of elites connected to the communist successor party. The rule of the BSP in Bulgaria from 2005 to 2009 has been widely described as intensifying corruption in all levels of Bulgaria's state administration. The rule of the PSD in Romania from 2000 to 2004 did the same, although, as is characteristic of Romania, the details are much more murky. The new, centre-right party GERB of Boyko Borissov came to power in 2009 in Bulgaria with a campaign that was almost entirely about fighting corruption. Similarly, in Romania, Traian Basescu from the Liberal Democrat Party (PDL) won the presidency in 2004 on a vehement anti-corruption platform.

The Czech Republic and Slovakia are the hardest cases to classify in relation to the corruption hypothesis. In the Czech Republic the social democratic party (CSSD) has lost two successive elections in 2002 and 2006. What is unusual is that the party polled substantially fewer votes in 2006 than in 2002, dropping from 32% to 22% of the vote. This would tend to contradict the simple 'pendulum' argument in this case, as we would expect to see the party recover its support in 2006. Instead, support for both the social democratic party and the main right-wing party, the Civic Democrats (ODS), declined quite dramatically as voters shifted to two new parties. As Sean Hanley argues, this suggests that some of the voting was not just anti-incumbent, but also against established parties that have been tainted by years of corruption scandals. The new parties are both centre-right, and campaigned heavily as 'new' parties, untainted by the corruption that is endemic in Czech politics (Hanley 2010).

In Slovakia, too, some voters abandoned the social democratic party Smer in 2010 due to concerns about corruption. Smer's four years in power were punctuated by scandals involving various government ministers – often, but not always, from Smer's two small coalition partners. Smer presented itself as an anti-corruption party during the election campaign of 2006, but by 2010 it was weighed down by the corruption scandals that ultimately removed the HZDS from parliament and squeezed the SNP down to one seat. Kevin Deegan-Krause has dissected the 2010 Slovak election results, and shows that while Smer gained voters from its two discredited coalition partners, it also lost voters to the centre-right parties (Deegan-Krause 2010). These voters left Smer because of corruption concerns, and poll evidence suggests that at least some of them went to a new libertarian right party, Freedom and Solidarity (SAS). Two years later, however, Smer won in the 2012 elections – and the so-called 'Gorilla' scandal played a role, implicating the established centre-right parties more than the social democrats (see Šimecka 2012a).

While we cannot take on the expansive literature on the determinants of electoral volatility in post-communist countries here, we can see that the strong anti-corruption agenda of a substantial portion of the voters helps push them toward new parties (Deegan-Krause and Haughton 2009). Recent studies also show that press coverage of corruption in post-communist countries is much greater than in the 1990s, and also greater than in other regions with comparable or higher levels of corruption (Grigorescu 2006; see also Ceka 2012). In the most recent elections, new and relatively new parties have gained sizeable vote shares in the Czech Republic, Hungary, Slovakia and Bulgaria. As elections continue, voters frequently search for new alternatives instead of voting for established parties (Pop-Eleches 2010). Whether this search for new and 'clean' parties is undermining established social democratic parties more than their established competitors requires further study. But social democratic parties that are direct descendants of the old communist parties in the region may have an especially difficult task cleaning up their image. We see in Poland, for example, that while the pendulum started to swing away from right-wing parties in the October 2011 elections, voters did not return to the SLD but instead supported a brand-new party called 'Palikot's Movement' (RP). This anti-clerical, anti-corruption, libertarian, centrist party has a vague economic programme but is making a play for dominating the left. It emerged just a few months before the elections that made it the third largest party in the Polish parliament (see Stanley 2012).

### The economic crisis: voting against the Greek model or against the IMF?

There has been much speculation about the relationship between social democratic policies and increased competition stemming from rising globalisation. Rothstein and Steinmo frame the paradox in Chapter 6 of this volume: 'Why are social democratic parties doing so badly in recent elections when the countries that have been most influenced by the social democratic model of society are, according to available measures, doing so well?' They add that the countries with a social democratic type of politics (Denmark, Finland, the Netherlands, Norway, Sweden, Austria) with higher spending on social services and social insurance systems have their public finances in good order. The trade-offs put forward by neo-liberalism thus turn out to be false: we do not need to choose between 'fairness' and 'effectiveness', and large public expenditures are not necessarily damaging to the economy. Iversen and Stephens similarly find that social democratic social policies bring investment in human capital that gives countries a competitive advantage, especially in the globalised knowledge economy (2008).

Yet the link between the global financial crisis and the political disfavour of social democratic parties is not a straightforward one in East Central Europe. Mitchell Orenstein has gathered data showing a great variation in the impact of the crisis, with Poland never even entering into recession. According to his 'aggregate crisis index' the best performers in the region are, in order, Poland (2), the Czech Republic (5) and Slovakia (5). The worst performers are Hungary (7), Romania (8) and Bulgaria (8) (Orenstein 2011).

The three countries that have performed well – Poland, the Czech Republic and Slovakia – all elected governments that are economically right (and also socially *gal*) soon after the crisis hit. An interesting hypothesis is that the economic crisis has strengthened the hand of these parties because they use the spectre of Greece's financial meltdown to equate social democratic policies with disastrous spending and borrowing. Once in power, these right-wing parties use the financial crisis to push through austerity measures and cut state spending on welfare, education and active labour market policies. The Czech Republic and Slovakia arguably have a lot to lose: in 2009 they were ranked as having the fourth and fifth lowest levels of social inequality in the world (after Denmark, Japan and Sweden).

This hypothesis is supported by the behaviour of the ruling economically right parties in the Czech Republic and Slovakia. Even though Czech public finances were in a reasonably good position, the right-wing parties have argued the opposite: the economic crisis requires putting in place tough austerity measures.[3] Beyond the spectre of Greece, some right-wing parties in the Czech Republic are adept at linking social policy with 'socialism' and communist practices in public debate. This discourse makes it much more difficult to weigh the relative merits of various social policies based on empirical outcomes across Europe today (see Hanley 2004 and 2007).

Invoking the Greek crisis after an austerity budget was passed by the Slovak parliament in December 2010, the Finance Minister Ivan Mikloš declared that the budget was very good news for Slovakia 'because over the past years, Slovakia had taken a very dangerous path, a path walked by Hungary and Greece. Now this dangerous path has ended' (quoted in Balogová 2010). The leader of Slovakia's social democratic Smer party Robert Fico argued instead that the winners from the budget are banks and monopolies while the losers are all other groups in Slovakia, especially the middle class. Rhetoric aside, this Slovak budget was quite modest and also attracted substantial neo-liberal criticism in Slovakia because it raised taxes in order to protect spending on social services. In other words, the centre-right was not attacking popular aspects of the welfare state.

The relationship between Hungary's ruling Fidesz party and the economic crisis is complicated. Fidesz is officially 'right wing' and located in *tan*, engaging in authoritarian and nationalist policies since taking office in 2010, but it has embraced a steadily more left position on economic policy. After the collapse of Hungary's state finances, the previous social democratic government implemented a series of IMF-supervised austerity packages. Fidesz has instead rebuffed the IMF, lowered taxes and increased spending to cater to its economically left voters. In other words, in Hungary the social democratic party is under attack for bowing to the neo-liberal strictures of the 'foreign' IMF – the exact opposite of the situation of the social democratic parties in the Czech Republic and Slovakia. Interestingly, to pay for all of this, the Fidesz government has levied 'crisis' taxes on banks, telecoms and retail and financial services dominated by foreign businesses – and then moved on to new taxes on various kinds of consumption. It has also forced Hungarians to transfer private pension savings back into the public sector (Buckley et al. 2011). The fate of opposition parties, including the social democrats, at the next elections (in 2014) will hinge in large part on how this 'improvisation' pans out for the Hungarian economy (which looked disastrous in 2012) – and, as discussed below, whether Hungarians will tire of Fidesz's concentration of power, sweeping corruption and intense Hungarian nationalism. The trend in 2012, sadly, was growing disillusionment and xenophobia – and an exodus of the young.

Overall, as the economic crisis drags on and austerity becomes unpopular, voters are inclined to punish incumbents. Following in the path of the social democratic party Smer in Slovakia, the social democrats in the Czech Republic and Romania are well positioned to benefit from this. In Bulgaria, Hungary and Poland, however, voters may look to new centrist parties instead of the old social democratic ones.

### Voting for nationalism?

A final hypothesis is that social democratic parties are losing support as the combination of economically left and socially *gal* positions becomes less attractive to voters. On the one hand, social democratic parties are losing middle-class and professional voters to right and *gal* parties. Centre-right parties offer positions that embrace individual rights, innovation and entrepreneurship without suggesting any fundamental unravelling of the welfare state. They may score easy points by campaigning against benefits for the undeserving and against government waste. As discussed above, they may also brand themselves as more skilled in managing the economy, especially in the midst of the economic crisis.

On the other hand, social democratic parties are losing working-class voters to left and *tan* parties. These parties may be known as 'right wing', but they combine leftist appeals for economic redistribution with strong authoritarian and nationalist positions. The details vary from country to country, but the nationalist appeals include the subversion of the national culture by foreigners and the EU, the protection of co-ethnics abroad, hostility toward ethnic minorities, and scaremongering about the consequences of immigration.

The Polish social democratic party, the SLD, appears to have suffered the most from these twin desertions. In the 1990s it was supported by workers and also by socially liberal professionals who wished to vote against the socially conservative positions of Poland's right-wing parties and the immodest role they afforded the Catholic Church in Polish politics. In the 2005 and 2007 elections, however, many working-class voters supported the left and *tan* 'right wing' Law and Justice Party (PIS) (see Szczerbiak 2007). For their part, professionals and young people supported the Civic Platform (PO), a right and *gal* party. Together the PO and the PIS enjoyed the support of up to 70% of the electorate by the end of the 2000s. On the eve of the October 2011 elections, the new party 'Palikot's Movement' (RP) emerged as a strongly anti-clerical, liberal party that quickly attracted the support of strongly *gal* voters, mainly professionals and young people. It has been much more outspoken (in, at times, outlandish ways) about limiting the role of the Catholic Church and about conferring equal rights to the LGBT community than the SLD. For the moment, then, the SLD has lost its nationalist working-class voters to the PIS, its entrepreneurial voters to the PO, and its socially progressive voters to RP. Perhaps the SLD can regain some of these constituencies over time. While the RP is casting itself as a social democratic party, its economic agenda so far has been vague and the commitment of the party leadership to social democratic values is questionable (Stanley 2012).

The Hungarian social democratic party, the MSzP, also suffered massive desertions – but almost all of the voters went to socially conservative/nationalist parties, including presumably some professionals. The MSzP lost voters to two right-wing parties in the 2010 elections that are both socially *tan* but economically left. Even more striking, the extreme right party 'Movement for a Better Hungary' (Jobbik) obtained 17% of the vote, compared to only 2% in 2006. This is a hard left party with strong anti-capitalist overtones. It is also a hard *tan* party peddling extreme Hungarian nationalism.[4] Together, Fidesz and Jobbik received some 70% of the vote, raising questions about how so many Hungarians could vote for such strongly nationalist parties. The Hungarian social democrats have a better chance at revival than the Polish ones: currently they are one of only two moderately right and moderately *gal* alternatives to Fidesz's *tan* policies that have been openly described as authoritarian in the European media. Moreover, given its economically left promises and Hungary's current fiscal condition, the Fidesz government is bound to disappoint. The MSzP could be positioned when the pendulum swings back – unless a new green, liberal party, 'Politics Can Be Different' (LMP), expands its support.

In the Czech Republic the social democratic party appears well positioned for the next elections when voters will have tired of the austerity message. Like Smer in Slovakia, it is likely to rely on left but also mildly *tan* appeals. Also like Smer, it will face challenges from new, centrist parties with 'clean hands' – but these could become convenient coalition partners. The Czech social democrats are stymied by an unusable hard left and *tan* unreformed communist party that polls well but cannot be invited into a coalition.

Smer has used mild nationalism effectively to boost its popularity. As Deegan-Krause argues, Smer's coalition with the HZDS and the SNP before

2010 was 'anti-market left' and 'Slovak national' (2010). Smer's former coalition partners organised a significant part of their agenda around anti-Hungarian and Slovak nationalist appeals. Smer is also a nationalist party, but its appeals are more diffuse and its party programme more diversified. It appears that most SNP and HZDS voters moved to Smer, which would share their economically left views and offer sufficient nationalism. Smer, however, is an eclectic party including cultural liberals, and it is unclear whether it will be able to hold on to both left-*gal* and left-*tan* voters (see Deegan-Krause and Haughton 2012 and Šimecka 2012b). Still, it is an accomplishment for Smer to have removed the HZDS and the SNP from parliament – first by revealing their incompetence after Smer included them in a ruling coalition, and then by providing a moderate alternative in future elections.

## Conclusion

In this chapter I have explored four hypotheses that try to explain why social democratic parties found themselves out of power and, in some cases, deeply out of favour in six East Central European states in the late 2000s and early 2010s. We see that social democratic parties in the six ECE countries differ in quite striking ways in how they position themselves on the dimension that we have labelled *gal-tan*. What I have not explored, however, is whether the electorate itself is becoming more or less supportive of social democratic policies such as the social safety net and spending on education and active labour market policies. I now turn briefly to the evidence supporting these four hypotheses.

First, the simple 'pendulum' hypothesis finds only weak support since five out of the six social democratic parties have already been – or are likely to be – out of government for two or more election cycles. Second, the 'voting against the Greeks' hypothesis, suggesting that the financial crisis has strengthened the hand of right parties, finds some support in the Czech Republic, Slovakia and Poland. But this seems quite limited in time – and as the crisis wears on and austerity budgets take their toll, the social democrats in Slovakia have already won power and the ones in the Czech Republic and Romania are likely to do so soon largely due to the unpopularity of recent spending cuts.

Third, the 'voting against corruption' hypothesis finds broad support: voters in all six countries punished social democratic parties for corruption scandals during their terms in office. In most countries, the search by voters for parties with 'clean hands' has propelled several new parties into the parliament. Social democratic parties appear to be suffering more from this than their established competitors. Whether social democratic parties that are direct descendants of communist parties are more corrupt than their competitors is unknown for Poland and Hungary – but rather obvious for Bulgaria and Romania. Nevertheless, the Polish and Hungarian social democratic parties face greater challenges in cleaning up their image after a corruption scandal since it is so easy to tarnish them with the communist label.

Fourth, the 'voting for nationalists' hypothesis also finds strong support. The Polish and Hungarian social democratic parties that have adopted the most socially liberal or *gal* positions are also the least popular. In both cases, working-class voters have turned to parties that are economically left but socially conservative or *gal*. Meanwhile, both parties have lost many of their professional voters as well. In Poland, these voters went first to PO, a centre-right and *gal* party that resembles the West European centre-right, and then shifted to 'Palikot's Movement', which is fiercely *gal* but economically unde-fined. In Hungary, some have gone to a left and *tan* party, and may swing back either to the social democratic party or to the small liberal or the small green party. This same dynamic has played itself out in the Czech Republic and in Slovakia, except that these two social democratic parties embrace some nation-alist positions that perhaps allow them to hold on to more of their traditional voters. In elections in 2012, Slovakia's Smer won 44% of the vote, and this earned it a majority in parliament. It benefited from all four factors explored in this paper. Voters wanted to vote against the incumbents, against the crooks, against austerity and for a sort of dignified Slovak nationalism.

This brings us to an interesting question: is Eastern Europe still becoming more like the West? It appeared in the early 2000s that gradually many parties were moving out of the left and *tan* quadrant – the quadrant that, in the West, has been completely empty. Today, however, it looks like major parties in Poland, Hungary, Bulgaria and Romania have settled there permanently. In the case of Bulgaria and Romania, these major parties *are* the social demo-cratic ones – which prompts the question as to whether they should actually be considered socially democratic. In Poland and Hungary, the social democratic parties are losing voters to left and *tan* parties. In the Czech Republic and Slovakia successful social democratic parties are flirting with *tan* positions to shore up their support.

This situation mirrors the debate in the West about the rise of parties that offer economically left but socially conservative, anti-immigration platforms, and how social democratic parties should respond. It also opens up the ques-tions of whether and how much Western European party systems are instead becoming more like the East. Some Western European parties were already on the cusp of moving into the left and *tan* quadrant in the 2006 dataset, and the 2010 dataset is likely to see further movement. And as we see across the Eastern cases, coalition partners are important: are left-*gal* social democratic parties willing to form coalitions with left-*tan* conservative parties? Finally, the threat from new parties is as strong in East Central Europe as it is in the West – only in the East the new parties are less likely to be green and more likely to win votes just for being 'clean'.

## Notes

1. Many thanks to Erica Edwards for constructing the figures in this paper, and to the entire CHES team. For post-communist Europe, the dataset for 2006 includes Poland, Hungary, the Czech Republic, Estonia, Lithuania, Latvia, Slovakia, Slovenia, Bulgaria and Romania. The dataset for 2002 includes all of the same countries except Estonia. Dataset and codebook are available from <http://www.unc.edu/~hooghe> (last accessed 21 February 2013).

2. Since electorates in post-communist states tend to vote out incumbents even if they have a good economic record, this may heighten the incentives to engage in corruption. As Andrew Roberts puts it, 'if incumbents know they will lose, then they may decide to enrich themselves when in power rather than produce good policies' (2008: 545).

3. I am indebted to Jacques Rupnik for this point, and for his careful description of how it plays out in Czech politics today. See <http://www.centrum-cesta.cz> (last accessed 21 February 2013) for transcripts of recent debates on social policy.

4. According to one observer it has 'switched from anti-Semitism to anti-Gypsy rhetoric, which resonates with the electorate on both right and left and is more acceptable in mainstream political discourse' (Dujisin 2010).

# RETHINKING PUBLIC EXPENDITURE FROM A SOCIAL DEMOCRATIC PERSPECTIVE

David Heald[1]

## Introduction

There are waves of public mood about public expenditure; it seems to be in fashion or strongly out of fashion. This contributes to alternating periods of plenty and famine in some countries, of which the United Kingdom provides a striking example. There is not only strong polarisation in periods of famine but also inadequate scrutiny during periods of plenty. Contemporary UK commentary, for example, exhibits conflicting narratives:

> Labour's fiscal policy [1997–2010] amounted to little more than bribes to cultivate a client state of public sector employees and the feckless underclass. (Mowbray 2012)

> Over a generation, social security has been rebranded as welfare, an undeserved gift rather than a right. (Clark 2012)

> I think there's a very deliberate policy across all of the public sector to roll back the achievements that have been made in this country [United Kingdom] since the second world war – including the [National Health Service] – and that financial austerity is being used to pursue an agenda aimed at dismantling the state. (Gabriel Scally, quoted in Campbell 2012)

These quotations – quite mildly expressed compared to what can be found in the media and on the Web – contextualise this analysis of public expenditure from a social democratic perspective.

Social democracy presupposes a degree of confidence in the competence, legitimacy and accountability of state institutions. It requires a sense of common purpose and of belonging and inclusiveness, which together underpin social solidarity. Yet social democracy is also about 'halfway houses', sometimes uneasy compromises between reliance on 'the market' and on 'the state', whose necessary periodic refurbishment can be problematic. The foundations of social democracy are therefore vulnerable to attack from multiple directions (as in the slogans 'shrink the state' or 'take public ownership of all the means of production'). It is difficult to write stirring rhetoric about the crafted or accidental compromises that social democratic policy stances sometimes involve. Faced with contemporary free-market radicalism, social democracy can appear deeply conservative in defence of inherited social settlements.

This chapter does not argue from first principles against attacks on public expenditure levels in OECD countries as wasteful and counterproductive (Schuknecht and Tanzi 2000). Rather, it covers ideology, public policy and technical issues of public expenditure definition and management. A degree of sympathy towards the use of public expenditure for economic, political and social objectives is assumed.

An approximation is that socialist parties have emphasised public ownership of the means of production whereas social democratic parties have emphasised high levels of public expenditure – with or without high public ownership of industry and infrastructure (Crouch 1981). As historically with public ownership, there are substantial country differences in the importance that political parties regarding themselves as social democratic attach to the size and scope of public expenditure. However, within a particular country at a particular date, such parties tend to prefer larger public expenditure/GDP ratios than do parties to their right.

Whereas privatisations have greatly reduced the size of public enterprise sectors, the debate on high public expenditure (often attacked as 'big government') is both continuing and more ambiguous. A social democratic position on public expenditure can be held by parties with other names or not held by parties with a social democratic label. Conservative and Christian Democratic governments have in the past expanded public services and the populist extreme right has a welfare tradition (as shown in the programme of the *Front National* in the 2012 French elections). Such breadth of political support for public expenditure suggests that there are complicated political, social, demographic and economic factors at work.

Public expenditure/GDP ratios might be taken as a preliminary indicator of big government. However, 'big' and 'strong' are not synonyms: indeed, public expenditure could be high in countries with weak governments unable to control interest group pressures to spend. The power of government to command and its relationship to society depends on many factors other than public expenditure ratios; Gamble (1988) drew attention to the link between the 'free economy and the strong state', the latter making the former possible.

Public expenditure is not the only instrument of public intervention, making valid cross-country comparisons more difficult than they would seem at first sight. Political argument may revolve around whether the public expenditure/ GDP ratio should be 20% or 30%, rather than 40% or 50%. However, two caveats are required. First, there is a profound distinction between proposals that substitute instruments (e.g. compulsory private healthcare insurance instead of public provision) and those under which government sheds responsibility on to individuals/households/families. Social democratic objectives might be achieved through the use of surrogates for public expenditure that do not require tax financing. Regulatory powers impose costs on private actors in relation to disability, historic buildings and health and safety. However, surrogates are often characterised by low transparency and unmonitored efficiency costs and equity impacts, especially when used to circumvent controls on recorded public expenditure (Heald 2012). Second, there is the issue of whether cash benefits are taxed, as this affects the interpretation of the public expenditure/GDP ratios (Adema et al. 2011). There are wide cross-country variations in the competence of public institutions, owing much to culture and traditions, and this may influence the choice of policy instruments.

Rethinking or rejustifying public expenditure, its objectives and mechanisms, is required from a social democratic perspective. Except where explicitly stated, this chapter focuses on ideas and policy priorities, not on party agendas and programmes. The next section discusses changes in the policy environment. Section three addresses the objectives of public expenditure through Musgrave's (1959) trilogy of allocation, distribution and stabilisation. Section four considers the neglect of tax policy-making, which has made public expenditure more difficult to finance and hence to defend. Section five responds to the identified challenges. Many of the examples used to illustrate particular points relate to the United Kingdom, reflecting the author's zone of confident knowledge. Albeit with different specificities, the issues discussed have general applicability.

### Changes in the policy environment

From 1945 to circa 1973, most democratic political parties operated within the context of the Keynesian social democratic state (Heald 1983), albeit with some marked country variations. Subsequently the monetarist critique of macro-economic policy, which de-legitimised stabilisation policy, evolved into a more general free-market critique of big government, which has been labelled as 'neo-liberalism'.[2] In relation to public expenditure, neo-liberalism can imply a preference for small government or for making extensive use of market-like mechanisms to improve the efficiency of government. Under the 1997–2010 UK Labour Government, neo-liberal styles such as outsourcing and Public-Private Partnerships (PPP) were accompanied by large expansions in public expenditure.[3]

Although the 1970s can reasonably be portrayed as a period during which governments lost control of public expenditure totals, the background to the 2010s is generally different. The private sector global financial crisis of 2008 translated into a public sector fiscal crisis, most obviously seen in relation to eurozone countries but also seen in the austerity programme of the 2010 Conservative-Liberal Democrat UK Coalition. The genuine requirement for medium-term fiscal retrenchment in response to GDP levels far below trend projections, and to the doubling of the net debt/GDP ratio, has been seized upon as a window of opportunity for a transformation of the role of the state, imposing policies that would otherwise have been politically inconceivable. This 'do not waste a crisis' tactic has significant implications for debate in a policy environment that differs drastically from 1945 to 1973.

First, social democratic compromises between the state and market were originally within national economies much less integrated into the global economy than is the case today. To varying extents, these compromises have been undermined by globalisation even where not unpicked by government policy. There can be two reactions within social democratic parties: one that accommodates change while offering generous protection; and one that resists economic change. Post reunification, Germany became contentiously labelled in the 1990s as the 'sick man of Europe'. Subsequently, the 1998–2005 SPD-Green Coalition of Chancellor Gerhard Schröder has been credited with labour market and pension reforms that were undertaken in a reasonably consensual way, without destroying the 'national bargain'. In contrast, Greece illustrates that resisting change is catastrophic in the medium term. Nevertheless, negotiating change while maintaining social consensus and trust in public authority is problematic for many countries.

Second, demography has changed dramatically in ways that threaten the social democratic consensus even in the absence of explicit policy attacks. Life expectancies far beyond previous expectations have significant expenditure consequences, as shown by the work of the European Council Economic Policy Committee's Working Group on Ageing Populations and Sustainability (see <http://europa.eu/epc/working_groups/ageing_en.htm> (last accessed 22 February 2013)). The effects on healthcare and pension costs alone threaten fiscal sustainability (Fiscal Affairs Department 2011). Such issues are difficult for democratic politicians to deal with, as ageing groups have greater attachment to political processes through voice and electoral turnout. Equally fundamental, the heterogeneity of European populations has increased dramatically, resulting from migration from the Third World and from the operation of the EU internal labour market. These developments have created pressures in labour and housing markets, limiting wage growth and pushing up house prices and rents.

The earlier safety valve of upward social mobility is less available, reflecting the fact that social mobility in the 1945–73 period was mostly one way as a result of the expanding pool of managerial and professional jobs. In the second decade of the twenty-first century, downward social mobility is more of a threat and affluent parents have both greater capability and greater inclination to protect their children. Examples include: housing moves into the catchment areas of prestigious state schools or claims to false addresses; gaming means tests; arbitraging nationality in response to differential university fees; tactical use of private facilities to speed up access to National Health Service treatment; and unpaid internships as a means of access to the professions. There can be less reliance either on self-restraint by economic and social actors, who have been encouraged to be more assertive and individualistic, or on social pressures against opportunistic behaviour. A culture of gaming rules and regulators complicates public governance at all levels. In these circumstances, achieving the social democratic value of equality of opportunity becomes more elusive.

Third, a factor weakening the social democratic position has been the ending of the widely held twentieth-century assumption that economic growth leads to less income inequality. Channelling some of the fruits of growth through the public budget into public services and the tax/benefit system was relatively pain-less for parties and governments; UK inequality reduced significantly between 1910 and 1979 (Dorling 2012). It was central to Anthony Crosland's formula-tion of social democracy (Crosland 1956). When the pre-tax/benefit distribu-tion is widening, the tax/benefit system has to work ever harder to achieve any given post-tax/benefit distribution. A much-quoted statistic is that real US median earnings have been stagnant for twenty-five years while GDP has doubled (Plunkett 2011). Various explanations have been advanced: globalisa-tion; technological change that puts premiums on certain skills; the weakening of trade union power; and unchallenged rent-seeking in key economic sectors.

A fourth change relates to the sheer scale of contemporary fiscal prob-lems. Whereas episodes of fiscal stress occurred after 1945, the post-2008 circumstances do merit the term 'fiscal crisis' and analogies with the 1930s have become commonplace. Consequences have included budget reductions unprecedented in scale during universal suffrage. It is unclear how much fiscal austerity various countries can sustain without unpredictable social conse-quences and the destruction of political legitimacy. While the 1930s involved social distress and political traumas of an entirely different scale from those of the 2010s, the potential damage from contemporary economic, political and social dislocations should not be underestimated. Examples include: long-term output loss; failure to absorb younger generations into the labour market; heightened social and economic inequalities; civil disorder; and the growth of extreme political parties, some of which lack democratic commitment.

## Objectives of public expenditure

Rethinking public expenditure from a social democratic perspective requires a fundamental examination of its objectives. Richard Musgrave's (1959) trilogy of allocation, distribution and stabilisation remains a valuable framework. These elements cannot be treated separately in actual policy, as the objectives are interwoven and instruments aimed at one will have implications for the others. However, this decomposition brings valuable discipline to the analysis.

Policy positions on each are separable but, in practice, often overlap. Some hold that private markets are highly efficient at allocating resources; that the market-determined distribution of resources meets the fairness criterion; and that fiscal policy is destabilising or ineffective. Others hold that private markets are inefficient; that fairness requires extensive redistribution via the tax/benefit system; and that fiscal policy can be effective and stabilising. There are hybrid positions: for example, Samuel Brittan and Martin Wolf of the *Financial Times* are strongly Keynesian in arguing for deficit financing during the post-2008 global recession, yet strongly market-oriented in allocation and distribution, reflecting suspicion of big government. There are complications: big government usually leads to high automatic stabilisers, through the effects across the cycle of progressive taxation and the benefit system. Consequently, Keynesian deficit financing needs more discretionary countercyclical fiscal policy in a (relatively) small-government country such as the United States. While social democracy traditionally subscribes to the interventionist view in relation to the redistribution of income and wealth, it exhibits a range of positions on the allocative efficiency of markets and on the relative weight to be placed on monetary and fiscal instruments for the purpose of keeping the economy on a growth path close to full employment.

## Allocation

The allocation problem in relation to public expenditure has two dimensions. First, there is the split between allocation through the market and non-market allocation through the state, principally through public expenditure. Further questions arise when the lines between public and private activities become less well defined: for example, does it matter for public policy that the US health sector accounts for 18% of GDP as distinct from the government-financed component being 8% of GDP? Much depends on the implications for access to healthcare and for cost control, and how healthcare financing impacts on other sectors. When policies are said to be 'unaffordable', there should be clarity about whether this claim refers to service configurations (e.g. en suite single rooms or dormitories in residential homes for the elderly) or whether it refers to who pays.

The second dimension refers to the composition of public expenditure: (a) between exhaustive public expenditure (when government is the decision-maker) and transfer payments (which add to the incomes of households operating in private markets); (b) by function, as between, for example, defence and healthcare; (c) by economic category (e.g. pay); and (d) by geographical location.

At a conceptual level, an efficient allocation of public expenditure is when the net marginal benefit from each type of expenditure is equalised. Operationally, that is of limited help because important attributes, outputs and outcomes are not credibly quantifiable. The practice of public expenditure allocation is intensely political in both ideological and bureaucratic senses. For example, social democratic parties have traditionally stressed expenditure on welfare state services whereas parties to their right have given higher priority to defence and law and order. Even though social democracy points to higher total public expenditure, difficult trade-offs within those totals are inevitable. On functional composition, there can be big surprises in relation to earlier projections, such as new spending pressures on housing and pensions.

For allocation through public expenditure, at least three persistently tricky issues are raised: the determination of eligibility for services and benefits; the pursuit of productive efficiency; and the validation of Value for Money (VfM).

*Determining eligibility*

The broad choice is between universalism (services or benefits are attached to citizenship/residence) and targeting (access is conditioned on satisfying a means test that specifies income and/or wealth levels). There is an important distinction between *exclusion* (e.g. income limits on access to social housing) and *self-exclusion* (e.g. voluntary use of private facilities for health and education). Beyond an imprecise threshold in terms of participation in publicly provided services, exclusion and self-exclusion are likely to generate a drift from an inclusive form of welfare state to a residual model of welfare (Esping-Andersen 1996). There can be different configurations in education, health, housing, pensions and social care, but the effects interact.

In gross public expenditure terms, universalism is always more expensive as benefits and services go to the 'affluent' who could 'afford' to pay for themselves or not receive the benefit. Where the benefit is in cash (as with old-age pensions) the net expenditure cost depends on whether these are taxable in the hands of the recipient.

While always cheaper in gross public expenditure terms, means-tested benefits encounter severe implementation problems, including high administrative and compliance costs, low take-up rates and vulnerability to fraud. Multiple means tests lead to marginal rates of taxation/benefit withdrawal that damage labour market incentives and discourage saving, and, in some societies and circumstances, generate social stigma. Moreover, there may be less middle-class voice articulating demands for high-quality services and less support for the taxes required to pay for them. Public services can become tainted as 'only for the poor', sometimes unintentionally or deliberately inferior in quality to private substitutes. Services not accessed by the bulk of the population are likely to lose taxpayer support (Flynn 1988).

Taxed UK old-age pensions contrast with hitherto untaxed child benefit. Arguments for the latter being untaxed have revolved around child benefit being paid to the mother (as the person most likely to have child-rearing responsibilities) and the existence of separate taxation of married couples and civil partners. The UK income tax system focuses on individuals whereas the benefit system focuses on households, making for some uncomfortable joins. However, from January 2013, an income tax charge will be imposed to the value of child benefit received if the adjusted net income of either partner exceeds £60,000 (with tapered withdrawal from £50,000). Alternatively, child benefit can be renounced. This is a landmark change, in relation to the gender-sensitive issue of separate taxation and to the recognition of child-rearing costs by the tax/benefit system. Small breaches may later expand.

*Securing productive efficiency*
There is a widely purveyed image of the 'bloated public sector', whether or not the characterisation is valid in a particular country or at particular times. This image of 'private good, public bad' may have little relationship to the actual quality of public sector performance. This is part of the denigration of the public sphere (Marquand 2004).

This context emphasises the importance of productive efficiency, yet also highlights several problems. First, there is ambiguity as to what is 'efficient'. If productive efficiency is conceptualised solely as least cost, there are certain actions denied to public organisations that may be used by some private organisations: those involving illegality include breaking immigration laws, disregarding health and safety laws, and evading taxes. There are uncertainties about the acceptability for public organisations to undertake certain legal actions: for example, in relation to the treatment of existing employees, off-shoring activities to low-wage economies, shuffling costs on to other public bodies, and tax avoidance. Second, what may seem in the short term to be least cost may prove more expensive in the long term: for example, outsourcing hospital cleaning, or the neglect of physical infrastructure whether through inadequate maintenance or non-replacement of life-expired assets. Third, in an economy with macro-economic maladjustment or problems of regional structure, there may be public policy reasons why governments pay above local market wage rates in some locations.

The international spread of market-like techniques that are analysed under the label of 'New Public Management' (NPM) has shifted the emphasis on modes of governance within the public sector from hierarchy towards contract. Under this umbrella came techniques such as accruals accounting, agencification, purchaser-provider separation, quasi-markets, outsourcing, PPPs and privatisation. The jury is still out on the NPM package, in part because it is a bundle of different tools. That makes evaluation particularly difficult; the evidence seems to be contradictory and often appears to conform to the *a priori* views of the evaluator.

From the perspective of social democracy, there are dangers in blanket condemnation of NPM prompted by overstated claims on its behalf or by the neo-liberal label attached to it. Public service production has always been a hybrid, for example, with private sector firms constructing fixed assets. Rubbishing what the public sector does, and how it currently does it, is more comfortable territory for those without commitment to social democratic objectives. Performance is both substantive and symbolic: it is possible for public sector performance on the ground to be improving whereas its image declines.

*Validating Value for Money*

Notwithstanding these complexities, continuous striving for productive efficiency through effective public management is vital for the sustainability of social democratic positions on public expenditure. Effectiveness must be assessed relative to policy objectives, a relationship that causes difficulties if policy objectives are poorly articulated and/or unstable. Value for Money requires that public expenditure programmes be effective in achieving policy objectives and do this in a cost-efficient way. Either by statute or by forbearance, public audit bodies do not comment on policy, only on the implementation of that policy. However, policy objectives are often not articulated clearly, especially in a form that leads to well-defined operational objectives. Governments conceal their objectives, including 'doing good by stealth', and policy objectives may change when governments change.

Two separate meanings of VfM become entwined. First is *cost effectiveness*, where the difficulties stem from ambiguities about outputs, outcomes and cost. Although the context is political, these questions are essentially technical. Second is *worthwhileness*, a little-used word that better captures the everyday understanding of 'value for money'. Whether spending public money is worthwhile is always value-laden and thus political in the broad sense.

Into this discussion comes the complicated concept of public waste. Whether something is waste can depend on how the policy objectives have been conceptualised and specified. What may look like waste might derive from disputed policy objectives, social or employment or territorial objectives that override cost minimisation, or redundant resources that have no social or policy justification. Differentiating these is likely to be controversial. A familiar tactic is to characterise as waste the spending on policies of which one disapproves: an excellent example is UK defence expenditure on the wars in Iraq and Afghanistan. What may look like efficiency improvements may derive from reductions in service quality, cost shifting to third parties, or genuine improvements in cost efficiency.

During the long period of UK public expenditure growth under the

1997–2010 Labour Government, what the expenditure was actually achieving received inadequate attention, as did questions of absorptive capacity. Paradoxically, it may require 'hard times' to raise the profile of systematic evaluation and to focus attention on choices at the margin between different expenditure types. Whatever the validity of the data, the Office for National Statistics' productivity series for education and healthcare attracted much media coverage in the run-up to the 2010 General Election. Reported falls in public sector productivity, both absolute and relative to the private sector, ran strongly in sections of the media, but largely disappeared after the election. These data fitted the narrative of a bloated public sector and the waste of billions of additional expenditure in the 2000s, to be rectified by fiscal austerity.

## Distribution

Welfare states shift massive amounts of money – interpersonally and geographically – and have huge resource implications intergenerationally: these often reflect complex and fragile distributional coalitions. Redistribution through the public budget, a tenet of social democracy, has become more problematic. Income dispersion is higher, whether measured at the individual or household level. Paradoxically, it is easier to build consent for redistributive policies and to implement them in relatively equal, homogeneous societies.

Sometimes it is argued, even within social democratic parties, that individuals and households should be left more exposed to market forces, which have now intensified through globalisation. However, this runs counter to Rodrik's (1998) conclusion that public expenditure is higher in internationally open economies; governments cushion the effects, through risk pooling, and thereby can achieve greater economic flexibility.

Although there has to be enough economic inequality to motor a market economy that works through aspiration and incentives, this inequality must not destroy the social fabric that underpins its functioning (Hirsch 1977). The degree of pre-tax/benefit inequality is substantially outside policy control, though the distinctiveness of Scandinavia shows that tradition and culture may constrain inequality.

A popular sense that something is 'unfair' can have powerful political effects. However, attitudes about fairness can be opportunistic and/or confused, rather than consistent. Equity has interpersonal and territorial dimensions: removing unacceptable differences in living standards and public services for individuals/households within a country; and addressing inequalities between regions (a provision in the 1949 Basic Law of Germany). Social democracy presumes a normative commitment that supports both interpersonal and territorial redistribution. However, the domain over which that commitment applies has become more contested. More geographically mobile and socially differentiated populations make explicit redistribution more difficult to achieve and undermine the stability of implicit intergenerational contracts (e.g. in relation to social security). This may reduce the sense of responsibility for others: with much greater knowledge about conditions elsewhere in the world, why should one care for geographically close neighbours if not for others with much worse suffering?

Moreover, there may be a 'revolt of the rich' at the individual/household level, taking the form of tax avoidance, threatened emigration or strengthened political opposition to financing public services and redistribution. There are powerful public finance arguments for making cash transfers when the objective is poverty reduction. This confronts claims that market-generated rewards are 'deserved' by the recipient and that government transfers are inferior. Such 'cash versus kind' questions are unlikely to have final answers, answers being contingent on circumstances. For example, the US Federal Government runs a massive food stamps programme whereas EU countries predominantly use cash benefits for poverty relief.

These tensions are mirrored at the level of the political collectivity. Within the eurozone, Northern Europe does not wish to transfer resources to Southern Europe. Prosperous regions within states such as Catalonia and Flanders wish to cut back transfers to the less prosperous, and those, like Scotland, which have tax revenues from natural resource rents such as oil may wish to prevent them going to the national budget.

Managing these dilemmas becomes particularly difficult when the market distribution of rewards disperses further and a non-negligible proportion of the population is unable, because of disabilities or lack of skills, or unwilling, because of cultural attitudes or a dysfunctional tax/benefit system, to generate sufficient resources in the marketplace for what their society considers an acceptable living standard. Public services do not operate in silos. What happens in housing, for example enforced moves because of housing benefit cuts, will have effects on population location and school achievement. Such circumstances have complicated effects: for example, child poverty will increase; educational and health indicators may deteriorate because of what is happening at the bottom of the income distribution; fecklessness will be attributed to those to whom it is certainly not applicable; and there will be a drag on economic productivity.

The residualisation of public services is a threat to social democracy. There may be tipping points in exit rates beyond which public sector services are reputationally devalued; rubbishing them as inferior then contributes to a political climate that stigmatises use, validates exit and supports expenditure cuts. Being inside the social networks developed through the use of private facilities may create competitive advantages in the labour market and in cultural and sporting achievement. Residualisation will lead to falls in electoral support for public spending on those services and to proposals that there should be tax deductibility of private fees. More extensive exit from public provision threatens the approach to 'limiting the domain of inequality' that extracts certain goods and services from the market, allocating instead on some indicator of 'merit' or 'need'. Such specific egalitarianism (Musgrave 1959; Tobin 1970) sometimes emphasises the distribution of outcomes; in other cases the sole objective is that everyone has the opportunity to step on the ladder.

Intergenerational issues are rapidly acquiring greater salience: the expectation that each new generation would be better off than their parents has been dashed, not least because of reduced affordability of private house ownership and the decline of occupational pension schemes. These add to the effects of higher education fees and labour markets in which it is more difficult to gain a foothold. Inheritance has resumed an economic importance not generally possessed in the post-1945 period. In the background are concerns about long-term developments such as the economic impact of climate change. These developments contribute to pressures to unbundle the welfare state, for example in relation to young people, often without regard for direct and indirect ramifications for other parts of the welfare state.

### Stabilisation

The 2008 financial crisis constituted a landmark in stabilisation policy, breaking a broad policy consensus established in the early 1990s that fiscal policy should be set with regard to the medium and long term, with monetary policy being used for short-term macro-economic management. The tools and instruments would be measurement of the output gap, fiscal rules and independent central banks. These were regarded as largely matters for non-political experts, with limited concern for the public accountability of those experts.

Several arguments coalesced against discretionary fiscal policy. First, there was the problem of lags: by the time additional public investment occurred the economic cycle had moved on, making the effect counterproductive. Moreover, economic cycles were not symmetrical and hence difficult to map in real time. Second, 'stop-and-start' changes damaged the efficiency and effectiveness of public expenditure programmes. Third, while governments might enthusiastically increase deficits during recessions, there was a singular lack of enthusiasm to run surpluses during booms – the pressures to spend or cut taxes were irresistible. These asymmetric reactions have contributed to secular increases in debt/GDP ratios. Fourth, there was an implicit ideological preference for monetary policy, seen as 'less interventionist' and less dependent on untrusted political processes. Social democratic parties mostly bought into this consensus because it seemed to solve the macro-economic problem while generating the taxation to finance public services.

Since 2008, discretionary fiscal policy has revived, though with conflicting purposes. Some have argued that governments should try to balance their economy rather than their short-term public finances. Others take the view that market economies are automatically stabilising if left alone, or the view that all intervention makes things worse. A critical question has been whether the automatic stabilisers should be allowed to run their course, thereby increasing the fiscal deficit in the years when the economy has failed to recover. If not, the effect of the automatic stabilisers will be suppressed, either by weakening the underlying policies (e.g. reducing tax progressivity or benefit generosity) or by imposing expenditure reductions or tax increases of the same size as the automatic stabilisers. Near-zero interest rates have negated the interest rate tool of conventional monetary policy, leading to what has become known as 'Quantitative Easing'.[4] Fiscal austerity is combined with lax monetary policy, with the latter partly intended to protect the real economy from the effects of the former.

In the context of this chapter, four observations are appropriate:

1. The ideological preference for monetary policy is misplaced, with there being a strong case for pragmatism on the basis of 'what works' in particular circumstances; indeed, the distinction between monetary and fiscal policy has been blurred by 'unconventional monetary policy' (Miles 2012).
2. The potential damage to coherent spending priorities and programmes that can be caused by fiscal fine-tuning, in either direction, should not be underestimated. Disruptive changes damage the actual and perceived efficiency of public institutions.
3. Intergenerational issues are pressing, a consideration which adds to the 'policy flexibility' case for containing and reducing debt/GDP levels and for monitoring both sides of the government balance sheet (Heald and Georgiou 2011).
4. The problem with fiscal rules is the incentives they create to find policy instruments that bypass those rules; this is likely to do damage to VfM and to breed cynicism that condones other rule-breaking. Setting budgets and taxes is central to political authority: removing or restricting this through the exercise of external authority has unpredictable and potentially far-reaching effects.

### The neglect of taxation

On the assumption that social democracy does involve higher public expenditure than political positions to its right, higher-than-otherwise taxation is required. This is a difficult political message to convey, leading to exaggerated claims about future efficiency gains and to excessive reliance on the fruits of economic growth. The pressures on private consumption from widening pre-tax inequalities and the impact of the 2008 recession are hardening social attitudes (Park et al. 2012).

A depressing feature of the 1997–2010 Labour Government was its neglect of the taxation system during fiscal plenty. A compulsive tendency to micro-manage, often for short-term media gains, was combined with failures not only to address structural issues but also to defend the purposes of taxation and to stress its relationship to political accountability (Bräutigam et al. 2008). There was no challenge to the remarkable levels of public ignorance about the operation of the UK tax system. Moreover, the ambitious but flawed implementation of tax credits suffered legitimacy problems because of a Treasury political style characterised by media spinning and a desire to do good, for example to reduce child poverty, but only by stealth.

The UK tax system is a prodigious machine for generating tax revenues: over the period 1965–6 to 2011–12 the ratio of public sector total receipts to GDP has never fallen below 35%. However, revenue generation is only one criterion. Most taxes impose efficiency costs on the economy: potential exceptions are externality-correcting taxes such as those designed to reduce environmental harm. These costs are analysed by economists in terms of 'excess burden' and the Marginal Cost of Public Funds (MCPF) (Dahlby 2008).[5] The policy objective should be to raise the target revenue and to achieve redistributional goals, while minimising unintended impacts on the functioning of the market sector of the economy. There undoubtedly are 'fiscal termites' (Tanzi 2001), such as avoidance, technological change and globalisation, which threaten governments' capacity to generate tax revenues at historic ratios to GDP. Nevertheless, the scale of the resulting problems needs to be kept in perspective, especially if the 2008 recession has genuinely stimulated coordinated international action through bilateral information exchange and OECD monitoring of tax havens, and stricter domestic enforcement.

The Mirrlees Review (2011) provided a road map for UK tax reform but timing issues have thus far limited its practical impact: it missed the period of fiscal plenty in the first decade of the century, and took too long from its commissioning in 2006. Its proposals for broadening the VAT base were marred by an unfounded belief in the credibility of offsetting tax/benefit measures and an inadequate recognition of the political problems of tax base broadening. The Review lacked clarity about whether differentiated VAT rates were simply distortions to the spending choices of consumers (*anomalies*) or whether, in part, they represented *policy encouragement* of particular patterns of expenditure such as books and newspapers. Public policy objectives might legitimately be progressed through either side of the government budget.

Increasing income inequality has made governments more dependent for taxation revenue on potentially mobile earners/consumers, thereby increasing revenue risk and adding to problems caused by capital mobility and tax havens. Inadequate attention has been paid to maintaining the legitimacy and integrity of taxation, for example by widespread failures to revalue the tax base for the residential property tax. This neglect of the taxation system (both operationally and in active defence of the purposes of taxation) has left public expenditure exposed to populist and free-market attacks.

The crucial point is that the public expenditure levels typical of social democracies can only be mainly financed through the income, consumption and property taxes paid by the bulk of the population: proposals to finance them through taxes on the 'rich' are delusionary. The interaction of tax design with legitimacy is neatly illustrated by the controversy surrounding Mitt Romney's denigration as 'victims' the 47% (actually 46.4%) of the US adult population who do not pay federal income tax (Whipp 2012). This figure is heavily influenced by the fact that US old-age and veterans' pensions are not taxable.

From administrative and compliance cost perspectives, there are arguments for limiting income taxpayer numbers. From a legitimacy perspective, there are strong arguments for bringing citizens within the income tax net. Also, a wide income taxpayer base facilitates the operation of tax credits. In contrast, the Liberal Democrat (2010) UK General Election manifesto envisaged a personal allowance of £10,000 that would eliminate the income tax liability of 3.6 million taxpayers. This well-intentioned proposal, involving dangers for legitimacy, emphasises the importance of thinking about the taxation system as a whole and how that is portrayed.

## The public expenditure challenge for social democracy

The distributional coalition supporting high public expenditure is a complex one. Instead of a reasonably clear left-right political spectrum, a more fragmented electorate runs along multiple spectra: for example, statist versus market liberal, social liberal versus social conservative, and internationalist versus nationalist. It has become more difficult to hold a pro-spending coalition together and it has become more difficult to negotiate with governments, for example about changes to retirement age and pensions. In particular, social groups expect that governments will come back for more concessions in a race to the bottom, and negotiators fear losing the confidence of their constituencies.

In these circumstances social democratic parties may lose votes (a) because these are taken by other social democratic parties (whatever their names), and/ or (b) because economic and social developments lead to a decisive shift of political values to the right. A social democratic party may become seen as the party of welfare recipients, not as the party of workers.

De-unionisation of the private sector has pushed the centre of trade unionism into the public sector, leading to allegations that unions are merely defending vested interests in a way that is unfair to private sector employees who have lost entitlements. These tensions are accentuated by suspicions of there being (hidden) agendas about (a) de-unionising the public sector, via outsourcing, competitive markets and the break-up of national bargaining, and (b) eventual service privatisation. While outsourcing might free political leaderships of certain difficult managerial tasks, there is ample evidence that outsourcing delivery does not necessarily divest responsibility, as evidenced by the security lapses in the run-up to the 2012 London Olympics. Notwithstanding advocacy of mutual or social or charitable enterprises as alternatives to direct public sector delivery, there are big questions as to what the eventual configuration of privatised suppliers would look like: UK buses, now dominated by an oligopoly, contrast markedly with the 1980s' projection of local and employee-owned firms. Procurement and regulation bring their own difficulties, as does direct production.

In this complex setting, social democratic thought needs clarity about the top-level issues. First, the optimal level of public expenditure for a particular country at a particular time depends critically upon 'big' decisions on the role of the state and on the choice of instruments. If healthcare is publicly financed, the aggregate level of public expenditure should be higher than if (a) the government compels private healthcare insurance, or (b) the government accepts no policy responsibility for healthcare. An excellent example of mismatching expenditure to policy commitments is UK defence expenditure in relation to foreign policy goals and commitments. The macro-economic imperative of restraining public expenditure commitments that are 'too high' relative to the present and future productive capacity of the economy and feasible tax revenue must be differentiated from the view that the expenditure is intrinsically undesirable.

Second, the 'how to tax' question is fundamental to the legitimacy and sustainability of 'high' levels of public expenditure. If public expenditure (after netting off charges to users) is relatively high, then aggregate taxation must be relatively high. Attention must focus on the efficiency costs of taxation and on the redistributional effectiveness of the tax/benefit system. Consent and compliance cannot be assumed. The rationale for a broad-based tax system, with the lowest tax rates consistent with targeted yield, has to be clearly articulated. Although parties in opposition will oppose government tax policy, those committed to high public expenditure should avoid populist positions on tax. Those wishing 'low' levels of public expenditure might see advantages in an inefficient tax structure and administration and in the erosion of governments' ability to raise revenue.

Third, there must be strong commitments to productive efficiency and to VfM. For this to hold, there has to be a recognition that these can cause difficulties with employees and beneficiaries, part of the distributional coalition supporting high public expenditure. Having established a clear view on the big picture, there should be pragmatism on 'what works'. Crucially, this means evidence-based policy, not the commissioning of policy-based evidence. There has been a damaging proliferation of advocacy masquerading as economic contribution/impact calculations, which, *inter alia*, neglect displacement effects (see Kay 2010 for a witty critique). Techniques of economic analysis should be deployed in a manner that opens up debate (such as in the Dilnot Report (2011) on options for financing long-term care), not closes it down in a way that breeds public and practitioner cynicism.

Fourth, the distributional issues are complex. A sceptical eye should be cast on economic rents in privileged parts of the private sector, not least because these have contributed to the adverse distributional trends. Policies other than taxation and expenditure can have distributional impacts; consider the effects of interest rate policy on the incomes of retirees and those living off their fixed-income investments and the wider position of borrowers versus lenders.

Given the likely duration of public expenditure restraint, intergenerational issues will become more prominent. Universal benefits to the elderly, such as bus passes, winter fuel allowances, prescription charges exemption, and free personal care, are often criticised as wasteful because of the proportions going to the non-poor. However, the addition of new means tests aggravates the existing problem of ludicrously high marginal rates of tax/benefit withdrawal at certain points in the income distribution. Central governments will be tempted to push the pain 'downwards' via inadequately funded mandates to lower tiers of government, and 'outwards' by fall-back reliance on charities, bringing their own explicit or implicit means tests. Proposals for new charges, fees or tolls should always prompt the question as to whether these will be waived on income or other grounds. If so, these would accentuate existing problems. Where means tests are used, they require to be designed at a sufficiently centralised level so that coordination is possible and data are verifiable.

Looking at the redistributional effects and trends as a whole is emphatically important (Hills 2010). Paradoxically, while the cultural values underpinning concern about inequalities may be weakening, awareness of the economic costs attached to increasing inequalities may be growing (OECD 2011). These economic costs are sometimes subtle, particularly in programme interactions and second-round effects. The development of a detached underclass may: put pressure on the benefits system; damage the productive potential of the economy; and lead to higher expenditure and worse performance in education, healthcare and criminal justice. For example, there are remarkable inter-country differences in the proportion of males under thirty who are expensively imprisoned, serving as a reminder that cutting social expenditure can prove a false economy.

Fifth, from the perspective of 2012, the stabilisation issues look different as a result of the 2008 global financial crisis. The surge in debt levels since 2008 urges caution on debt levels in 'normal times'; there has to be sufficient fiscal room to allow for the full operation of the automatic stabilisers, however bad the recession. It is now less clear what would be a cautious debt/GDP ratio. The political difficulties associated with a policy of lowering debt levels are obvious: one government having taken the pain (foregone public services or tax reductions), the following government might benefit politically by running debt levels back up.

Sixth, the achievement of substantive policy objectives in relation to public expenditure requires an open debate: securing fiscal transparency is imperative (Heald 2012). This might partly counteract the damaging obsession with 'scoring' (see Portes 2012) which elevates form over substance: for example, manoeuvring activities to just outside general government or just outside the public sector; using PPPs for reasons other than VfM; and pretending that government guarantees to privately undertaken public infrastructure are costless. Such devices add to country fiscal risks (by temporarily disguising the macro-economic position) and can result in inappropriate amounts and mixes of infrastructure. The default position should be suspicion of attempts to achieve desirable policy objectives by stealth, not least because this approach is unlikely to be sustainable.

In summary, the levels of public expenditure required to sustain the welfare state that is a central tenet of social democracy require a well-informed defence. Threats come from long-term factors such as globalisation and more complex social structures and from the current fiscal austerity which has been seized upon as an opportunity for far-reaching reforms by some governments. That defence requires not only the articulation of social democratic values in relation to the objectives of public expenditure but also open-minded yet hard-headed analysis of alternative public expenditure programmes within constrained totals.

## Notes

1. The author wishes to thank the Royal Society of Edinburgh for his 2010–11 Scottish Government Support Research Fellowship on 'Improving the quality of public expenditure'. Sole responsibility for the contents of this chapter rests with the author.
2. 'Neo-liberal' is often a term of abuse, directed at particular policies and programmes by those who are hostile. In self-description, preference is given to labels such as 'free market', 'market liberal', 'liberal' or 'conservative', largely dependent on linguistic usage in their own communities.
3. From 1996–7 to 2007–8, the Treasury's measure of UK public expenditure (Total Managed Expenditure) grew in nominal terms by 85% and by 46% in real (i.e. GDP deflator-adjusted) terms. Over that period, the TME/GDP ratio increased from 39.5% to 40.7%, as GDP was growing strongly. The 2011–12 ratio was 46.6% (Treasury 2012, Table 4.1).
4. This involves the Central Bank creating electronic money in order to buy government securities in the market, thus forcing bond prices up and interest rates down. The expectation is that improved bank balance sheets will then result in more bank lending to the commercial private sector.

5. Excess burden is the loss of economic welfare caused by taxes beyond the realised tax revenue, which is a transfer to the government sector. This results from the way in which taxes create a wedge between prices faced by buyer and seller. The MCPF is therefore greater than 1, often thought to be in the range 1.2 to 1.3. A more efficient tax structure will lead to a lower MCPF than an inefficient one, thereby increasing the economically optimal size of public expenditure.

CHAPTER

6

# SOCIAL DEMOCRACY IN CRISIS? WHAT CRISIS?

Bo Rothstein and Sven Steinmo

### Has the social democratic model of society stopped working?

This chapter addresses the following question: can the weakening of the social democratic political project in Europe be explained by the fact the social democratic model of society no longer performs? In other words, can the recent electoral crisis in social democratic parties be seen as a rational response from an electorate saying goodbye to a socio-economic model? If you want to compare social democratic policies with some kind of utopian political programme, you will certainly be disappointed. As pointed out in the introductory chapter to this volume, social democracy was never a utopian political project and its earlier success can therefore not be seen as a result of fulfilling a nirvana type of society. In contrast to the utopian models historically launched by communists and anarchists, social democracy has traditionally been firmly anchored in a concrete, down-to-earth pragmatism based on a realist vision that politics must be based on what is 'possible'.

Our argument is that the most reasonable way of judging the performance of the social democratic 'model for society' is to compare it with other existing macro-models. The most relevant in a European perspective is the centrist Christian democratic model and the political right's neo-liberal model. The questions are these: what should count as success for such macro-models and which countries should be seen as the best representatives of the social democratic model of society? We will start with the latter question.

### What is the social democratic model of society?

In order to discuss the current situation of social democracy, it is of course important to define the subject itself. The label 'social democratic' is sometimes used to identify a large assortment of polities and left political parties. In our view, this is a misuse of the label which leads to some rather fundamental misunderstandings about social democratic systems in practice. We instead use the term social democracy to depict a certain type of social (and economic) model, which finds its roots in the ideology of social democracy. Quite simply, social democracy is a political economy built on the ideas of universal social solidarity, modernity and the belief that society can be changed by 'enlightened politics'.

The social democratic model of society, as we define it, contains three main commitments.[1] The first aims to provide all people in society, regardless of their background, with a set of general social rights to certain kinds of service and economic support.[2] Such programmes are not targeted on specific vulnerable groups or distinct minorities in society but cater to 'all' or very large segments of the population (Rothstein and Uslaner 2005). The classical 'universal programmes' such as healthcare, universal child allowances, free public education, elderly care and broadly based tax systems are examples of this approach. It is important to understand that these universalistic polices are different from both the targeted tax and social policies more typically found in the United Kingdom and the United States, and also from the wage-based social insurance systems typically found in many European welfare states. These universalist policies are based on the idea that everyone should pay and everyone should benefit as equally as possible, rather than the idea that the state should compensate losers and punish winners. Although these principles developed along different intellectual paths, it is interesting to note the extent to which these social democratic ideas align with leading liberal mainstream political philosophers. For example, Nobel laureate Amartya Sen's idea that social justice demands providing all citizens with 'basic capabilities', as well as John Rawls's similar argument for equal access to a set of 'primary goods', can be seen as arguments for the type of universal social policies that have become the hallmark of social democracy (Rothstein 1998).

The second commitment in social democratic politics can be described as an ambition to tame, but not replace nor control, the market economy. To the surprise of many who do not know these systems, social democratic polities are remarkably pro-market. These systems, however, combine a positive attitude toward free trade, free labour markets and economic competition, with a realisation that a well running market economy demands a wide range of public regulations to function properly. Social democracy's goals are thus obviously different from those of state socialism (or communism). But, more interestingly, social democratic policies are also quite distinct from the populist/leftist policies regularly witnessed across the twentieth century which are motivated by a desire to redistribute income and wealth directly from one class to another. From its beginning, typical social democratic regulations were directed mostly towards the labour market (the eight-hour working day,

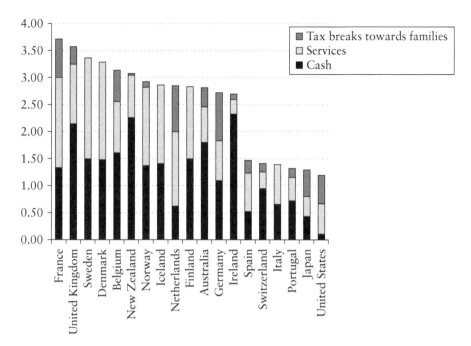

**Figure 6.1** Public spending on family benefits in cash, services and tax measures, as per cent of GDP, 2007

*Source:* OECD, iLibrary <http://www.oecd-ilibrary.org/social-issues-migration-health/social-issues-key-tables-from-oecd_20743904> (last accessed 6 March 2013)

pensions, unemployment insurance, work safety, child labour laws, union rights) and were later expanded to many other areas such as environmental protection, gender equality and regulation of financial markets. In contrast to neo-liberals, social democrats do not believe that markets have the capacity to serve 'the common good' if left unregulated. In contrast to populists, social democrats do not aim to directly redistribute from the rich to the poor. While it would be incorrect to say that social democracies have no targeted social welfare policies directly focusing public spending on the poorest and most vulnerable in society, to the surprise of many, classical social democratic countries spend relatively *less* on targeted poor relief and direct cash transfers to the poor than many other advanced welfare states. The following figure gives an example of this. Here we see public social spending on 'families' in several OECD nations. Notice that the classical social democratic systems are among the largest spenders here, but not the highest. More significantly, however, note that the levels of direct cash transfers to families is *lower* in Sweden, Denmark and Norway, for example, even though these countries give a universal cash payment to all families with children. Where they are 'big spenders' is in services (including for child care and early primary education).

It is important, above all, to understand that social democracy is not a populist movement. Social Democratic parties have built large, universalistic social welfare systems often by taxing their own voters heavily. They have not attempted to finance their social welfare systems though confiscatory taxation or government appropriation of individual or corporate wealth (Steinmo 1993).

The key logic underlying delivering social programmes and services 'universally' is not simply that this will ensure their political/electoral success.[3] Instead, as Sheri Berman points out, 'social democrats translated communitarianism, meanwhile, into an emphasis on social solidarity and policies designed to strengthen social unity and solidarity' (Berman 2006: 206). The eventual consequence of this logic was the financing of social programmes that benefited even society's most well-off individuals. Social solidarity eventually came to mean solidarity among all the people, not just the working class.

Finally, social democratic polities have made a commitment to socially progressive policies. By this we mean that these systems do not attempt to hold their societies stable or in some idealised equilibrium. On the contrary, social democratic polities have intentionally and explicitly pushed their societies forward. Whether it is in the arena of women's rights, labour rights or even children's rights, social democratic states can be distinguished from other democracies and welfare states by the fact that the state has been an explicit agent of social change. In many different arenas, these states have specifically attempted to improve the life choices for individual citizens independently of family background, gender or ethnicity. Social democrats have instead attempted to enhance the individual's life choices. It is curious to many that social democratic states have, in this sense, been some of the most liberal states in the modern world.[4]

### Having a big welfare state does not a social democracy make

We argue that it is the structure of the welfare state that distinguishes social democratic systems, not the level of public spending. Many large welfare states are not social democracies. In fact, by the early twenty-first century, it is probably more accurate to call several of Europe's large welfare states 'pension states'. It is well known that the social democratic welfare states in Northern Europe have comparatively high taxes and high levels of public spending. It has often been incorrectly assumed, however, that the high levels of economic and social equality that these countries have achieved have been the result of highly redistributive tax systems and heavy social spending on the poorest in society. On the contrary, the Social Democratic Policy Model has developed in quite another direction with relatively flat tax structures and largely universal social spending programmes (Steinmo 1993). The paucity of targeted programmes specifically designed to help to lift the poor above the poverty line or to provide them with special subsidies is really quite remarkable – especially when contrasted with countries like the United States or the United Kingdom (Steinmo 2010).

### Social democracy in practice

Where do we actually find social democracy in practice? Clearly, social democracy has been on the agenda in many periods in Europe, and most democratic countries have had political parties who have called themselves Social Democratic, or at least fought for social democratic ideals. But if we ask which countries have consistently implemented and sustained social democratic policies, we find that arguably only the four Scandinavian countries, Sweden, Denmark, Finland and Norway, are today what one might call thoroughgoing 'social democracies'.[5] By this statement we do not mean to suggest that social democratic ideas are unique to the Scandinavian countries. Nor do we mean to argue that the left in these Scandinavian countries has always consistently pursued a social democratic agenda. Our point is instead that it does appear that only a very small number of relatively unique polities have created social democratic welfare states. While there have been elements of social democratic ideology within the left in many other welfare states – including the United States during the New Deal – in only a few countries did these principles become foundational to the system itself.

We argue, then, that we can look at these four countries as having built distinctive sets of policies and that they can be understood as a distinctive social model. If we examine these four countries as a set distinct from the other advanced democratic polities, a remarkable pattern begins to emerge. As the collection of figures below indicates, these countries have: high levels of taxation; high levels of social spending – within which a high percentage of spending goes towards families and young people rather than simply towards pensioners and the old; low levels of public debt and relatively small budget deficits; high spending on education and public health; high levels of social equality; high levels of gender equality; high levels of private investment; highly educated citizenries; a higher degree of interpersonal trust; low levels of corruption; high levels of population health; and even high levels of self-reported 'happiness' within society.

Certainly one could argue that if our point is that only a small number of countries actually embraced social democracy, then the very question of the 'crisis of social democracy' is irrelevant to the rest of the advanced capitalist world. We think not. First, as we show here, *social democracy* is not failing. In fact, social democratic systems are thriving in the era of intense global competition. It is not social democracy that is failing. Instead it is the populist policies offered by the left which appear to be failing.

*The crisis of social democracy in Europe*

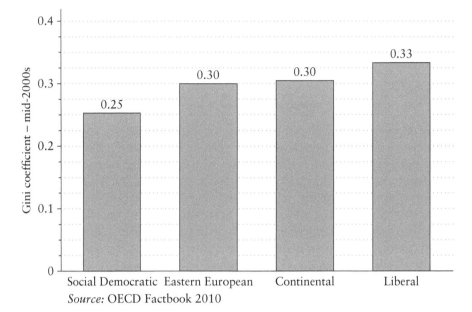

Figure 6.2  Inequality

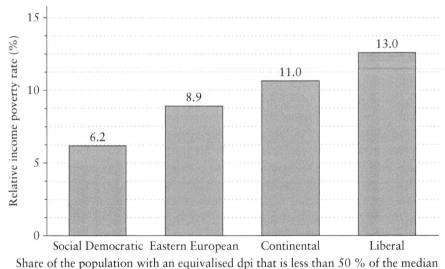

**Figure 6.3**  Poverty mid-2000s

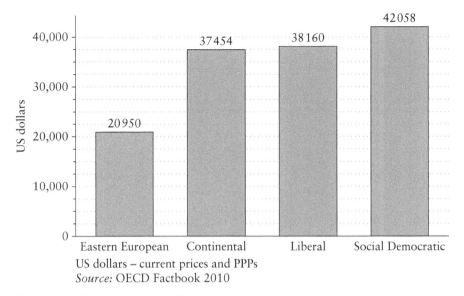

US dollars – current prices and PPPs
*Source:* OECD Factbook 2010

**Figure 6.4** GDP per capita 1998

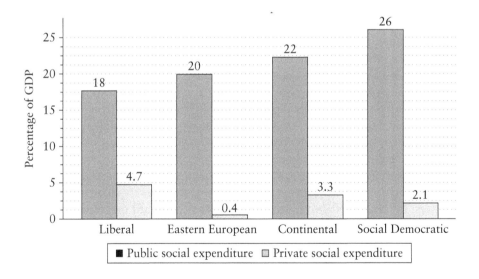

**Figure 6.5** Social expenditure 2005 or latest available year

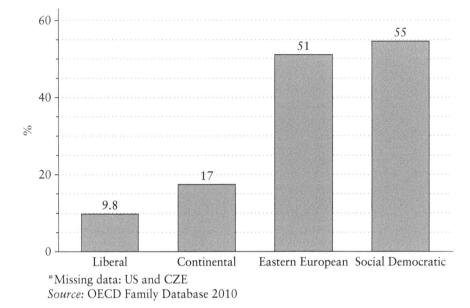

*Missing data: US and CZE
Source: OECD Family Database 2010

**Figure 6.6** Maternity leave and parental leave payments per child born

In Figures 6.1 to 6.6 we demonstrate through a wide variety of measures that the four social democratic countries form distinctive patterns in policies and outcomes. It is certainly possible to say that one country or another helps explain any particular outcome, for example, that Norway's recent oil wealth weights the scales in budget outcomes. But taking Norway out does not change the general pattern.[6] In sum, we think it is virtually impossible to look at this collection of data and not see a pattern – a pattern that by most accounts must be considered a description of a group of unusually successful societies. But for our purposes here, this pattern also fits with the kinds of social democratic ideals and policies we identify above.

There can be little doubt that when evaluating a political model, it is meaningful to compare countries that have been influenced by this model to varying degrees. In the figures above, we use a number of standard measures of human well-being such as the health of the population (child mortality, life expectancy), individuals' satisfaction with life, different measurements of 'human progress', economic equality, absence of corruption, and economic standards. In these measurements, countries that have been most influenced by what we have defined as the social democratic model fare particularly well and, put together, clearly outperform the countries characterised by neo-liberal or conservative politics. Additionally, when international business organisations, such as the World Economic Forum (WEF), conduct their annual ranking of countries' economic competitiveness, the social democratic countries are

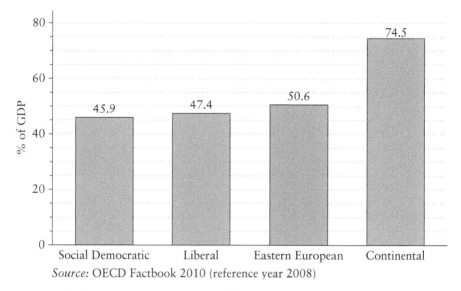

Source: OECD Factbook 2010 (reference year 2008)

**Figure 6.7** Government gross financial liabilities

placed at the top, as high as, and often higher than, the 'neo-liberal' countries (Schwab 2011).

The picture that emerges from available measures of policy performance (see Figures 6.7 to 6.11) is, for once, unequivocal – namely, that if one were to use the title of the recent book *Successful Societies* by Peter Hall and Michelle Lamonte (2009), countries with social democratic politics end up on top regarding measurements not only of economic and social equality but also of social development in general, as well as on human well-being and population health. It also comes as a surprise to many that these high-tax and high-public-spending countries outperform other countries in economic efficiency.

### The social democratic universal welfare state: four common misunderstandings

There are many misunderstandings, even by sympathetic commentators, about the logic of the social democratic welfare states. The most common is that the social democratic welfare state is a very costly undertaking, with a high level of taxation that becomes a hindrance to economic growth. This reveals a misconception regarding the form of the welfare state. Its main feature is not the benefits to poor people, but universal social insurances and social services (like healthcare, pensions, support to families with children, and public education) that benefit the whole, or very large segments, of the population. These goods are in high demand by almost all citizens and research shows that having these

*The crisis of social democracy in Europe*

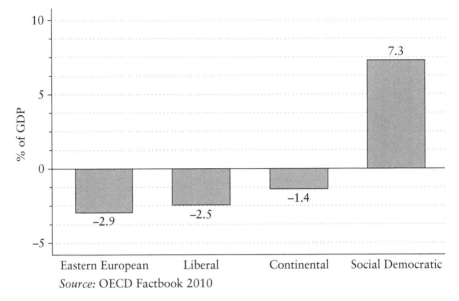

**Figure 6.8** Government net lending and net borrowing 1998

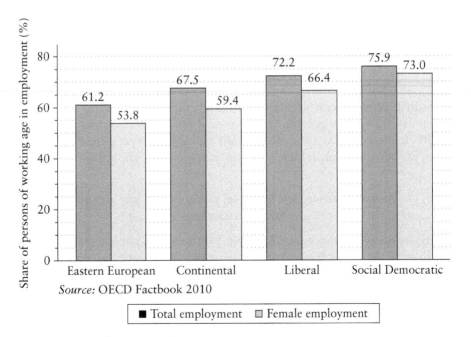

**Figure 6.9** Employment 1998

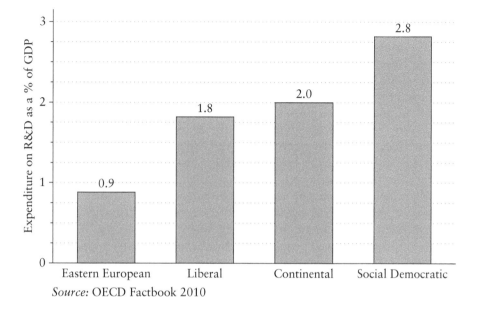

Figure 6.10 Gross domestic expenditure on R&D 2007 or latest available year

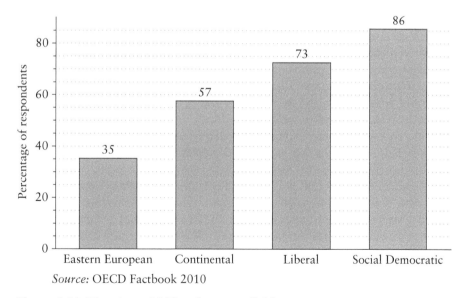

Figure 6.11 Happiness 2009 or latest available year

demands covered by universal systems in many cases becomes more cost-effective. In private health insurance systems, for example, the administrative costs for insurance companies alone (in screening out bad risks, the costs for handling legal problems about coverage) can become very high – as seems to be the case in the United States.[7] Universal systems, on the other hand, tend to be more cost-effective for the simple reason that risks are spread over the whole population and the incentives for providers to overcharge or use costly but unnecessary treatments are minimal. As the British economist Nicholas Barr has observed, due to what economists call 'asymmetric information costs', universalist policies 'provide both a theoretical justification of and an explanation for a welfare state which is much more than a safety net. Such a welfare state is justified not simply by redistributive aims one may (or may not) have, but because it does things which markets for technical reasons would either do inefficiently, or would not do at all' (Barr 1992: 781; see also Barr 2004). Simply put, if middle-class people in the Nordic welfare states are deprived of their universal systems for social protection and social services (not to speak of free college education for the children), they would in all likelihood decide to buy these services on the market.

The second misunderstanding is that such welfare states by necessity come with heavy-handed bureaucratic intrusion and paternalism ('the nanny state'), and that they cannot be combined with freedom of choice for various services. This is, for the most part, wrong. An example is the publicly financed school systems in Denmark and Sweden that are fully fledged charter systems. Public schools compete with private charter schools that are run on public money and have to accept that they work under the same national regulations and education plans. For example, they have to accept students without any discrimination concerning their learning abilities (Björklund 2005). This can be compared with the intrusive inquiries and testing used by many private schools in the US in their admission procedures.

A third general misunderstanding about the universal welfare state system is the neo-liberal argument that high public expenditures are detrimental to market-based economic growth. As shown by the economic historian Peter Lindert (2004), and also in a recent book by Nobel laureate Douglass North (together with John Wallis and Barry Weingast, 2009), this is simply not the case. From a global perspective, rich states have a level of taxation that is almost twice as high as that of poor states. And when the rich Western states are compared over time, the evidence that high public spending is negative for economic growth is absent. The reason, according to North et al., is that large parts of public spending go to the provision of public goods that are necessary for economic growth but which markets cannot provide, partly on account of the information problems stated above. Interestingly, among those public goods North and his colleagues include not only the usual things like infrastructure, research and the rule of law, but also education, social insurance and social services.

**Table 6.1** The redistributive effects of flat taxes and universal benefits

| Pre-tax income | Tax rate 30% | After tax income | Benefit per individual | Final income |
|---|---|---|---|---|
| 10,000 | 3,000 | 7,000 | 16,000 | 23,000 |
| 50,000 | 15,000 | 35,000 | 16,000 | 51,000 |
| 100,000 | 30,000 | 70,000 | 16,000 | 86,000 |

* 3,000 + 15,000 + 30,000 = 48,000/3 =16,000
Income ratio before taxes and benefits    1 to 10    (10,000 to 100,000)
Income ratio after taxes and benefits    1 to 3.7    (23,000 to 86,000)
*Source:* Steinmo 2010

A fourth common misunderstanding is the notion that targeting welfare benefits on the poor is the best way to achieve economic redistribution. Intuitively, one would assume that redistributive policies that tax the rich and give to the poor would be the most efficient way to reduce poverty, while universal policies that give everyone the same service or benefits would not have a redistributive effect. But the facts demonstrate the opposite to be the case. The technical reason as to why universal systems are more efficient in reducing economic inequality is that taxes are usually proportional or progressive, but services or benefits are usually nominal: you get a certain sum or a certain type of service. The net effect of proportional taxes and nominal services/benefits results in comparatively high redistribution from the rich to the poor (Moene and Wallerstein 2001; Rothstein 1998; Åberg 1989).

In Table 6. 1 we offer an idealised version of how such a system can work. Here we have three classes of people, in which there is a hypothetical income distribution of 1 to 10. In other words, lowest income earners have a before tax and benefit income of 1 unit, and the highest income earners have a before tax and benefit income of 10 units. Following the logic of a purely flat tax and a purely universal spending regime, we see that the initial income distribution goes from 1 to 10 to a final income distribution of 1 to 3.7.

In point of fact, no tax system is perfectly flat and no social spending system is perfectly universal. But, as this model implies, a purely flat tax system, if combined with universal benefits/services, is likely to be more progressive in its effects than the targeted systems found in many real world countries. Again, the redistribution is achieved by taxes being paid as a percentage of the income while universal benefits are nominal. Thus, in a universal system where 'everyone pays the same' and 'everyone receives the same', a huge amount of redistribution is taking place.

The political reason as to why universal policies are more effective in alleviating poverty is that if a state is going to tax the rich and give to the poor, the rich and semi-rich (that is, the middle class) will not agree to pay high taxes because they perceive that they do not get enough back from the government (Korpi and Palme 1998). They will perceive social services and benefits programmes as policies only for 'the poor'. The middle class in particular (who are usually the 'swing voters') will turn away from political parties that argue for an increase in taxes and social policies (Rothstein and Uslaner 2005).

Many have argued that the social democratic states are under threat from the economic forces of globalisation. The argument is that high levels of taxation and social spending – and indeed economic equality itself – are simply not sustainable in the modern competitive world. Looking at the facts, however, it is difficult to sustain such a simplistic argument. What is at issue is not how much the government taxes and spends, but rather how it taxes the private economy and spends that money. Social democracies, as we have seen, have done notably well economically just as economic competition has heated up in recent years. Second, there is no coherent or consistent correlation between tax or spending levels and economic performance across the OECD (Steinmo 2010: 207–14). Third, as Werner Sinn and others have pointed out, public spending is not necessarily bad for the economy not only because it pays for education and infrastructure, but also because much social spending can be considered insurance. Insurance lowers individual risk, and in a dynamic environment lowering individual risk can contribute to innovation and productivity (Sinn 1994: 1; Steinmo 2010: 213–17). Finally, as Rothstein and Uslaner (2005) have argued, a high level of equality is strongly correlated with high levels of social trust. Social trust, we submit, lowers transaction costs in the social economy, and in the context of an increasingly competitive and fast-changing world, those systems that can lower transaction costs have many competitive advantages.

### Why does social democracy work?

Perhaps neo-liberals or classical conservatives will find the data presented above difficult to accept. They will not like the fact, or will not believe, that countries with high levels of taxation, social spending and economic equality can do so well in economic performance, budgetary finance, and/or social trust/satisfaction and happiness. Perhaps such sceptics will argue that there is something about these countries that makes them so successful other than the distinctive public policies they have pursued; or perhaps that they are successful despite the social democratic policies they have pursued (Bergh 2006). We suggest that the key to the outcomes demonstrated here is that social democratic states have been able to strike a balance between equity, inclusiveness and personal choice or freedom. Social democracies have pursued policies that, first, attempt to build and support the whole of society, rather than simply their voters and/or class supporters, and, second, attempt to give

**Table 6.2** Public social expenditure on income tested programmes, selected OECD countries, 2007

|              | % GDP | % Soc X public | Soc X public in cash |
|--------------|-------|----------------|----------------------|
| Australia    | 5.6   | 34.9           | 75.9                 |
| Denmark      | 1.6   | 6.2            | 13.0                 |
| France       | 4.1   | 14.5           | 24.1                 |
| Germany      | 3.3   | 13.1           | 22.5                 |
| Ireland      | 4.3   | 26.3           | 48.4                 |
| Italy        | 1.2   | 5.0            | 7.3                  |
| Japan        | 0.6   | 3.0            | 5.3                  |
| Netherlands  | 3.6   | 18.1           | 36.1                 |
| Norway       | 1.4   | 6.8            | 14.1                 |
| Sweden       | 1.1   | 4.0            | 8.5                  |
| UK           | 5.0   | 24.1           | 50.0                 |
| US           | 1.2   | 7.5            | 15.2                 |
| OECD Avg.    | 2.0   | 10.6           | 21.2                 |

*Source:* Adema et al. 2011, available at <http://dx.doi.org/10.1787/5kg2d2d4pbf0-en> (last accessed 6 March 2013)

individuals more life choices within that community. As a result transaction costs in social and economic relations are lower than they would otherwise be.

Table 6.2 shows the amount of social welfare public spending that is delivered via income-tested benefits in several OECD countries. We see that the anglophone countries in particular rely heavily on targeted 'poor relief' programmes, whereas countries dominated by social democratic policies use these targeted policies much less.

Neo-liberal regimes also emphasise individual choices, but instead of improving life choices, including heavy investment in human capital, within a community, these regimes pit individuals against each other. These societies can well achieve high levels of competitive success, but at the cost of social cohesion, interpersonal trust, broad-based high-quality education and, in the end, increased anomie. More explicitly redistributive welfare states have often built large and expensive social programmes, but these systems champion the interests of the organised and politically powerful, resulting, for example, in what we would call 'pension states'. Thus, the critical difference between classically redistributive welfare states and social democracy is that whereas social democracy is universalist, the more common type of welfare state like those found in many European countries and most obviously in the Anglo-American world are targeted. Certainly it is true that even the most universalistic social democratic state, Sweden, has several programmes that are designed to aid particular target groups. But in the continental welfare state virtually all programmes are targeted to specific groups. Social programmes in these countries, especially in the social insurance sector, usually cater to specific (employment-based) segments of the population that are therefore treated differently by the state. Ironically, in this way they are more similar to the liberal states like the US.

### Continued support for the social democratic welfare state

We have highlighted many of the strengths of the social democratic model of society and shown how it has been the foundation of some of the most successful political economies in the advanced democratic world. Still, many analysts believe that the election of centre-right governments in countries like Sweden surely spells the death of social democracy in these countries. We are sceptical of this argument. Public opinion evidence demonstrates that the foundational principles and policies of social democracy are highly popular in these countries. In other words, it would be political suicide for the centre-right parties to make a head-on attack on the social democratic state, something that these parties also have realised. The table below gives some indication of the level of support the voting public, in Sweden at least, have for some of the basic features of the welfare state. It also demonstrates that they are increasingly willing to pay taxes to finance these programmes. Stefan Svallfors, Sweden's leading expert on public attitudes to the welfare state, summarises his findings as follows: 'There are two remarkable findings [in Table 6.3]. One is the sharply increased willingness between 2002 and 2010 to pay more taxes ... The second finding is that for all listed policies, the proportion that is willing to pay more taxes is actually *larger* than the proportion that want to increase overall spending for that policy' (Svallfors 2011: 9).

In short, we do not believe that the major threat to social democracy in social democratic states comes from the pernicious undermining of the social welfare state by mass political parties. We cite Svallfors's conclusions from his most recent analysis of Swedish attitudes:

> Hence, no corrosive feedback effects from changing welfare policies may be detected in the Swedish public. It seems rather that the changes in institutional practices and political rhetoric that have taken place in the 1990s and 2000s have further strengthened middle-class support for the welfare state. In an ironic twist of fate, market-emulating reforms of the welfare state and the changed political rhetoric of the political right-of-center completed the full ideological integration of the middle class into the welfare state. The electoral base for any resistance against a high-tax, high-spending, collective welfare state now looks completely eroded. While the Social Democratic party suffers, the Social Democratic welfare state thrives. (2011: 15)

**Table 6.3** Attitudes towards public spending in Sweden 1997–2010
Individual willingness to pay taxes for welfare policies
Willingness to pay more taxes for . . . (per cent answering 'definitely' or 'probably')

|  | 1997 | 2002 | 2010 |
|---|---|---|---|
| Medial and health care | 67 | 65 | 75 |
| Support for the elderly | 62 | 60 | 73 |
| Support for families with children (child allowances, child care) | 42 | 39 | 51 |
| Social assistance | 29 | 25 | 40 |
| Comprehensive and secondary schooling | 62 | 61 | 71 |
| Employment policy measures | 40 | 31 | 54 |
| Base | 1,290 | 1,075 | 3,800 |

*Source:* Svallfors 2011: Table 2

### Challenges for social democracy – from the right and the left

Having noted that there continues to be widespread support for the social democratic welfare state amongst strong majorities of voters, we are not so sanguine as to believe that there are no challenges ahead for social democratic societies. Our argument has been that one of the core principles of social democracy is that of universality. In our view, there are two potential threats to this fundamental principle emerging in several social democratic states. Curiously, these threats come from both the political right and the left in these countries.

The first, and certainly most obvious, challenge to the universalistic principles underlying social democracy comes from an emerging anti-immigrant sentiment in several of these countries. In the most recent elections in Sweden, for example, the anti-immigrant Sweden Democrats (SvD) party won 5.7% of the popular vote and entered the *Riksdag* for the first time. Similar populist parties have been a feature of Danish and Norwegian electoral politics for a much longer time. However, it should be underlined that these parties are not anti-welfare, or anti-social-spending, but are instead right-wing anti-immigrant parties arguing that immigrants overuse and/or abuse the social programmes or that, because they are immigrants, they have no right to benefit from these programmes (Rydgren 2012a). Recent analysis shows that increased ethnic heterogeneity is not necessarily a major problem for the underlying social solidarity on which the social democratic type of welfare states are built. Repeated surveys on the level of social trust among the population in the Nordic countries show that despite the high level of immigration in particular in Sweden and Denmark, the level of social trust remains notably high and stable.[8] Moreover, Dinesen (2011a and 2011b) and Kumlin and Rothstein

(2010) show that immigrants that come from countries in which the level of social trust is very low often increase their level of social trust by a considerable extent. The most important factor for this to happen is if they perceive that they have been fairly treated by the government authorities. And since universal programmes are not plagued by intrusive means-testing, such institutional fairness is easier to achieve in a typical social democratic welfare state. Thus, the 'new liberal dilemma', as it has been called, stating that increased ethnic heterogeneity spells problems for social trust and social solidarity, may not be as set in stone and as problematic for the social democratic type social solidarity as has been portrayed (Kumlin and Rothstein 2010: 77). One reason may be that since universal social services and social insurance programmes are less prone to 'overuse' or 'abuse', social democratic parties are not as easily forced into the politically awkward position of defending misdirected public services.

Another interesting challenge, in our view, comes from the radical left within these countries. Here we see a new politics arising in which particular groups, interests and identities are to be championed and given special attention or treatment. We submit this is dangerous for social democracy as well. In recent years there has been considerable pressure from the left within the social democratic movements towards various forms of identity politics. Ethnicity, sexual orientations and various lifestyle issues have been proposed as mobilising factors that have become grounds for making specific demands for targeted policies for these identity groups. We believe that this political discourse is difficult to combine with universalism (Dahlström 2004).

We argue here that, for the social democratic project to be sustainable, it is essential to keep and maintain the general welfare systems, and not to conduct a politics directed at 'the most vulnerable'. The reasons for this are threefold. Firstly, general welfare systems need to encompass the middle class, without which it is impossible to reach a majority in favour of such politics, or to generate a sufficiently large amount of tax revenues in order to carry out general welfare politics. Secondly, general systems prove more efficient in achieving redistribution to resource-weak groups, compared to politics immediately directed at these groups. The third reason is that programmes directed toward especially vulnerable groups tend to stigmatise these very groups, rendering the programmes partly counterproductive.

## Conclusions

As the other chapters in this volume point out, there are many plausible explanations for why we are currently witnessing a crisis at the polls for European social democracy. What we have suggested is that one cause can be dismissed, namely that, compared to other socio-economic models, the social democratic one does not deliver. As we show, based on a large set of standard measures of what should be counted as a 'successful society', the social democratic model outperforms not only the low tax/low public spending neo-liberal model but also the more centrist Christian Democratic model to a surprising degree. There may be many reasons why several leading social democratic parties have still not been able to convert this into electoral success and struggle to find a politically viable strategy. But the fact that social democracy as an idea or as a viable model has failed is clearly not one of them.

It is all the more strange since one can argue that social democracy's main ideological adversary, namely neo-liberal market fundamentalism, is in serious trouble. The October 2008 financial crash has made the idea that markets ought not be regulated quite controversial. We note, for example, that even the call for 'austerity' so common in the early half of 2012 is already breaking down towards demands for more equal sacrifices across all groups and classes in society.

While some extreme politicians on the right in the US may still espouse some version of a neo-liberal doctrine, believing that markets left to themselves would take care of any 'imperfections', for most economists and politicians alike this argument has lost a large part of its credibility. It is worth noting that while the Nobel Economics Prize Committee at one time donned their seal of approval to free-market ideologies, more recent winners such as Joseph Stiglitz and Paul Krugman have argued that the Chicago school of economics needs to be passed to the landfills of history.

The recent (May 2012) success by the French Socialists in the presidential election and the dramatic increase in the polls for the Swedish Social Democrats may indicate that the tides are turning. One historical parallel may be put forward as an answer to why the deep economic downturn of 2008, which at least to some extent has discredited neo-liberalism, has not resulted in an immediate political gain for social democratic parties. In a recent study, Johannes Lindvall shows that the 1929 economic crisis, which resulted in the even more dramatic economic depression of the 1930s, did not result in any immediate political gains for left-wing parties. He shows that it took the social democratic parties in the Nordic countries quite some time to come up with a new political-economic model that resulted in their long-term political success. The electoral successes of the left came three or more years after 1929. As Lindvall shows, the pattern is to a large extent the same in the current crisis, which implies that voters do not immediately swing to the left when market economies collapse. It is when the parties to the left present a credible programme for handling the crisis that this shift may occur. This would imply that the current difficulties for European social democracy are more of an intellectual and strategic problem than a problem of performance.

## Notes

1. We note the very similar definition offered in McCrone and Keating 2007.
2. For some of the very best analyses of this idea see Berman 2006.
3. As was the case for FDR's Social Security Program (Derthick 1979).
4. We would like to thank Stefan Svallfors for this observation.
5. Of course this raises the interesting question about whether there is something about being Scandinavian that makes these countries socially democratic, with social democratic policies the products of some deeper historical or cultural facts. Without going into depth on this issue, let us say here that we are sceptical of this line of reasoning due to the fact that many of the key historical facts of these nations' histories have in fact diverged dramatically. For example, while Sweden and Denmark were once powerful imperial regimes, Norway and Finland were colonies. Similarly, the structure of social relations, land tenure and the very nature of feudalism differed significantly in these countries. Finally, their wartime experiences in the twentieth century were also nearly polar opposites, with Denmark and Norway defeated and occupied by the Nazis, Finland siding with the Germans in order to fight their long historic battle against Russia, and Sweden remaining neutral in both wars. It is certainly the case that there was a great deal of policy learning and sharing between these countries in the second half of the twentieth century. But the focus here, then, should be on the policies and not some vague cultural or historical narratives. It is the policies that have made these four countries social democratic, not some kind of primordial cultural attributes.
6. Moreover, having large natural resources is arguably a recipe for all kinds of economic and social disasters that in development literature is known as the 'resource curse'.
7. For a brilliant journalistic analysis of these problems, see Gawande 2009.
8. Social trust, also known as generalised trust, is measured by answers to questions such as 'in general, most people can be trusted'.

# CAN THE SWEDISH SOCIAL MODEL SURVIVE THE DECLINE OF THE SOCIAL DEMOCRATS?

Henry Milner

## Introduction

This chapter begins with a contention dating back more than twenty years (see Milner 1989): in Sweden, social democracy is not merely the programme of a party, but constitutes a way of life incorporated into the institutions of society. Despite some overreaching in the 1970s, and the ensuing backlash in the early 1980s, the social democratic way of life had become entrenched in what had come to be known as the 'Swedish model'. The model consisted of a logically coherent set of policies and institutions instituted over half a century by the Swedish Social Democratic Party (SAP) and its allies in and beyond the labour movement. The model withstood the wide-reaching challenges to the welfare state identified with globalisation, the neo-conservative policies of Reagan and Thatcher and the public choice ideas underlying them (Milner 1994). Adaptations to these challenges, not only in Sweden but also in Finland, Norway and Denmark, did not undermine the fundamentals of the model. Indeed, the policy choices effectively defied the stark logic of public choice: supporting the welfare state constituted a rational choice for Scandinavians.

While, as we shall see, it was never only a matter of having social democrats in power, the predominance of the SAP during this period was an enduring and seemingly eternal part of the Swedish landscape. This is no longer the case. In the last decade a significant change has taken place in Sweden, the cradle of twentieth-century social democracy, with possible repercussions elsewhere in Scandinavia and beyond. The SAP's dominant political role has come to an end. Emerging generations do not necessarily associate supporting the policies and institutions the Social Democrats created during their years in power with voting for them in elections.

The erosion of the SAP's position seems to fit a wider sense that social democratic parties may have outlived their usefulness. As suggested by Keating and McCrone in Chapter 1, 'the social support base of social democracy is eroding, so that it is no longer possible to put together the coalitions of interests that underpinned social democratic projects in the various states of Europe in the past.' Put more widely, that erosion is seen as reflecting developments in a globalised world in which the dominant factors are no longer those of class and state but rather of new communications-related technologies. Swedish social democracy successfully adapted to technological and sociological changes over more than half a century. This chapter asks if it can continue to do so under current conditions without a powerful social democratic party at or even near the helm.

## The new political situation

In September 2010, the Swedish Social Democrats suffered an unprecedented defeat. The SAP, in power for over 80% of the period from 1932 to 2010, marked its worst results since 1914, with 30.6% of the vote, a mere 0.6 percentage points ahead of the Moderates (Conservatives). The outcome, observers agreed, was the final nail in the coffin of SAP hegemony. Swedish exceptionalism, as based on a social democratic party perpetually in or near power, is a thing of the past.

But how significant is this development? Such hegemony has long been absent among Sweden's Nordic neighbours, where social democratic parties have been out of government as often as they have been in power, and in power only in coalition. Nevertheless, in adopting key aspects of the model, the SAP's sister parties were able to take advantage of policy developments under SAP hegemony. Moreover, the implications transcend Scandinavia. Social democracy in practice in the form of the Swedish model has provided a meaningful alternative to practice elsewhere. A viable Swedish social democratic welfare state undermines the claim that in the globalised IT world in which we live the only durable and effective socio-economic system is one based on market fundamentalism. Its erosion signifies the contrary.

In looking at recent developments in the Nordic world, Sweden in particular, this chapter takes an approach somewhat outside the mainstream of work on the social democratic welfare state. It focuses less on social and economic policy choices, and more on the institutions and the shared understandings that underpin them, especially those concerned with what is termed civic literacy (the capacity of citizens to make sense of the political world and thus choose effectively among alternatives).

In past work (Milner 2002), I have shown that Northern European, especially Scandinavian, countries are higher in civic literacy than comparable countries, and that this correlates with levels of political participation. In countries high in civic literacy, informed political participation is more common especially among those elsewhere often excluded from effective participation in the democratic political process. Their needs and interests, thus, attract the attention of policy-makers and find their way into policy outcomes. Among modern societies, high civic literacy is attained through non-material redistribution, reducing disparities in not only material but also intellectual/cultural resources. Bringing those on the lower rungs of society to higher levels of knowledge not only augments their economic opportunities, it enhances their capacity to exercise political influence through informed political participation. By enhancing citizenship skills and knowledge through non-material redistribution, the countries high in civic literacy spread well-being more widely, evidence of which can be found in the various cross-national indicators of life expectancy, infant mortality and life satisfaction (see Wilkinson and Pickett 2009).

Non-material redistribution was a key dimension of the political culture of the Social Democratic Party and its partners in the labour movement during the years that they dominated Swedish political life (see Milner 1989). Andersson (2009) shows that while, like its policies in power, the ideas of the movement evolved with the changing economic, technological and communications context, this evolution constituted not a rejection but a 're-articulation' of the traditional discourse. In particular, she notes the stress on popular education as a means of achieving one's potential as a free individual through mastering the skills required by emerging workplace technologies, up to and including the development of policies to meet the challenge of the knowledge-based IT economy.

If indeed the political culture of the labour movement is at the core of the Swedish model, the question posed is whether it can be sustained over time in the absence of a hegemonic SAP. To begin to address this question we need to place this cultural dimension in context, to situate it among what may be termed the seven pillars of Scandinavian social democracy. This is not the place to address the wider question of whether the Scandinavian form of social democracy is exportable, but it should be clear to the reader from the discussion below that certain aspects are more the exception than the rule outside Scandinavia.

## *Pillars of Scandinavian social democracy*

1. Strong trade union and other popular representative organisations with structured input into relevant social and economic policy decisions.
2. A strong social democratic party linked to the above, committed to low disparities in income, wealth and power.
3. Political institutions that are administratively decentralised and based on the principle of proportional representation, so that the strength of partisan representation reflects support in the population, and necessitating some

degree of structured cooperation in policy-making and administration at every level.

4. Productive industries capable of maintaining good but internationally competitive salaries and working conditions (driving out low-paying jobs, thus resulting in wage solidarity – the Rehn-Meidner model), necessitating a high level of structured cooperation between employers and trade unions in the labour market.

5. An education and training system that provides and upgrades the skills needed for employment in rapidly changing industries.

6. Social and labour market policies based on the principle of universal services, in health, pensions, unemployment insurance and child care, along with education and training, to complement retraining and mobility.

7. An emphasis on the 'non-material' side of redistribution via adult education, subsidies for study circles, support for public service media, newspaper subsidies and popular libraries.[1]

The erosion of political support for the SAP weakens the second pillar. We return to this factor below. The next section first briefly describes the situation with regard to the other pillars in the light of political and socio-economic developments. It then turns to recent developments that affect the non-material dimension that forms the seventh pillar. The final section returns to an analysis of recent political developments in light of the above.

### The socio-economic context

It is first worth noting the absence from the above list of certain elements that have been associated with the Swedish model. Full employment, considered a fundamental element of the model in the post-war years, is a thing of the past, unsustainable in the globalised world that emerged in the 1980s. Unemployment in Sweden at the end of 2011 was a respectable but not overly impressive 6.7%. The same is true of the major role played by state-owned industries especially in services, transportation and communication. Here, change came about due to globalisation, but also as a backlash to efforts among certain leading elements in the labour movement in the 1970s to challenge the structured cooperation underlying the fourth pillar. The idea was to use state intervention in the labour market rather than structured cooperation to attain egalitarian goals, most notably via wage-earner funds, but also through several laws that sought to impose forms of industrial democracy. By allowing them to raise the threat of confiscation, these initiatives played into the hands of those employers who sought to weaken labour's capacity to attain its objectives by diluting the process of structured accommodation.

As the tendency toward confrontation on the labour market eased in the latter part of the 1980s, policies that gave a greater role to market-based

**Table 7.1** Union density by age and category in Sweden 1990–2007 (%)

| Age/category | 1990 | 1993 | 2000 | 2006 | 2007 | 1990–2007 | 1993–2007 |
|---|---|---|---|---|---|---|---|
| 16–24 | 62 | 69 | 52 | 46 | 40 | −22 | −29 |
| 25–29 | 78 | 81 | 74 | 68 | 64 | −14 | −17 |
| Sum 16–29 | 69 | 76 | 64 | 58 | 53 | −16 | −23 |
| 30–44 | 85 | 86 | 82 | 77 | 74 | −11 | −12 |
| 45–64 | 88 | 89 | 88 | 85 | 82 | −6 | −7 |
| Sum 16–64 | 81 | 85 | 81 | 77 | 73 | −8 | −12 |
| Blue-collar workers | 82 | 86 | 83 | 77 | 74 | −8 | −12 |
| White-collar workers | 81 | 83 | 79 | 77 | 73 | −8 | −10 |

*Source:* Kjellberg 2009

institutions were introduced, confirming that, unlike elsewhere, state owner-ship is not one of the pillars of Swedish social democracy. An example of inte-grating market solutions was that, after long discussion, in 2000 the pension system was reformed with the support of five of the six parties. Within the public scheme, private individual pension accounts could be set up, with the retirement benefits they generate depending solely on the contributions (up to 2.5%) made into them and the actual returns they earn. By 2008, 785 private investment funds were registered (Marier 2010).

Another factor underlying these developments has been a decline in union density (see Table 7.1), a decline that particularly affected the blue-collar, SAP-affiliated LO, whose members constituted 74% of trade unionists in 1960, but

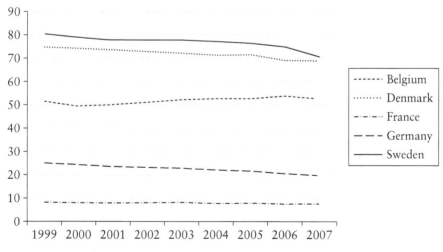

**Figure 7.1** Trade union membership rates 1999–2007
*Source:* Bergstrom 2009: 43

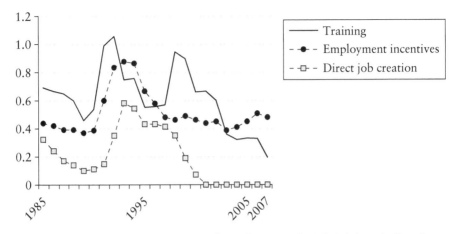

**Figure 7.2** Measures to support workers threatened with job loss in Sweden
*Source:* Bergstrom 2009: 39

only 49% in 2007 (Kjellberg 2009). Nevertheless, as we can see in Figure 7.1, despite the decline, union density is still comparatively high in Sweden. Because of its position, organised labour has been able to adapt to a situation in which its political ally is out of power. In the labour market and the economic sphere generally, the labour movement has been able to use its publicly recognised place in the institutions of structured cooperation to preserve the key elements of the model as set out in the relevant pillars. This includes the municipal and regional level of politics and administration (pillar three), where, in key instances, the SAP has proven better able to maintain its position.

Such strategies, it will be argued below, potentially preserve the accomplishments of the social democratic regimes with the SAP out of power. While it is not possible to provide – or indeed see – anything like a comprehensive picture, it seems fair to suggest that the overall situation is one in which the economy and labour market pillars remain solid. Sweden remains a small open economy, dependent on relatively large exporting companies and highly vulnerable to external factors, to which it must adapt. It continues to do so through a relatively centralised collective bargaining system, which keeps wage levels aligned across industries, thus allowing efficient and advanced export industries to successfully compete – pillar four (and support the redistributive social policies through taxes – pillars five and six), forcing less productive companies to rationalise production through investment in new production technology or workforce reduction.

Such restructuring is accepted by and large by the partners in the labour market and entails a set of agreed-upon measures to support workers to find new jobs in more productive industries. Though short-term job creation measures by government are used during recessions, the emphasis is on training and incentives arranged by the partners in job security councils (see Figure 7.2). Just as non-productive industries in textile and related manufacturing sectors were eliminated in the post-war decades, in recent years we have seen a fundamental restructuring of Swedish industry, from a heavy dependence on manufacturing towards more knowledge-intensive high-tech industry, which has resulted in a solid record of economic performance. Productivity levels have remained stable, partly by abandoning low-productivity jobs and sectors, partly by investment in new technologies and high value added sectors. Instead of maintaining the existing production structure, public policy is oriented toward developing the infrastructure and resources that stimulate new industries and investments.

This approach is illustrated by the government's treatment of the ongoing crisis in the automotive sector (see Bergström 2009). Unlike in North America, there was no question of direct government bail-out: Saab was allowed to go bankrupt (though it may still be revived by a foreign buyer). Instead, in accordance with the model, the basis for the programme lay in collective agreements implemented at the company level. The 'Agreement on temporary lay-offs', concluded in March 2009 for blue-collar manufacturing workers and extended to professional technical staff, provides for compensation of losses in income resulting from working-time reductions. The agreement has been implemented via job-saving agreements, most prominently at Volvo and Scania. At Volvo, jobs were saved by reducing working time, mainly via flexible working-time accounts, with wages almost fully maintained. At Scania a similar agreement limited losses in pay to 10% (with a reduction of working time by 20%) and provides for training funded by the European Social Fund (see Glassner and Keune 2010). The fact that Volvo, along with many of the biggest names in Swedish industry, are no longer Swedish owned suggests that the model does not depend on the existence of national capitalism.

## The cultural/attitudinal context

The technological world today is dramatically different from that of the post-war decade when the economic model was first developed. On balance, it would appear that the fundamental principles, differently applied to be sure, are still in place. To understand this, we must give due weight to the final – cultural – pillar, the non-material side of redistribution via adult education, subsidies for study circles, support for public service media and popular libraries. These strengthen the underpinnings of the entire model. Indeed, they potentially constitute a basis for its continuity among a generation that does not necessarily link supporting the principles of the social democratic welfare state with voting for the SAP and is somewhat less predisposed to joining trade unions.

*Civic literacy*

I argued in earlier work that the capacity of the Scandinavian social democratic welfare state to adapt policy to achieve relatively egalitarian outcomes reflects the quality of the information that enters the decision-making process. This relationship holds not just at the elite level, but also at the level of 'ordinary' citizens, since informed individuals are better able to identify the appropriate policies – and the actors to implement those policies – in order to achieve desired welfare outcomes. In the context of appropriate institutions – the 'supply side' of civic literacy – citizens are also more knowledgeable about the effect their individual choices will have on the institutional arrangements themselves. In a complex, economically interdependent world, it is by no means self-evident what the effects of particular choices will be. To make choices that reinforce the capacity to redistribute without undermining the capacity to adapt requires appropriate information linking actors, policies, institutions and outcomes. If informed individuals can better identify the effects that alternative policy options have upon their own interests and those of others, societies with a larger proportion of informed citizens can be expected to be more egalitarian in their outcomes.

An important, if indirect, indicator of civic literacy is participation in education, especially adult education. The figures here are clear. In 2009, in its report entitled 'Key Data on Education in Europe', the European Commission's agency on Education, Audiovisual and Culture noted that 'In Sweden, 72.3% of those aged 3–29 were in school, the highest in Europe, with average for the EU 27 of 62.9%' (2009: 92). A year later, the Eurostat Yearbook reported that in Sweden, 32.4% of those aged 25–64 were in continuing education, the highest in Europe, with average for the EU 27 of 9.6% (2010: 273).

Consistently high electoral turnout without compulsory voting is another indirect indicator that civic literacy remains high. Having declined to a still comparatively very high 80% in 2002, Swedish turnout rose to 82% in 2006, and in 2010 to 85%, matching Denmark's highest level. The turnout reflects high levels of political attentiveness. Sweden was placed first among the ten countries in the Roper/National Geographic survey of the political geographical knowledge of 18–24-year-olds which assessed the knowledge of political geography of 3,250 young adults in 2002.[2]

Grönlund and Milner (2006) calculated the dispersion of political knowledge using the political knowledge questions in the national electoral surveys assembled by the Comparative Study of Electoral Systems (CSES). Given the absence of common questions,[3] the overall means of correct answers varied widely, from 31% correct in Israel to 64% in the United Kingdom. Hence rather than using this score, the analysis was based on comparative variation from the national mean (F score) for each of three groups broken down by education level attained (incomplete secondary or less; secondary or post-secondary; university undergraduate or more), providing a comparative indicator of the education-based dispersion of political knowledge. Sweden and Norway were found to have a much lower F score than other CSES, notably Anglo-Saxon, countries.

Analysis of the Swedish election survey 1985 to 2010 (see Table 7.2 overleaf for the data up to 2006) shows no overall decline in political knowledge (though we should note that analysing knowledge-level changes across time is a very challenging task, since the difficulty of a single indicator will vary across time). Nevertheless, it is fair to conclude that overall, in countries comparable to Sweden there has been a decline in levels of political knowledge (see Milner 2010, Chapter 5). One empirical indicator of this is provided by the Institute of Economic Affairs in its study of political knowledge, although admittedly it refers to fourteen- and fifteen-year-olds. As we can see in Table 7.3, of the countries participating in both its 1999 survey and its 2009 survey (known as ICCES), Sweden is among the few that did not see a drop in average score.

*Attitudes toward the welfare state*

What of public opinion toward the welfare state? Does reduced support for the Swedish Social Democratic Party indicate reduced support for the welfare state that it founded and nurtured; or, rather, does it reflect the fact that the now powerful Conservatives (Moderates) have moved toward a much greater acceptance of the welfare state? An answer is to be found in the recent work of Stefan Svallfors, who has been conducting surveys on attitudes toward the welfare state in Sweden for several decades. In a recent paper which reports on Swedish attitudes toward the welfare state from 1981 to 2010, Svallfors finds overall a large degree of stability in attitudes in the last three decades. Indeed, whatever change there has been in recent years tends to go in the direction of increasing support, for example in the willingness to pay higher taxes toward welfare state programmes. The proportion of Swedes 'definitely' or 'probably' willing to pay more taxes if those taxes went to welfare state purposes was stable from 1997 to 2002, but rose dramatically between 2002 and 2010 (Svallfors 2011).

Another indicator with similar results is the support for the collective financing of social insurance (unemployment, pensions and health) as opposed to via insurance fees combined with lower taxes and employer contributions. The greatest increase in such support (and in the case of unemployment a reversal from the decrease in support between 1992 and 2006) takes place from 2006 to 2010. A similar trend is noted in attitudes toward negative aspects of the welfare state, such as cheating, as well as perceptions of 'moral hazard' and 'over-consumption'. In response to whether the unemployed really want a job,

**Table 7.2** Political knowledge in Sweden

| | 1985 | 1988 | 1991 | 1994 | 1998 | 2002 | 2006 | |
|---|---|---|---|---|---|---|---|---|
| *Factual knowledge of current state-of-affairs 1985–2006* | | | | | | | | |
| Open unemployment in Sweden is today lower than 5% | 40 | 59 | 58 | 92 | 87 | 45 | 26 | varies |
| Denmark is a member of the EU | – | – | 88 | – | – | – | – | true |
| Spain is a member of the EU | – | – | – | 69 | 75 | 80 | 83 | true |
| A euro is today worth more than 10 Swedish kronas | – | – | – | – | – | 77 | – | false |
| The sickness benefit is today 90% of the wage/salary from 1st day of sick leave | 76 | 82 | 65 | 81 | 83 | 81 | 83 | varies |
| About 10% of all who live in Sweden are born abroad | – | – | – | 45 | 59 | – | – | false |
| Price increases (inflation) have so far in [year] been higher than 9% | 57 | 56 | – | – | – | – | – | false |
| There is a wage earners' fund in each county | 56 | 45 | 43 | – | – | – | – | false |
| Last year, about 20,000 people applied for asylum in Sweden | – | – | – | – | – | 42 | – | true |
| Swedish foreign aid to developing countries is 1% of gross national income | – | – | – | – | – | 34 | 44 | false |
| Last year, Sweden received more than 50,000 refugees from other countries | – | – | 33 | – | – | – | – | false |
| The state budget deficit has increased during the past year | 26 | – | – | – | – | – | – | false |
| *Factual knowledge of the political system and its workings* | | | | | | | | |
| You must cross a candidate on the party list, otherwise your vote will be invalid | – | – | – | – | 88 | – | – | false |
| The Swedish *Riksdag* has 349 members | – | – | 69 | 69 | 74 | 72 | 74 | true |
| The *Riksdag* voted to store abroad highly radioactive waste from nuclear power stations | – | 52 | 46 | 58 | 72 | – | – | false |
| During the period 1998–2002, Sweden had a social democratic one-party government | – | – | – | – | – | 47 | 45 | true |
| *Affiliation of candidates and party officials* | | | | | | | | |
| Anna Lindh | 81 | – | – | – | – | 83 | – | sd |
| Karin Söder | – | – | – | – | – | – | – | c |
| Erik Åsbrink | – | – | – | – | 80 | – | – | sd |
| Bosse Ringholm | – | – | – | – | – | 78 | – | sd |
| Åsa Domeij | – | – | – | – | – | 76 | – | green |
| Göran Persson | – | – | – | 76 | – | – | – | sd |
| Ingvar Carlsson | 75 | 75 | 54 | – | – | – | – | sd |
| Thage G. Petersson | – | 75 | – | – | – | – | – | sd |
| Eva Goës | – | 69 | 75 | – | – | – | – | green |
| Birgit Friggebo | 65 | 71 | 68 | 68 | – | – | – | lib |

*Source:* Derived from Oscarsson 2007, supplemented by his recent data. The results show the percentage of all respondents providing correct answers to the questions indicated.

**Table 7.3** Average civic knowledge score in countries participating in both the 1999 IEA survey and the 2009 ICCES survey

| Country | Mean scale score 2009 | Mean scale score 1999 | Differences between 1999 and 2009 |
|---|---|---|---|
| Finland | 109 | 108 | 1 |
| Slovenia | 104 | 102 | 3 |
| Chile | 89 | 89 | 0 |
| Estonia | 95 | 94 | 1 |
| Lithuania | 94 | 94 | 0 |
| Italy | 100 | 101 | −1 |
| Switzerland | 94 | 95 | −2 |
| Latvia | 91 | 92 | −1 |
| Colombia | 85 | 89 | −4 |
| Norway | 97 | 103 | −5 |
| Greece | 102 | 109 | −7 |
| Poland | 103 | 112 | −9 |
| Slovak Republic | 97 | 107 | −10 |
| Czech Republic | 93 | 103 | −10 |
| Bulgaria | 88 | 99 | −11 |
| Sweden | 98 | 97 | 0 |
| England | 90 | 96 | −6 |

*Source:* Schulz et al. 2010

and whether those who report themselves sick are really sick, Svallfors found suspicion about welfare abuse to be at its lowest level ever in 2010, with the change since the mid-1980s especially salient – and all the more striking as it coincided with a widening political and media debate about welfare cheating and abuse. 'It would seem that whilst the worsening labour market situation may induce some voters to turn away from the SAP for solutions, they do not reject the fundamental premises of the SAP's welfare state policies' (Svallfors 2011: 819).

Interestingly, middle-class and working-class respondents differ less on these questions in 2010 than in earlier surveys, with 'middle-class non-manual groups gradually coming to resemble workers ... The lower- and middle-level non-manual groups increase index values continuously from 1992, and in 2010 the former group is on a par with the workers ... The middle class is now firmly included among the supporters of collective financing of the welfare state' (2011: 818). Svallfors's conclusion merits citing at length:

What seems to have taken place in the last few years is that since their main party – the Moderates – have embraced the core aspects of the welfare state, even the higher salariat and the self-employed have increasingly become supporters of a collective welfare state. The Social Democratic Party may be in dire straits electorally, but the

social democratic welfare state is more popular than ever . . . The changes in institutional practices and political rhetoric that have taken place in the 1990s and 2000s
have further strengthened middle-class support for the welfare state. In an ironic
twist of fate, market-emulating reforms of the welfare state and the changed political
rhetoric of the political right-of-centre completed the full ideological integration of
the middle class into the welfare state. While the Social Democratic Party suffers, the
social democratic welfare state thrives. (2011: 820)

The answer for Svallfors is clear. The decline of the SAP and the rise of the
Moderates reflect not changing attitudes towards the welfare state, but rather
the Moderates' embracing of the key aspects of the Swedish welfare state.
It may be ironic, but it is quite understandable why the acceptance by the
Conservatives of the basic premises of the welfare state should have in effect
won over otherwise reticent middle-class Swedes.

Svallfors does not ask whether this situation is likely to continue, but his
analysis suggests that this could very well be the case. If voters, especially
middle-class voters, are coming around to trust the non-socialists more than
the SAP with administering the welfare state, it does not bode well for the latter's electoral prospects. Svallfors does not pose the wider question of whether
the disconnection between support for the welfare state and support for the
party that established it entails no longer identifying with social democracy as
an alternative world view to the dominant neo-liberal view that is taking hold
elsewhere. It is a question that cannot be answered at this point, but the existence of the possibility – if not likelihood – suggests that (small-s) social democrats should not accept with equanimity the prospect of further SAP decline.

### Social democratic prospects and strategy in the current context

It would appear, thus far, that the erosion of the social support base for the
Social Democratic Party has not yet resulted in the erosion of the project realised over several generations. But we cannot presume that this will continue to
be the case. There are political choices to be made that could have more lasting
and profound implications.

In the 2006 election, the Social Democrats lost to a united 'bourgeois' opposition, the 'Alliance for Sweden' formed by the Moderates with the Liberals,
Centre and Christian Democrats. A key factor in the Alliance's victory was
that, unlike earlier non-socialist blocs, its spokespersons consistently presented
a common and coherent – and genuinely moderate – election platform. Indeed,
by 2004 the dominant Conservatives were imitating Tony Blair, restyling
themselves as the 'new Moderates' under the now Prime Minister Frederick
Reinfeld.

At first, it appeared like just another interregnum. Unpaid taxes led to two
ministerial resignations, and a number of early political decisions reflected a

lack of experience in government. Changes in the tax structure, ending the tax-exempt status of union membership fees, and tighter restrictions on social-security eligibility and sick leave, as well as a reform of the property tax system and abolition of the wealth tax, proved generally unpopular. As the popularity of the new Alliance government plummeted, the SAP under Mona Sahlin sat back and awaited its return to power.

Little thought was thus given to the implications of the Conservatives having reconciled themselves to the core components of the welfare state. Instead, the focus was on criticism of the new government's taxation policies. Yet the Alliance's tax reforms were more complementary than contradictory to the existing system. Moreover, the earned-income tax credit, which raised the disposable income of lower-paid groups, and thus served as an incentive to work, proved popular, and was reluctantly endorsed by the SAP – despite the vocal opposition of the Left Party. And one tax reform was very popular: that to the RUT, the tax deductibility of payments to people or companies engaged to do household repairs and child care. This measure had long been resisted by the Swedish labour movement as exploitation of workers. Failure by the SAP to act on this whilst in power had forced many otherwise law-abiding, pro-welfare-state Swedes to hire help 'in the black' to avoid the onerous charges they were expected to pay. It was a natural step for some of these urban middle-class voters to consider alternatives to the SAP.

An indicator of more profound change came in the creation of an alliance on the left to oppose the Moderate-led one. This was a new stance for the SAP, borrowed from the Norwegians, where the Labour Party governed with the Greens and Socialist Left Party. Sahlin's establishing such a Red-Green alliance constituted an acknowledgement of the end of SAP hegemony. While coherent cooperation with the Greens proved effective, the same was not the case with the Left Party, whose spokespersons accentuated those areas of policy that alienated middle-class voters in the bigger cities, the voters lost by the centre-left in 2006. It was only an intervention by the trade unions that blocked an effort by the SAP and the Greens to dump the Left Party from the alliance.

Sahlin's authority was undercut by such squabbles. In an effort to make up lost ground in the run-up to the 2010 election she made promises that appeared incoherent. According to a December 2010 report by an SAP commission tasked with an analysis of the election results, the main cause of the party's loss of support was its budget proposal which would raise the property and petrol taxes of its potential supporters, which appeared incoherent as well when Sahlin suddenly promised big tax cuts for pensioners.

More profoundly, the SAP's traditional claim to being the best economic manager was undermined in the process. This was not the case before 2006. The outgoing SAP government had maintained tight fiscal balance. Hence, when hit by the economic downturn, cash was available to the new government to speed up recovery – an opportunity not missed by the able young finance minister, Anders Borg. A remarkably articulate communicator and, apparently, administrator, Borg's reputation for economic competence steadily grew as the 2010 election neared. Indeed, the SAP would probably have done even worse if the populist Sweden Democrats hadn't surged in the late polls, polls which also showed that Sahlin had rallied lukewarm supporters around opposition to this threat in the last ten days of the campaign.

How real was the threat? The election marked the end of innocence on immigration and integration, with the Sweden Democrats entering parliament by crossing the minimum 4% threshold, winning 5.3% of the vote. But the result is not the 'nightmare scenario' of the radical right being in the driver's seat that Sahlin had evoked. For one thing, government and opposition were both explicit on refusing to allow the SD to use its balance-of-power position to win policy concessions, and this has proven essentially to be the case. Moreover, while early on some Sweden Democrats sounded like the old Nazi sympathisers portrayed in the first volume of Stieg Larsson's *Millennium* (entitled, in the original Swedish version, *The Men who Hate Women*), under its current 31-year-old leader, web designer Jimmy Akensson, the SD cleaned the house of overtly racist elements, insisting that the SD was 'not against immigrants, just immigration policy'. Too much immigration, they claimed, is undermining the Swedish welfare state, which they seek to secure, not tear down. Indeed, except in their position on immigration and harsher punishment for youth offenders, the Sweden Democrats' programme is not out of the mainstream.

Elsewhere in Europe the expression of such views is only to be expected, and would not provoke the shocked reaction to the SD breakthrough. With an effective new leader and real experience in local councils in southern Sweden, it was inevitable that they would improve their organisation and showing. It is this, rather than changing popular attitudes, that explains the Sweden Democrats' success. That their showing was widely seen among Swedes as a fundamental threat rather than a marginal development is due in good part to the fact that serious public debate about immigration and integration is largely absent. The crime, violence and other problems associated with immigrant-dominated suburbs are little covered in the media and ignored by mainstream politicians seeking to avoid any possible hint of racist attitudes – leaving the field open to the Sweden Democrats and their one-sided analysis.

Politically, Mona Sahlin's legacy – she announced her resignation soon after the defeat – may be one of placing anti-racism at the core of the SAP's identity. The political impact of this stance is unclear. The SAP reached out to immigrant groups, which account for 14% of the Swedish population, and a larger portion of its unemployed. The party has commendably sought to attract candidates from these communities, assigning important positions to individuals from an immigrant background, notably party secretary Ibrahim Baylan. Yet its shrill denunciations of the SD and of any hints of racism may prove counterproductive since political participation among immigrant groups is low, while it weakens the SAP's identity as the party of workers. The political problems inherent in this approach were manifested in the poor showing of the SAP in the regional and local Stockholm elections in which the Conservatives and their allies, especially the Centre Party,[4] strengthened their already strong position.

The net result is that the SAP came out of the election with few believing that it was still the party best suited to manage the economy. Yet rebuilding that confidence is not an impossible task. Developments elsewhere indicate that the SAP can still appeal to the urban voter. In contrast with the Stockholm region, in 2010 the SAP and its allies maintained control not only of their northern bastions, but also of Sweden's second and third largest cities, Gothenburg and Malmo, in the southwest. In both cities, far-sighted local administrations were able to retain their working-class base while appealing to a sophisticated emerging middle class with a well-articulated programme emphasising sustainable economic development based on research and development, especially in the new communications technologies. In the former, Anneli Hulthén has managed to follow in the footsteps of her predecessor, Göran Johansson, from whom she took over at the beginning of 2009. Johansson, an old-style SAP trade unionist, placed the role of the city's scientific and artistic communities at the forefront of its development. In Malmo, SAP Mayor Ilmar Reepalu has presided over its profound transition from the classic deteriorating smokestack city to a beacon of high-tech, sustainable development (Reepalu and Rosberg 2010).

In these regions, SAP-led administrations were able to link the labour movement to a high-tech project based on research and education. Yet, in the national election debate, it was the Alliance, and especially the Liberals, which made educational reform and modernisation their issue. Without such a clearly articulated project at the national level, the SAP did a poor job of distinguishing its position from that projected by its Red-Green allies. This has already been noted with regard to the Left Party, whose stance on taxes and economic issues and radical foreign policy scared off middle-class voters. The converse problem with reconciling the positions of the Greens with the SAP's traditional working-class base was well expressed in an article in October 2010 by Niklas Nordström, a social democratic member of the Stockholm Regional Council.

> The Social Democrats and unions have always agreed that the redistribution of wealth requires, well, wealth. The party has also contended that economic growth is the key to developing new and greener technology for a more sustainable future. Sweden's Greens, however, increasingly perceive economic growth to be incompatible with their lofty environmental aspirations. The global financial crisis only served to cement this view . . . The Green Party did improve its share of the electorate, but it mainly siphoned voters from the Social Democrats. The strategy to attract young,

environmentally aware, urbanites who would have traditionally voted centre-right simply never panned out. Distrust of the Green Party was especially high in historically Social Democrat strongholds. I have experienced this suspicion firsthand when talking to family and friends in northern Sweden. 'They want to take away our way of life. They want to close our factories, take our cars and our snow scooters. They want to restrict hunting and travel. We have absolutely nothing in common. Their values aren't my values. Why are we in bed with this party?'

## Conclusions

Sahlin was replaced as leader of the Social Democrats by Hakan Juholt, a virtual unknown. His lack of experience soon became apparent as he became bogged down in mini-scandals and internal party squabbles, leading to further drops in the polls (25% at the beginning of 2012), largely to the benefit of the Greens, who reached a record 12%. In late January 2012 Juholt was replaced by a member of the party executive, Stefan Löfven, a respected trade unionist from the north, president of the Steelworkers union (IF Metall) since 2005. Though he lacked a seat in the *Riksdag*, his selection increased the party's credibility. Combined with the selection as leader by the Left Party of another northerner, Jonas Sjöstedt, identified with the moderate wing of his party, the prospects of renewed Red-Green alliance increased substantially, a development reflected in the polls, which saw the three parties' combined support surpass that of the ruling coalition.

Still, these are untried leaders benefiting from the novelty factor. Prospects for a return to power by the SAP and its allies will be largely determined by the Alliance's record of economic management, which, so far, remains solid.[5] Still, longer-term prospects for Red-Green are not necessarily bleak. Overall, the three parties did better among young voters in the 2010 election. A poll three months before the election showed that it led among 18- to 29-year-olds, while all other age groups showed greater support for the Alliance.[6] The fact that, as the Swedish Election Survey's analysis of the results clearly showed, this was due not to the SAP's support, which was concentrated among older voters, but to that of its allies adds a certain urgency to the renewal of the Red-Green Alliance (Oscarsson and Holmberg 2011).

To conclude, then, we return to the main argument of this chapter. As noted above, the SAP and its allies, despite low support for their *Riksdag* lists, maintained control of Gothenburg and Malmo. Apparently a strategy of high-tech 'green growth' can be combined with an affirmation of the basic principles of the Scandinavian welfare state so as to attract young and not-so-young workers and professionals. This is the challenge. There is no returning to power on the basis of its past economic and social achievements. Swedes today cannot be counted on to go from supporting the policies and institutions that the Social Democrats enacted and created during their years in power to voting for them in elections. Nor will the SAP be able to go it alone. The immediate challenge is to ensure that the Swedish Social Democratic Party remain a potent political force at all levels of political life,[7] and thus guarantee that the institutional edifice that the Swedish labour movement built remains solid.

Overall, the 2010 election served to affirm the values and achievement of the Swedish welfare state and the desire to find innovative ways of securing that achievement. Not only did turnout attain 85%, according to Statistics Sweden's April 2011 report, the greatest improvement was among the young and foreign-born. And voters expressed a remarkably high level of political trust. In the exit poll, 70% stated that they trusted politicians – quite different from elsewhere, and from Sweden in previous decades. Ironically perhaps, since the outcome in partisan terms was dramatically different, the 2010 election takes us back to an earlier period of consensus around a shared model.

## Notes

1. Note that while Sweden and Finland are just at the OECD average in the percentage of 5- to 19-year-olds in school (data from 2007), they lead by far when it comes to those 20 to 29 and 30 to 39. The OECD average is, respectively, 25 and 6; for Finland it is 43 and 14, and for Sweden 35 and 13 (Swedish National Agency for Education 2010: 84).

2. Out of 56 total questions asked across the ten countries surveyed, the average young Swede answered 40 – compared to young Americans who answered 23 questions correctly, with young persons in Great Britain (28) faring almost as poorly.

3. A modicum of similarity emerges out of the stipulation that their content be chosen to try to have them answered correctly by roughly one-third, one-half and two-thirds of respondents respectively.

4. The Centre Party found a space vacated by the Moderates on the right wing, i.e. neo-liberal, side of the Alliance, seeking urban votes to replace those from its declining rural base. This has puzzled its supporters and activists in the periphery, some of whom are still involved in old-style cooperation with local social democrats.

5. In early 2011, Borg's accomplishments at steering Sweden's economy drew the plaudits of the OECD, its growth being described as 'as strong as Pippi Longstocking'. A month later, in its Global Competitiveness Report for 2010–11, the World Economic Forum placed Sweden second, after Switzerland, for having the world's most transparent and efficient public institutions, with very low levels of corruption and undue influence, and a government that is considered to be one of the most efficient in the world.

6. The poll showed that the centre-left Red-Greens had 56% support among 18- to 29-year-olds compared with 32% for the centre-right Alliance. The party with the highest youth support was the Social Democrats at 34%, with the Green Party at 16%, and the Left Party at around 6%.

7. One temptation will be for the SAP to push for a majoritarian system to replace the

proportional one. This is something that might appeal as well to the Moderates if their coalition becomes fractious. But this still unlikely plan would be unlikely to succeed: public opinion can be expected to side with the small parties in defence of the third pillar. The reality of the American two-party system is not very appealing from a European perspective.

# MULTICULTURALISM, RIGHT-WING POPULISM AND THE CRISIS OF SOCIAL DEMOCRACY

Susi Meret and Birte Siim

## Introduction

Globalisation and increased migration to and within Europe have led to a growth in nationalisms and anti-equality, anti-diversity and anti-human-rights agendas inside and outside the EU (Banting and Kymlicka 2006; Rydgren 2012b; Wodak et al. 2012). Migration from non-Western countries has changed the social and political landscape in the Nordic countries. Norway, Sweden, Finland and Denmark[1] have a democratic tradition of including peasants, workers and women in politics and society (Bergqvist et al. 1999). With their universal welfare states and strong egalitarian traditions, these countries are often included among the most equal societies in international rankings, particularly by class and gender.

Nordic welfare states have been successful in economic terms, and the basic components of extended welfare policies and redistribution are today supported by mainstream political projects. Since the 1970s, the countries have developed extended gender equality policies which are supported by the political left and the right. Social equality, democracy and gender equality have today become crucial elements in the Nordic sense of national belonging. Yet there are serious problems in relation to accommodating ethno-cultural and religious diversity and including immigrant minorities as equal citizens (Brochmann and Hagelund 2010).

Multicultural policies for accommodating 'complex diversity' point to social and political contexts in which diversity has become a multidimensional and increasingly fluid empirical phenomenon (Kraus 2011). The challenge that multiculturalism presents for social democracy – to renegotiate principles of economic redistribution with recognition of diversity – has entailed intense debates[2] within the Nordic contexts. Besides, the present economic and

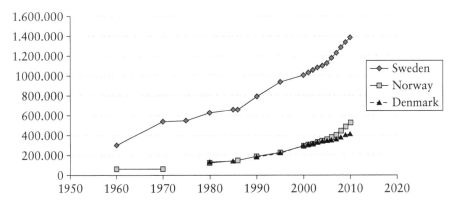

**Figure 8.1** The number of immigrants in Sweden, Norway and Denmark between 1960 and 2010

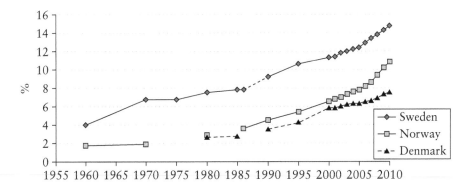

**Figure 8.2** The relative number (percentage) of immigrants of the populations in Sweden, Norway and Denmark between 1960 and 2010

*Sources:* Breidahl 2012. Breidahl's dissertation is based upon data from: Statistics Sweden, Statistics Norway and Statistics Denmark; Ministry for Refugees, Immigration and Integration, 2010, and Breidahl's own calculations.

financial crisis exacerbated the situation and amplified the need – particularly for the social democratic parties – to discuss and rethink their approach to fundamental principles of social solidarity, democracy and citizenship embedded in nation-states and welfare regimes under the present post-national conditions.

But the crisis of social democratic parties is not a recent phenomenon; studies in the past decade have analysed the changing electoral fortunes, constraints, opportunities and transformations faced by European social democracy (Kitschelt 1994; Kriesi et al. 2008). Most of this literature emphasises the difficulties encountered by European socialist and social democratic parties in tackling the changing class structures in advanced capitalist socie-ties. Working-class support for these parties started to shrink in the 1970s, a development further intensified by growing in-migration and by the increasing internationalisation of the labour markets. These transformations condensed into the emergence of new political cleavages on socio-cultural and religious issues, which gained increasing relevance in the restructuring of party systems, and of the political space and logics of party competition and voter alignment (Kitschelt and McGann 1995; Kriesi et al. 2008; Bornschier 2010). The result was a bi-dimensional political space defined by: an economic/redistributive/ equalitarian leftist vs neo-liberal/individualistic dimension; and a new cultural/ value dimension of postmaterialist/libertarian and universalistic vs tradi-tional (materialist)/authoritarian positions (Inglehart 1997; Kriesi et al. 2008; Bornschier 2010).

Social democratic parties generally reacted to these transformations by adopting a dual strategy: maximising their potential electoral support (mainly appealing to highly educated, public employed and professionals), and devel-oping left-libertarian and egalitarian positions on multiculturalism, gender equality, environmentalism and so forth. At the same time, under the guise of 'Third Way' politics, several social democratic parties began promoting neo-liberal-inspired reforms, justifying this choice with the need to create realistic balances between welfare state schemes and market economy require-ments. These programmatic responses not only resulted in a reconfiguration of the political space, but created opportunities for new political parties to fill the ensuing programmatic void, with respect to both traditional welfarist left-wing economic positions on the one side and traditional authoritarian values coupled with globalisation-sceptical positions on the other (Kitschelt and McGann 1995; Kriesi et al. 2008). It is in this context of structural and societal transformations and of new political opportunities that several contemporary studies locate and explain the rise and consolidation of the populist right. In the Nordic countries several of the challenges for the social democratic parties come today from this new political landscape and players.

This chapter will mainly focus on the relations between welfare and rec-ognition policies in relation to ethno-cultural diversity, which in our view represent the major political, theoretical and programmatic challenges to social democracies. It addresses the intersections between multiculturalism, right-wing populism and the crisis of social democracy from the perspective of Nordic welfare states. The objective is to analyse the specific challenge from multiculturalism[3] and complex diversity to Nordic social democracies. We will look at the 'crisis of social democracy' seen as a decline in popular support from voters and members traditionally loyal to social democratic parties, and discuss attempts to redesign public policies, discourses and strategies to address complex diversities and meet the competition from rivalling political projects, especially populist right-wing parties.

Neo-liberal and conservative political strategies aim at reducing public expenditure by cutting welfare services and increasing labour market participation, for example of immigrants, by means of economic inducements and coercive measures. Right-wing populist approaches differ, since they often combine anti-migration/anti-diversity policies with support for welfare state programmes and an anti-EU agenda with emphasis on national sovereignty (Betz and Meret 2012). In this sense, we suggest that right-wing populism in Nordic welfare states presents a particular and more direct challenge to social democracy today. Although the two belong historically and ideologically to very different political families, they both claim to support welfare policies, as well as gender equality, and the two political projects often compete for the working-class vote (Rydgren 2012b). This chapter aims to highlight the challenges from right-wing populism and to suggest the need to rethink, to redesign and to display the distinctiveness of a social democratic perspective in relation to welfare and equality.

### The multicultural challenge to Nordic equalities

The Nordic countries are often considered to belong to the same welfare regime: a large and generous public sector, with high levels of universalism and tax-financed benefits. Social equality became a core value in the Nordic welfare states during the twentieth century with the expansion of the welfare state supported by broad compromises between the major political parties and the social partners. As a result, the Nordic countries managed to build universal welfare states and strong democracies with a high degree of social equality. Denmark, Finland, Norway and Sweden have all been characterised as having a 'passion for equality', what Esping-Andersen defined as the 'Social Democratic Welfare State Regime' which emphasised the collective responsibilities of the state in order to ensure the rights of the individual (Esping-Andersen et al. 2002).

The countries, however, have different histories and institutions, and they have recently developed different approaches and policies towards the migration and integration of ethnic minorities. Sweden has adopted the most multicultural policies, whereas Denmark since 2001 has adopted relatively restrictive policies (see Hedetoft et al. 2006), with Norway and Finland positioned somewhere in between (Albrekt Larsen 2011). In spite of these differences, the countries face similar challenges in including immigrants and minorities as equal citizens in the labour market, in democracy and in society.

Brochmann and Hagelund (2010) argue that the founding and evolution of the Nordic welfare states can be interpreted as 'welfare nationalism' based upon integration with three central elements: democracy, citizenship and modernisation. Denmark, Norway and Sweden can be understood as one welfare model with three exceptions. The multicultural Swedish model represents a relatively accommodating response towards diversity, which is often contrasted with the restrictive Danish response, and the pragmatic Norwegian response positioned somewhere in between. Danish-Swedish comparisons of policies and discourses indicate that whether public and political discourse labels diversity as a threat or an asset is important, and whether the political majority manages to frame ethnic minority groups as 'them' and 'us', instead of perceiving diversity as an asset, is one of the key factors in shaping public policies (Hedetoft et al. 2006). The studies indicate that divergent integration discourses and policies may be combined with an actual convergence in the practical effects of integration policies (Hedetoft et al. 2006: 406).

Comparative studies demonstrate that the most fundamental similarity in the integration approach of the three Scandinavian countries is the growing emphasis on labour market participation as the route to integration (Brochmann and Hagelund 2010). According to Karin Borevi (2010a) all three countries conform to the ideal of civic integration, but the countries are clearly distinguished in their official requirements for immigrants. Only in Sweden do rights clearly come before duties, as in Marshall's classical citizenship theory (Borevi 2010a: 26–9). The most explicit differences can be found at the political-ideological level: Sweden has the clearest redefinition of a *demos*-based nation-state, with, for example, the right to dual citizenship. This contrasts with Denmark, which between 2001 and 2011 experienced a shift towards *ethnos*, with nine years' residence as a condition for citizenship. Norway has an unclear middle-position on official requirements for immigrants (Brochmann and Hagelund 2010: 356–7). It is not evident, however, what these political-ideological differences mean in practice, since accommodative cultural policies have not led to successful integration of immigrants on the labour market. The studies suggest that the three countries are de facto multicultural countries, which are presently being forced to redefine the national welfare projects faced with global mobility and a growing demand for labour. A comparative analysis demonstrates that traditional welfare state policies have not been successful in developing equality-based policies towards new immigrant groups (Brochmann and Hagelund 2010: 367).

In spite of this, Borevi (2010a) has shown that Sweden followed the general European journey from multiculturalism to civic integration, which is concerned with national cohesion and belonging rather than active accommodation of ethno-national subgroups. However, in spite of a greater emphasis on individual obligations in welfare policies, Swedish integration policies still tend to be based on individual 'rights' rather than obligations. Three examples illustrate how Swedish integration policies differ from the general European trends: (1) politicians have rejected citizenship tests, the obligation for immigrants to learn the Swedish language and history as a condition for citizenship; (2) programmes of introduction are still voluntary and not mandatory; and (3) immigrants have the freedom to choose where to live (Borevi 2010b: 116–30). The Swedish activation programmes, which tend to be general and voluntary, are based upon 'an individual rights model' (Borevi 2010b), and thus contrast with the similar Danish programmes which since 2002 have been increasingly premised upon 'an individual obligation model' with economic sanctions that target immigrant groups (Emerek and Bak Jørgensen 2009).

Nordic migration research has started to compare welfare and integration/ immigration policies and discourses and has shown that, in spite of different policies, there are important similarities related to a common perception of welfare, which can be interpreted as a form of 'welfare nationalism'. Arguably this welfare nationalism is based upon a strong historical tradition of social equality and a more recent belief in the principle of gender equality. This emphasis on redistribution combines with a relatively weak tradition for recognition policies and accommodation of ethno-cultural diversity. Studies find that the trend toward divergent immigration/integration policies is combined with a trend toward convergence on the practical and common responsibility of integrating immigrants as equal citizens. This is why understanding the challenge of migration/multiculturalism is fundamental in order to put gender equality in perspective and to acknowledge the need to redesign equality policies in a way that can include diversities among women.

### The intersections of ethno-cultural diversity and gender equality

Comparative Nordic research has shown that the Nordic countries share basic characteristics in relation to gender relations: (1) a dual breadwinner model combined with a system of public childcare services and generous maternity and parental leave; (2) a relatively high number of women in the national political elite; and (3) a strong discourse about gender equality as part of both public policies and the private lives of citizens (see Bergqvist et al. 1999; Melby et al. 2008). The level of trust in the state is comparatively high and led Helga Hernes in the late 1980s to coin the phrases 'state feminism' and 'women-friendliness' in order to capture the close relationship between feminist mobilisation and state responsiveness in Scandinavia, in relation to both work life and family responsibilities (see Borchorst and Siim 2008).

The increase in migration from non-Western countries has raised concerns about new forms of inequalities between native-born and foreign-born women, and has questioned the ability of the Nordic gender model to accommodate diversity among women (Melby et al. 2008; Siim and Skjeie 2008). Immigrant women are said to represent a special challenge for Nordic governments because of their low labour market participation compared to women from the ethnic majorities, who have had the highest employment rates within the OECD area for several decades.

Feminist scholars have started to address the new challenges of ethnic diversity for 'women-friendly' policies. Gender equality policies are criticised for neglecting diversities and the specific problems of immigrant women, thus making alternative meanings about gender and family relations invisible (Siim 2007; Siim and Borchorst 2010). Post-colonial theory has criticised the dominant trend in Nordic gender and ethnicity research, which limits welfare to native-born citizens, and produces a hegemonic picture of gender and femininity that makes power inequalities between the 'white' majority and immigrant women invisible (De Los Reyes et al. 2003: 31).

Migration and multiculturalism are highly politicised. Research has demonstrated that gender equality in many European countries is being used by anti-migration forces on the left and the right. Scholars have noticed that the dominant 'victimisation discourse', which contrasts gender equality in the (white) majority with the perceived patriarchal oppression of women in the Muslim minority, resonates especially well with the Nordic gender system (Gullestad 2006; Siim and Skjeie 2008; De Los Reyes et al. 2003). This discourse is often shared and further elaborated by mainstream parties and right-wing populist parties (Meret and Siim 2013). In the Danish case, the previous Liberal-Conservative government used gender issues such as forced marriages to legitimise stricter immigration control in relation to family members (Siim 2007; Emerek and Bak Jørgensen 2009).

Immigration has increased inequalities between native and foreign-born citizens, and has challenged the Nordic welfare states' self-understanding as the normative models for welfare, social justice and (gender) equality. Instead of Helga Hernes's grand vision of a society '(w)here injustice on the basis of gender would be largely eliminated without an increase in other forms of inequality, such as among groups of women' (1987: 15), research has pointed to the new inequalities among women. Siim and Skjeie (2008) suggest that the new forms of inequality represent a Nordic gender equality paradox between the white majority, who are included in politics and society, and ethnic minorities, who are marginalised both in the labour market and in politics. Right-wing populism successfully addressed the cultural oppression of women in patriarchal Muslim culture, in opposition to Nordic/national gender equality principles which they claim these societies have already achieved. Social democracy has redesigned egalitarianism to include gender equality. It has, however, failed to renegotiate equality with ethno-cultural diversity and to rethink universalism and egalitarianism so as to include immigrant and refugee groups and thus redesign visions of social justice, including ethnic equality.

### The challenges to social democracy from right-wing populism

In Nordic countries, social democratic welfare policies still find substantial support among the population (Albrekt Larsen 2011), and seem to represent one of the best antidotes in times of economic and financial crisis. In spite of this, actors that have striven to introduce and uphold social rights, equality and same welfare services for all people in society have been poorly rewarded when the fate of social democratic parties is historically considered (cf Rothstein and Steinmo, in this volume). Arguably, traditional social democratic policies have become mainstream policies, despite the fact that only Norway and Denmark today have governments headed by social democrats. On the other hand, social democratic parties seem to fail at elections because they have inadequately dealt with contemporary socio-economic and cultural challenges, such as increasing ethnic diversity and multicultural issues. We argue that these inadequacies partly relate to the fact that social democratic parties have failed to redesign welfare and cultural policies and to integrate immigrants as equal citizens, and that this must be understood in relation to the challenges coming from the populist right.

## Populist-right and working-class support

Working-class support for the populist right has given rise to different interpretations, often seeing a direct relationship between this trend and the social and economic costs of globalisation, particularly given its impact on the social groups considered more vulnerable to the recent economic and social developments (Betz 1994). Right-wing populist parties seem to do well in the economically more prosperous welfare-based Nordic region, which in itself is a factor raising some doubts about the explanatory potential of an approach emphasising the reaction from the globally marginalised. Our position is rather to acknowledge that different context, conditions and opportunities have made this possible, including the difficulties Nordic social democratic parties face in responding to the common challenge facing their welfare states and in dealing with new inequalities and solutions that can accommodate multiculturalism. This situation has been used by the populist right-wing parties, offering a combination of pro-welfare positions, anti-immigration politics and cultural nativist appeals to mobilise the working classes in particular. We propose to examine these challenges and tensions by looking at the 'supply' side of right-wing populist politics; at what these parties offer programmatically that might appeal particularly to blue-collar workers and more generally to lower-level employees.

The populist right-wing party with an undoubtedly working-class profile is the Danish People's Party (*Dansk Folkeparti*, DF); this profile has certainly affected the party's position on welfare issues. The DF is among the most successful populist parties in Western Europe and a paradigmatic case within the Nordic context. Since its launch in 1995 the DF has gained increasing electoral support, with peaks above 13% of the vote between 2001 and 2011. The previous Liberal-Conservative minority government elected in 2001 and in power until 2011 not only helped to legitimise the DF, but also depended on its parliamentary support for survival. This invested the party with influence and responsibility. It was in this phase that the DF demonstrated that it was a reliable and result-oriented political partner. Remarkably, the party also succeeded in another task that was conferred on it: the role of 'welfare guarantor' within the Liberal and Conservative project. At the 2011 elections the DF vote slightly declined from 13.9% to 12.5%, but the party remains the third strongest political force in the country. More than half of the DF votes come from skilled and unskilled manual workers, principally men and people with low levels of education (Andersen 2004; Meret 2010). Working-class support has clearly been achieved at the expense of the traditional left wing, especially social democrats, which in the past decade have lost a considerable share of working-class support. The pro-welfare orientation of the party became carefully and gradually part of the DF programme. Today the party leadership promotes the DF as the only genuine carrier of the classic social democratic welfare tradition. In 2006, the DF leader Pia Kjærsgaard declared that 'a real Social Democrat votes for the Danish People's Party' (*Dansk Folkeblad*, 2006, no. 5). Welfare is considered to belong to the deserving, who – according to the DF – are the native Danes, who have paid for it through generations. To strengthen this point the DF's 2007 campaign posters significantly captured 'tight immigration policy and real welfare', formalising the party politics around two central issues: anti-immigration and the welfare state, and at the same time maintaining a strong Eurosceptic position.

The 'firm and fair' migration/integration policy characterised the Danish Liberal and Conservative government, which in 2002 adopted several restrictive measures. One example is the Danish introduction benefit (*starthjælpen*), which is targeted towards new immigrants and is lower than the ordinary social benefit (*kontanthjælpen*) for Danish citizens. This differentiation was a clear break with the key principle in the universal welfare state: considering all individuals equally. Another example was the so-called '300 hour rule' targeted at married couples and providers above twenty-five years of age who had received social benefits in the last two years. According to the law, people would lose their right to social benefits if they had not been employed for at least 300 hours (later raised to 450) during the previous year. The rule was heavily criticised for targeting the most vulnerable groups, especially immigrant women, but the government insisted that it was a necessary economic sanction/inducement to integrate immigrants into the labour market. The results of these policies were contested and assessments divided over whether this was to be considered a success in terms of integration of immigrants into the labour market, or a failure that increased the poverty of immigrant families (Jønsson and Petersen 2010: 200–9). The present Social Democrat-led government promised a change in migration and integration policies to reassess citizenship laws and rights in compliance with EU legislation and resolutions of the European Court of Justice. However, the only significant initiative so far has been to remove the '450 rule', also known as the poverty trap, which had increased poverty among unemployed people highly dependent on social benefits. In Norway, social democracy has remained relatively strong, although conservative-centre governments have been in power in recent years (1997–2000 and 2001–5). The party leader Jens Stoltenberg has since 2005 led a Red-Green government coalition with the Centre Party (SP) and the Socialist Left Party (SV), and was re-elected in 2009. The party also did well at the last local elections of September 2011 (about 32% of the votes), although opinion polls had forecast declining levels of support.[4] Nevertheless, Norway is also a Scandinavian country with an electorally successful populist right-wing party that has registered increasing levels of electoral support over the years.

The Norwegian Progress Party (*Fremskrittspartiet*, FrP) has roots in the neo-liberal and tax protest wave of the 1970s (Andersen and Bjørklund 2000). Compared to its equivalent in Denmark, the FrP survived the new times, rethinking some of its positions on economic issues, but particularly developing anti-immigration and cultural protectionist standpoints, strongly critical of the multiculturalist politics pursued by the Norwegian governments. In 2009 the FrP became the second strongest party in Norway with 22.9% of votes, a significant share coming from less-educated, less-skilled workers (Bjørklund 2011: 285). Already in 2005 the FrP had gained votes among unskilled manual workers in Norway and was the second party among manual workers, just behind the Labour Party (Bjørklund 2009). These levels of working-class support are remarkable, particularly as the FrP continues to support economic liberalism at the core of party ideology (*Prinsipp- og handlingsprogram* 2005–2009; see also Mudde 2007). From the 1990s, the party leadership acknowledged its role as 'new working-class party', introducing ad hoc pro-welfare measures that appealed to this electorate. For instance, the party asked to 'use oil reserves to benefit the common people' and to employ the revenues to finance public infrastructures and improve social, health and schooling systems.

Another case in point is the Sweden Democrats (*Sverigedemokraterna*, SD). At the 2010 parliamentary elections, the party made their electoral breakthrough and with 5.7% finally crossed the threshold of representation in the Swedish national parliament. Sweden has ceased to be an exception within the Nordic and European context in relation to the role and challenges of the populist right. Despite its still limited political weight, the SD also gained a strategic parliamentary position between the winning centre-right coalition and the Left-Green opposition (with a weak and internally divided social democracy). The extremist origins of this party and its past associations with national-socialism constitute one of the major differences from the other Nordic cases (Lööw 2011). Marginalisation strategies by mainstream politics and media against the SD did not deter skilled and unskilled workers, the unemployed and the retired from voting for them (Oscarsson and Holmberg

2011). Hellström et al. (2012: 203–5) recently analysed the claims of nationalism in the public debate about Sweden Democrats (SD) and their voters, and found that the SD today plays a significant role in public debate in challenging the mainstream perception of Sweden as more tolerant and open-minded. They concluded that the reactions to the SD are themselves framed in a nationalist framework, since mainstream parties share common-sense nationalism – a benign and morally good nationalism, opposed to SD nationalism which is depicted as evil, malign and morally despicable. At the same time, the SD appeals to the widely accepted and well-established Swedish concept of their country as 'The Home of People', in Swedish *Folkehem*: a society that ensures welfare, work, equality and democracy for its citizens (Hellström 2010).

In Finland, the True Finns (*Perussuomalaiset*, TF) won more than 19% of the votes at the Finnish general election in 2011 and are today the third largest political force. The TF siphons off votes not only from the Finnish Social Democrats, but also from other mainstream parties. Nonetheless, a recent survey on party identification shows that about 40% of manual workers identified with the party (Rahkonen 2011). After the 2011 general election, the TF was invited to participate in coalition negotiations, but the party preferred to remain in opposition. Consequently, the TF is one of the two parliamentary parties in Finland that do not take part in the oversized coalition government; this is a position from which the party can draw advantage as it accentuates its difference and autonomy from the mainstream parties and the political elite.

On the socio-economic right-left dimension, the True Finns, like the Sweden Democrats and Danish People's Party, defend the Nordic social democratic welfare state, considered threatened by globalisation, increasing immigration, growing ethnic diversity in society, and European integration, all of which are seen to erode the country's national sovereignty. Redistribution through taxes and public support to weakest groups – pensioners, children – are very often advocated, but mostly targeted at natives. Non-Western immigrants and particularly Muslims are considered as undeserving recipients. All four parties are however only moderately against the privatisation of the public sector and services, with the Norwegian Progress Party having the most explicit neo-liberal agenda – an aspect that helps to explain their coalition agreements and support for centre-right policies. Virtually all these parties support protectionist policies that can safeguard national interest and national production systems from the threats of the globalised market.

The right-wing populist parties' claim to be the sole guarantors of Nordic welfare states is only partly true, as their welfare is interpreted within a narrow version of welfare-chauvinism in which a nativist approach, exclusionary politics and a sharp distinction between deserving and undeserving prevail. This understanding of welfare contrasts with the universal, egalitarian and inclusive approach characterising the Nordic social democratic tradition.

### Right-wing populism and gender equality

Gender issues have become a central theme of the immigration debate. One of the most significant political developments is the way the populist right wing, particularly in the Nordic countries, frames the issue within a discourse of the defence of liberal values, civil rights, individual liberty and gender equality and against intolerant, authoritarian, patriarchal and male chauvinist views attributed to immigrant cultures, and in particular Islam.

In Denmark and Norway, gender equality is an important part of the discourse and programmes of the populist right wing, and the Danish People's Party and the Norwegian Progress Party have used it for assimilative and anti-immigrant purposes (Meret and Siim 2013). Focusing on stories and concerns about the vulnerable condition which immigrant women suffer, these parties may have improved the legitimacy of their positions among part of the electorate and strengthened their respectability by combining it with discourses that emphasise equal gender roles and opportunities, at the same time discrediting multicultural perspectives and imbalanced gender approaches attributed to the left-wing parties, notably the Social Democrats.

While the question of gender was already part of the FrP agenda in the 1980s, this issue recently entered the programme of the DF (Meret and Siim 2013). Both parties hold an essentialist understanding of gender equality, considering it an almost accomplished condition in the Nordic countries. According to the two parties little needs to be done, and only by means of the free play of the market forces, without any involvement of the state and particularly without any need of quota thresholds or similar measures 'from above'. These parties have a very critical and overall negative view of recent waves of feminism, and consider the feminists' struggle for women's rights in society and on the labour market as a selfish, self-centred project provocatively compared with issues related to immigrant women's lack of access to basic rights. Their framing of gender equality also displays conflicting positions between what these parties claim to be their unconditional commitment to gender equality, and the strong emphasis given to the role of the traditional nuclear family, married couple with children – considered the 'bearing force of society' (DF *Arbejdsprogram* 2009) and the most suitable environment for a child (FrP *Prinsipper* 2009–2013).

Gender equality is used in the discourses and rhetoric of populist right-wing parties mainly to address the relationship between Islam and the West, where the Muslim way of life is seen as incompatible with Nordic liberal democratic values because it accepts 'male-chauvinism, violent upbringing, separation between sexes, forced marriages, genital mutilation, beating and brainwashing of children' (DF 2001: 190). Within this discourse, Muslim women wearing the veil have in the last decade become a symbol of their subordination and of discrimination as victims of sexist gender roles under Islam. To prohibit the use of the Muslim veil in public thus becomes a way of fighting against sexual discrimination, acting in support of Muslim women's emancipation, besides being a measure to avoid Islamisation in the Nordic democracies. Many of the populist right-wing parties' policy proposals are actually negative measures to enforce integration and/or restrict immigration, rather than positive ones promoting or facilitating gender equality.

Nordic social democracy often agrees with the discourse about the cultural oppression of immigrant women by their families, although not always on the proposed concrete solutions such as banning the Muslim veil in public institutions, restricting family unification or limiting welfare to citizens (Siim and Skjeie 2008). There are also national variations in the response to right-wing populism influenced by different gender equality policies. The Norwegian Labour Party defends existing parental leave policies with a reserved quota for fathers as well as gender quotas in politics, whereas the FrP wants to abolish all quotas. The policy logic is different in the Danish case, where gender equality policies have not achieved the same level of implementation. Here the DF is generally content with the existing gender policies and opposes any proposal of improvement, including the adoption of new parental leave policies with quotas reserved for fathers. However, this does not prevent the Nordic social democratic parties from having similar problems in addressing ethno-cultural diversity and multidimensional equality. They have failed to rethink the notion of equality to include ethnic equality and to redesign a Nordic gender equality paradigm so as to include immigrant women (Siim and Skjeie 2008).

## Conclusion

Rothstein and Steinmo argue in Chapter 6 that social democracy combines policy success with electoral failure. Our analysis suggests that this is only part of the explanation. To explain electoral failure, Rothstein and Steinmo hypothesise that social democratic parties have not been able to come up with policies for handling immigration that are acceptable to a fairly large segment of their traditional political supporters. Our analysis confirms that Nordic social democracy has indeed experienced policy failure in relation to the integration of immigrants in society. On this basis we suggest that one explanation for the failure to attract voters could be that the parties have failed to address ethno-cultural diversity as well as to rethink the principles of universalism and egalitarianism. One of the challenges for social democracy is thus to rethink and redesign welfare and equality policies to enable the inclusion of immigrants as equal citizens in the labour market and in society generally.

Our main argument is that Nordic right-wing populism, which combines forms of economic protectionism and cultural nativism, represents particular challenges to Nordic social democracy. The combination of criticism of Islam, support for working-class interests, gender equality and pro-welfare policies resonates today with mainstream politics. We suggest that what unites right-wing populism and social democracy is an approach to welfare which has been labelled 'welfare nationalism', combining principles of democracy, citizenship and modernisation. Social democracy has historically been a strong champion and defender of universal and egalitarian principles and social justice, but these were mainly, although not solely, attached to the citizens of the nation-state.

The struggle between social democracy and right-wing populism is often portrayed as a struggle between support for the welfare state on the one side and neo-liberal right-wing policies on the other. But the real competition derives from the social democratic failure to address migration issues and to seek solutions to the dilemma between policies of recognition and redistribution. We find that there is no evidence of the so-called recognition /redistribution trade-off in the sense that both the left and the populist right support the universal welfare state, although with substantial differences when it comes to distinguishing between in-group and out-group, deserving and undeserving. There are, however, important differences between the forms of social democracy within the Nordic countries. Danish social democracy has become increasingly critical of multicultural recognition policies because they fear these would increase the support for right-wing populism, whereas Swedish social democrats have continued to support a moderate version of multiculturalism. The governing Norwegian Labour Party again represents a middle position, with a strong rhetorical support for multicultural policies.

Right-wing populism is, in essence, anti-diversity and anti-Europe. There are tensions in the ideology of the populist right-wing parties between neo-liberalism and support for welfare policies – as well as between formal support for universal principles of gender equality on the one hand, and traditional (authoritarian) family policies on the other. There are also tensions between universalism and egalitarianism attached to national citizens and support for social justice and human rights principles at the global level, which include immigrants and refugees. Social democrats have been the champions of worker solidarity and human rights, but it is arguable how these rights can be defended at the transnational and global levels. Membership of the EU has been controversial, and the European Union was perceived as an economic union which would increase the mobility of workers and pave the way for continued welfare, economic growth and prosperity. Right-wing populism, which combines support for economic and cultural protectionism, thus represents a challenge to social democratic ideas and ideals about transnational governance of welfare and migration/integration. The present economic and financial crisis has contributed to accentuate the need to discuss and develop post-national principles of welfare, equality, solidarity and social justice.

## Notes

1. The chapter focuses on four of the five Nordic countries, namely Denmark, Finland, Norway and Sweden. It does not address Iceland.
2. Banting and Kymlicka discuss what has been labelled the 'progressive's dilemma': the claim that Social Democrats are faced with a tragic trade-off between sustaining their traditional agenda of economic redistribution and embracing ethno-cultural diversity and multiculturalism (2006: 4–5).
3. Banting and Kymlicka differentiate between different aspects of the debate about multicultural policies, the case of national minorities, indigenous peoples and ethno-cultural diversity related to migration. They argue that the retreat from multiculturalism is restricted to the domain of ethno-cultural diversity, i.e. immigration (2006: 7).
4. This changed after 22 July 2011 when seventy-seven people were killed, eight in Oslo and sixty-nine on Utøya, most of them young members of the Social Democratic Youth (AUF). After these tragic events Stoltenberg urged Norwegians to respond to the attacks with even 'more openness and more democracy'.

# LABOUR MARKETS, WELFARE STATES AND THE DILEMMAS OF EUROPEAN SOCIAL DEMOCRACY

Martin Rhodes

## Introduction

This chapter maps out the challenges facing social democratic parties deriving from the labour market and welfare state – areas in which the centre-left has traditionally built its organisational and electoral strength. The principal argument is that equality – which Kitschelt (1999), referring to the rise of 'left-libertarianism', argued would have to be played down in social democratic aspirations and strategies – has returned as the biggest issue facing social democratic renewal.

Although 'left-libertarianism' is now a well-established feature of the political landscape in Western countries, traditional distributive class politics are still extant – but in a form that social democrats find increasingly difficult to exploit. Growing levels of inequality pose broader challenges to democracy in terms of trust in institutions and the growing appeal of 'anti-system' parties (Schäfer 2010). Social democratic parties face their greatest challenges in countries where income inequality is increasingly connected with inequality of access to secure employment and welfare entitlements.

Part one considers the particular problems facing social democratic parties in coping with socio-economic change and engaging in labour market and welfare state reform. It also sets out a framework specifying the socio-economic and political-strategic challenges to social democratic parties. Part two considers in greater detail how social democratic parties are confronting – or failing to confront – those challenges across Europe's different welfare state regimes.

## Socio-economic and political-strategic challenges

### *A framework for analysis*

The crisis of European social democracy has been frequently announced. If there is a crisis of social democratic parties today, poll results reveal that it is also shared by other mainstream parties. In Germany, for example, recent discussion has centred on the crisis of the *Volksparteien*, following the decline of support to a post-war low for the Social Democrats (SPD) and Christian Democrats (CDU/CSU) in the 2009 federal elections. More generally, analysts of European party systems have long speculated about the demise of mass parties. It is now common to refer to the decline in class voting and party membership and the diminishing strength of flanking organisations such as unions, as well as the emergence and strengthening of single-issue parties and radical parties on the left and right.

Yet there may well be something particular about the predicament of social democracy. Its political parties are presently incumbent in only a handful of countries, and have seen a general decline of popular support over the last few decades. Exceptions to this trend are found only in Southern Europe – at least until the recent financial crisis. Party system analysts have often viewed the prospects of social democratic parties more pessimistically than those of the right. Mair (2003), for example, worried that the organisational and electoral weakening of political parties was especially problematic for the social democratic left for whom the model of the mass party was especially well suited. Adaptation on the right, by contrast, would likely prove easier because there was simply that much less to discard, referring to the left's traditional dependency on 'distinct social constituencies that were bounded by clear collective interests, and . . . represented through a more or less tight and hierarchical organisational network' (Mair 2003: 20).

Others have identified a specific set of dilemmas and trade-offs for social democratic parties. Some of these, in line with Mair's preoccupations, relate to the difficulties of transitioning from class parties to 'catch-all' parties and beyond, in dealing with 'embourgeoisement' and the emergence of left-libertarianism (Kitschelt 1994, 1999); with internal splits and competition between traditionalists (devoted to employment security and the 'social security state') and modernisers or pragmatists (supporting 'flexicurity' and the 'social investment state') (Korthouwer 2010); with the emergence of socio-political divides between labour market 'insider' and 'outsider' welfare preferences; and the rise of the 'welfare chauvinist' populist right (Schwartz 2010; Schwander and Häusermann 2011). In light of recent developments, one can add to that list the emergence of an increasingly successful radical left-wing challenge – as in Germany, Greece, the Netherlands and France. A deeper set of political-economic problems (discussed in Iversen 1999 and surveyed by

Table 9.1 Social democratic parties and their socio-economic and political-strategic challenges

| | Socio-economic challenges | | | Political-strategic challenges | | | |
|---|---|---|---|---|---|---|---|
| | WS/labour market weaknesses | WS/work and new divides | WS/work-immigration nexus | Political space dimensionality | Form of political competition | WS issue ownership | Links with the labour movement |
| LIBERAL (UK) – Mainly tax-financed – Loosely regulated labour market | Persistent poverty, high level of inequality; tax/debt constraints on public sector expansion | Less regulated labour market means there are no strong insider-outsider divisions | Immigrants more easily absorbed into loosely regulated labour market; Labour has liberal immigration policy | Majoritarian – median voter; opportunity-fear axis within main parties, but extremist options emerging | From liberal conservatives who pursue logic of Labour innovations; median voter limits on left moving left | Some ownership overlap with compassionate conservatism; New Labour can still 'own' major WS issues | Moderately strong, but unions not seen as active allies; unions as critics not partners |
| SOCIAL DEMOCRATIC (Scandinavian) – Mainly tax-financed – Flexible labour market in Denmark; moderately regulated in Sweden | 'Growth to limits'; tax constraints on public sector job creation; inequality rising; high youth unemployment in Sweden | Continued use of public sector to create employment and macro-corporatism restricts insider-outside divide | Problematic labour market inclusion of some immigrant groups ; risk of social exclusion for these groups if poorly educated | Traditional left-right axis strong, but growing competition from the welfare chauvinist radical right | Competition from WS-supporting conservatives and right – social democrats lose role as *the* party of the welfare state | Social democratic ownership loss as centre-right (and far-right) embrace welfare: social democracy without social democrats? | Active alliance between social democratic parties and labour movement; latter strong universal WS supporters. Unions strength is weakening |

| | | | | | | | |
|---|---|---|---|---|---|---|---|
| **CONTINENTAL-CONSERVATIVE (Bismarckian)** – **Mainly contribution-financed** – **Tightly regulated core labour market** | 'Growth to limits'; reform of WS and labour market provokes strong union/left opposition; still a 'welfare without work' problem | Very strong insider-outsider divisions as a result of two-tier labour market reforms; very little re-regulation of core labour market | Problematic integration into core labour market; largely restricted to outsider status; poor levels of education and skills; social exclusion | Left-right axis weakening with value axis (fear-opportunity) fuelling competition from the radical left (*Linkspartei* in Germany) and right (FN in France) | With move to centre, loss of SD initiative to conservatives who have also modernised; both challenged by new parties on the fear-opportunity axis | Germany – both social democrats and Christian democrats have liberalised on WS; leaves more space for far-left/right incursion on social issues | Medium but weakening: German labour movement split between SD and *Die Linke*; in France, weak links and 'social movement' unionism |

Van Kersbergen 2003) derive from the loss of social democratic government capacity to reconcile efficiency and equality goals through centralised industrial relations, flexible and centrally coordinated macro-economic policy, a generous welfare state and public sector employment.

This chapter is limited to a schematic treatment of those issues. Table 9.1 sets out the challenges facing social democratic parties operating in countries broken down according to Europe's different welfare regimes: liberal, social democratic and continental-conservative, as defined by Esping-Andersen (1990).[1] Two kinds of challenges to social democratic parties are presented. The first are socio-economic, and break down into three categories: (1) those relating to welfare state/labour market characteristics including unemployment and inequality – outcomes that especially concern social democratic parties – and taxing and spending constraints that may limit their attempts to tackle them; (2) the relationship between welfare and work and new socio-economic divides, namely 'insider-outsider' divisions in the labour market and attendant shifts in social policy preferences, that threaten to undermine the traditional support base of social democratic parties; and (3) issues raised by the interaction between welfare, work and immigration: deficits in migrant integration are creating a serious problem for many European employment and welfare systems, and pose a particular challenge to those parties defending traditional social democratic notions of equality and solidarity.

The second set of challenges is more precisely political-strategic, breaking down into four categories: (1) the changing dimensions of political competition – the extent to which the 'opportunity-fear' axis (Azmanova 2004) or the 'egalitarian-conflict discourse' axis (Elchardus and Spruyt 2012) is moving into an orthogonal position in relation to the traditional left-right axis of political competition; (2) the form of political competition facing social democratic parties: the first challenge is more problematic for those parties competing in PR electoral systems, where new dimensions of political competition are less easily contained within the political mainstream than in majoritarian, first-past-the-post systems (e.g. the United Kingdom); (3) welfare state 'issue ownership', that is, the extent to which social democratic parties are still able to use the welfare state 'brand' as a resource in political competition, as other parties seek to use the political salience of welfare for their own ends – either by defending it more strongly, proposing to reform it more effectively, or retrenching it to solve other (e.g. budgetary) problems; and (4) the extent to which Mair's 'hierarchically organised social constituencies' – class-based flanking organisations, primarily industrial unions – remain an asset or have become a 'liability' for social democratic parties, as unions weaken or challenge the positions of those parties, sometimes by shifting their allegiance to political competitors further to the left.

## The 'crisis' of social democracy and the politics of welfare state/labour market reform

Much has been written about the respective vulnerabilities of the different welfare state regimes in Europe. Alongside ageing populations and declining birth rates, technological change – linked in part to globalisation, and the outsourcing of standardised tasks – and the rise of the service economy are also challenging the welfare state and the socio-economic status quo by creating new inequalities and skill-biased patterns of social exclusion: the low-skilled and unskilled (including many immigrants) are subject to a decline in demand and a loss of wage-sustaining power.

At the same time, a weakening of families as traditional providers of welfare and new sources of immigration and labour market segregation pose an ongoing threat to social cohesion – generating a series of 'new' social risks and exacerbating existing ones, including income inequality which has increased everywhere in Europe over the last decade or so (OECD 2011). The budgetary constraints of existing commitments (in pensions, education, health and unemployment) and the defence of entitlements inherited from the so-called 'golden age' of welfare by various benefits-based constituencies constrain and shape policy innovation (see Hemerijck et al. 2006 for a survey).

As Paul Pierson (1998) put it, irresistible forces (pressures for reform) have come up against immovable objects (entitlements-linked veto groups), generating policy responses that range from stasis to sometimes quite profound reform. One way of mitigating the power of the 'immovable objects' has been to lessen or avoid the impact of politically difficult reforms (e.g. in pensions and employment regulation) on core 'insider' constituencies, at the expense of 'outsider' groups – especially younger workers, women and migrants. Although conservative governments have typically pursued these reforms (Ochel 2008), social democratic parties, as in Germany in the 2000s and Spain in the 1980s, have also been responsible for producing these divisive labour market outcomes (Rueda 2005).

Regulatory solutions to high levels of unemployment in the past have led to greater employment inflows into non-standard work contracts and, in the recent recession, to disproportionate outflows from such contracts into unemployment. Tito Boeri (2009) argues that the employment success in Europe over the decade or so before the financial crisis disguised a substantial deterioration in employment quality and a significant increase in labour market risk for outsider workers. If between 1995 and 2007 the number of unemployed in the EU declined by almost four million, and long-term unemployment was almost halved, this was because of much greater inflows out of employment into fixed-term and other kinds of precarious contracts. The result, argues Boeri, has been growing insider job dissatisfaction due to elevated employment risk, and growing outsider job dissatisfaction due to a decline in labour productivity linked to the expansion of employment and stagnant or declining wages.

The political consequences of these trends are especially acute for social democratic parties, due to the interaction between the socio-economic and political-strategic variables referred to above. There are three general kinds of interaction effect: the contribution of social and employment policies advocated by social democratic modernisers to socially divisive outcomes that fragment the centre-left's electorate; the link between a socially and economically divided working class, the dualisation of social and employment preferences between 'insider' and 'outsider' workers, and social democratic parties' neglect of the latter group's interests; and the migration of support by the 'losers' from cultural and economic modernisation from social democratic parties to both populist right and left-wing competitors.

The first of these interaction effects derives from the failure of the two 'big ideas' embraced by social democratic 'modernisers' – labour market 'flexicurity' and the 'social investment state' – to deliver on their promises due to unexpected consequences, poor implementation or the sheer force of socio-economic change. Regarding 'flexicurity' – the notion that labour markets can be made both more flexible and more secure by reducing employment protection and activating unemployment benefits (that is, increasing training and education) – the evidence suggests that flexibility has increased for outsiders but not for insiders, and that the security side of the deal has not been met (Van Vliet and Nijboer 2012). At the same time, certain continental-conservative welfare states (the Netherlands, France, Germany and Belgium) have seen a substantial polarisation of employment since 1995, with high growth in the lowest and highest income quintiles but little growth in between (Fernández-Macías 2012).

In these circumstances, it is not surprising that the 'social investment state' (investment in training, education and child care) has failed to capture the electoral imagination. As discussed below, it is much less attractive to low-skilled, low-income workers than their higher-skilled, better-paid counterparts. As Cantillon (2011) argues, by shifting political and policy attention away from redistribution, social investment state policies may also have added to higher poverty rates and falling real incomes for those out of work – developments to which other factors (notably trade and technology-driven demand for highly skilled workers, and growing wage dispersion between the latter and the unskilled) have also undoubtedly contributed (Van Kersbergen and Hemerijck 2012).

A second set of interaction effects relates to the political consequences of widening socio-economic divides. As Pontusson and Rueda argue, there is something of a vicious circle that links growing inequality with lower voter turnout and greater voter apathy among low-income workers: 'increasing inequality makes their preferences for redistribution stronger, but decreasing mobilisation makes their demands less relevant to left parties, which in turn make these parties less distributive when they get to power, and so inequality grows further' (2010: 699). Other evidence (see Anderson and Beramendi 2012) suggests that increases in inequality are indeed associated with a growing number of labour market 'outsiders' and declining political engagement on the part of those at the extremes of the income distribution: only in the presence of a left competitor are social democratic parties now likely to pay attention to low-income groups.

In the background, the capacity of social democratic parties to sustain a political coalition spanning low-skilled and high-skilled workers has substantially declined with the end of Fordism and the rise of low-skilled services, especially in continental-conservative welfare regimes (Iversen and Soskice 2009). That coalition, underpinned by union membership of both groups, was critical for equality-oriented collective bargaining and public policies. The decline of the industrial union that traditionally led in establishing better wages and conditions for all workers and not just union members or skilled workers (Visser 2012) reflects and contributes to this trend.

There is further recent evidence that fragmentation of the traditional social democratic electoral base brings with it a dualisation of attitudes and preferences regarding welfare policies. Schwander and Häusermann (2011) demonstrate that labour market dualisation is a socio-structural divide with powerful political implications, reflected in stronger preferences on the part of 'outsiders' than 'insiders' for income redistribution, publicly supported job creation and publicly funded child care. The dualisation of welfare preferences, which is especially marked once again in the continental-conservative welfare regime, creates the potential for political conflict over policy priorities and provides electoral openings for left- and right-wing competitors to social democratic parties.

The third set of links between socio-economic and political-strategic dilemmas is related precisely to this latter point – the extent to which the socio-economic developments make the demands of low-income workers less relevant for centrist social democratic parties and their votes available for populist left and right-wing parties instead. As René Cuperus (2010: 21) puts it, referring to the problems facing the Dutch Labour Party and German Social Democratic Party, 'left-wing populism (*Die Linke* of Oskar Lafontaine, or the Socialist Party in the Netherlands) is our biggest threat, although in the Netherlands, unlike in Germany, right-wing populist movements are also seducing the classical social democratic electorate [leading to] the end of the left-wing working class.' This is where the new 'cultural value cleavage' (Henjak 2010) or 'opportunity-fear' axis (Azmanova 2004) comes into play. But as Häusermann (2010a) argues, the emergence of cultural conflicts interacts in complex ways with more traditional distributive ones, in large part because they are closely linked to social and economic policy issues.

Thus, there has long been speculation, revived by recent developments, that immigration would eventually begin to undermine European welfare states via the erosion of the normative consensus on which they are based, and the emergence of 'welfare chauvinism' and an 'us-versus-them' welfare politics. The centre-left has particular problems dealing with this development, precisely because of the importance it attributes to national solidarity and community (Freeman 1986, 2009; Schwartz 2010). Bornscheier argues that welfare chauvinist right-wing political parties are able to gain the support of the losers from both cultural and economic modernisation and are able to 'articulate these grievances predominantly in cultural, not economic, terms' (2010: 200). Elchardus and Spruyt (2012) also argue that the orthogonal dimensions of the new 'cultural/distributive' political space create a complex new playing field for all political parties but especially for social democrats. For as Van der Brug and Van Spanje (2009) note, there is now a large group of voters with left-wing positions on socio-economic policies and right-wing positions on the cultural value dimension, that provides new electoral recruits for social-welfare-supporting, anti-immigrant, right-wing populist parties.

Reflecting on the ways in which these socio-economic and political-strategic challenges interact, it is important to note the following. First, social democratic parties are not necessarily moving to the right on immigration issues in response to the emergence of a cultural value cleavage. Although in certain cases social democratic parties have strongly and consistently advocated restrictions on immigration – the Swedish Social Democratic Party (SAP) has opposed open immigration not for ethno-nationalist reasons but out of fears that it would undermine the regulated labour market and generous welfare state – right-wing parties have largely been responsible for restrictive immigration policies. Even the SAP has worked hard on the integration of migrants into Swedish society, and has joined other Swedish political parties in opposing the right-wing xenophobic Sweden Democrats who entered parliament for the first time in 2010 (Hinnfors et al. 2012). Most left-wing parties still appear committed to a distinctly liberal immigration and integration policy and have not embraced or advocated welfare chauvinism themselves (Akkerman 2012). But that does not prevent the loss of their former supporters to newer welfare chauvinist parties.[2]

### Three worlds of European social democracy

The ways in which socio-economic and political-strategic variables interact will depend greatly on the nature of the welfare regime, the extent to which it encourages or mitigates welfare state and labour market dualism, and the ease with which immigrants integrate socially or economically. It will also depend on the nature of the electoral system and party competition. Keman (2010) demonstrates that if, in general, social democratic parties are moving to the electoral centre of gravity, individual social democratic parties are making that move in idiosyncratic ways and at different speeds by reducing their commitment to the social security state, embracing 'Third Way' policies and altering their appeals to traditional welfare state constituencies. That variable movement depends in large part on political context and dynamics: social democratic governments will feel more constrained in retrenching social policy and embracing the market if they face another centrist competitor or fear the loss of welfare state 'ownership' to the far right or the far left (Kitschelt 2004: 17–18).

## Social democratic parties in liberal welfare states: the UK

Liberal welfare states are less costly and face fewer problems of financial sustainability than their continental European counterparts. Labour market flexibility, combined with high rates of economic growth, has helped boost employment, especially in private-sector services, since the early 1990s (Fagan et al. 2005). Compared to continental countries, there has been little recent income polarisation or formal labour market dualisation in the UK: the distribution of employment by income and educational quintiles since 1995 has seen an increase at the upper end, explaining growing inequality, but little increase in the lower quintiles – a consequence of an already substantially deregulated labour market (Fernández-Macías 2012). The UK also manages to avoid the major differences in employment participation and unemployment between nationals and non-nationals found in most European countries (Kahanec and Zimmerman 2011).

Against this socio-economic background, the political-strategic challenges for New Labour in a majoritarian, first-past-the-post electoral system are quite different from those in other parts of Europe – and much less problematic. The traditional left-right distributive axis is still strong, with little success for political parties campaigning on 'cultural' (anti-immigrant) themes.[3] In addition to electoral constraints, that failure can be attributed in part to the absence of entrenched labour market divisions between insiders and outsiders, or migrant worker labour market exclusion, which blunts the appeal of anti-immigrant politics.

The logic of majoritarian competition for the electoral middle ground led New Labour in government after 1997 to focus on middle-class, median-voter concerns, and to turn the compensating welfare state into a more coercive workfare state. New Labour's appeal to the median voter worked to attract disillusioned Conservatives as well as independents unsympathetic to old Labour style policy. It was based on a broad strategy of 'Third Way' reform. Trade unions, which have weakened significantly outside the public sector since the 1980s, had meanwhile lost their erstwhile influence over New Labour policy orientations (Bryson and Forth 2010).

Indeed, Labour's shift to the 'radical centre' has been more extreme than any other European social democratic party (Keman 2010: 676) and has delivered considerable electoral success. As Moschonas (2011) shows, when comparing the electoral performance of social democratic parties for the period 2000–9 with their best decade since the 1950s, those in liberal welfare states with first-past-the-post systems do best. The British Labour Party loses a relatively low 17.9% of the vote. As for product differentiation, much like the Conservatives before them, Labour's approach has been to minimise intervention and regulatory burdens on a well-functioning, deregulated labour market. But its 'welfare-to-work' strategy differs substantially from Conservative workfare policies. The most distinctive feature has been a reliance on work and employability to address poverty and social disadvantage.

The consequence has been a considerable transformation of the UK welfare state, with much attention being paid to youth and long-term unemployment. The main target of the 'New Deal' launched in 1997 was young people in search of their first job, but it later extended to the long-term unemployed and single parents. It included training initiatives to help the unemployed to find a job or attend an interview, an offer of a publicly subsidised job or a further training experience, and a loss of benefits if a job offer was rejected. Another form of activation, tax credits, was introduced in 1998, targeted at working families and single parents to prevent voluntary exit from the labour market. Between 1999 and 2002, the Blair government introduced a statutory national minimum wage and revised the rules on unfair dismissals and workers' rights in the workplace. In 2002, 'Jobcentre Plus' was created by merging benefits offices with job centres where the unemployed register for work opportunities with largely positive outcomes: between 1998 and 2007 over 1.7 million people returned to work. A major emphasis was also placed on poor families, with a pledge to halve child poverty by 2010. As part of the workplace reforms, maternity rights were improved from the late 1990s, and childcare policies were linked to the New Deal and tax credits.

In the late 1990s and 2000s, Labour thereby successfully redefined British social democracy and its relationship with labour markets and the welfare state. Its current challenge is to provide an alternative to the present Conservative-Liberal Democrat coalition government's austerity policies in an economic recession, with a greater stress on social solidarity and a centrist social investment strategy (Taylor-Gooby 2012). And it can do so without fear of challenge from a radical left or an anti-immigrant, welfare chauvinist far-right.

*Social democratic parties in continental-conservative welfare states: Germany*

Social democratic parties in continental-conservative systems are in a quite different situation. They face growing inequalities in the labour market, involving both their own national citizens and difficult-to-integrate migrants, coupled with a loss of support from traditional constituencies and growing political-strategic challenges from alternative left- and right-wing parties. The occupational fragmentation of these welfare systems and their potential for social exclusion and socio-economic dualism make them especially vulnerable to such attacks.

'Insider-outsider' divides in these systems risk creating impervious divides between workers who are young, migrant, female and less skilled, employed on various kinds of 'precarious' contracts (and often with reduced access to welfare entitlements, including unemployment benefits and pensions), and core workers who retain much higher job protection and an array of welfare supports (Hinrichs and Jessoula 2012). As Fernández-Macías (2012) notes, the extent to which there has been an accentuated dualisation of the employment structure and job quality in the Netherlands, France, Germany, Belgium and Austria is quite distinctive in Europe. Entrenched employment divides are also coupled with a growing divergence of welfare preferences, with outsiders consistently more supportive of redistribution than insiders (Schwander and Häusermann 2011). Growing insecurity and perceptions of vulnerability among lower-income groups, coupled with much lower participation rates and higher unemployment rates for non-nationals than nationals (Kahanec and Zimmerman 2011), can readily be exploited by anti-system parties (Swank and Betz 2003).

These problems derive in part from the way that the 'post-industrial employment trilemma' (identified by Iversen and Wren 1998) has played out over time. In its original formulation, liberal welfare states could secure both fiscal discipline and employment growth more easily than the other welfare state regimes, but would continue to sacrifice income equality. The Nordic welfare states could achieve both employment growth and higher levels of equality than elsewhere, but only at the cost of fiscal deficits, since much employment growth would be in the public sector. The Christian democratic (continental-conservative) countries could try to control income inequality and maintain fiscal discipline, but only at the cost of low employment growth.

Over the last decade or so, the Nordic countries have maintained a social consensus (though not one immune to challenges) behind a high-expenditure, high-taxation model. The liberal welfare states have allowed income inequality to rise, and the continental-conservative countries have adopted a quite different strategy – sacrificing income equality by heavily stratifying entry to the labour market in order to boost job creation, reduce unemployment and improve very low employment rates. The political-strategic consequences can be quite dramatic, as the German case reveals.

Politically, there have been two major social and employment policy trends in Germany. The first has been for both the SPD and the Christian Democratic CDU/CSU to embrace a 'Third Way' strategy, in pensions (decreasing the generosity of the system by reducing replacement rates, increasing the retirement age and encouraging investment in private pensions) and labour market regulation. A significant deregulation of the lower end of the labour market occurred under the SPD-Green coalition in the early to mid 2000s, notably under the 'mini-jobs' scheme aimed at the unemployed and those with jobs but very low incomes, whereby workers paid up to €400 per month were exempted from social security contributions and paid almost no income tax. Temporary work was extended to the construction sector and fixed-term contracts were further liberalised, producing an increase in the share of temporary contracts to 14.5% of total employment by 2009, over half of which were held by workers under twenty-four (Gualmini and Rhodes 2011). In the federal elections that year, *Die Linke* won 11.9% of the vote, and the Greens 10.7%, while the SPD's share fell from 34.2% in the 2005 elections to 23%. Its electoral support in the 2000–9 period was 27.8% below its best decade after 1950 (Moschonas 2011).

If the left-libertarian Greens and the traditional socialist *Die Linke* are working like a pincer movement in subtracting from the SPD's vote, a serious threat from a welfare chauvinist popular right has yet to materialise, unlike in France, the Netherlands and Belgium. The CDU/CSU's opposition to opening the German immigration system to new high-skilled labour has contained some of the 'fear' (and xenophobia) found among a swathe of its right-wing supporters, and the far-right *Republikaner* have not made much progress, remaining below the 5% electoral threshold. The 'fear' factor on the left, however, has helped lift support for *Die Linke*, while the SPD itself has found it increasingly difficult to reconcile the aspirations of its middle-class professional voters with those of its older, blue-collar constituency.

## Social democratic parties in Nordic welfare states

The greater success of Nordic welfare states in dealing with the above socio-economic problems, especially in avoiding the emergence of acute 'insider-outsider' divides, in theory leaves those countries' social democratic parties in a much better position to compete with political-strategic challenges. In fact there are serious questions as to whether the Nordic social democratic parties retain their legitimacy as the primary defenders of the welfare state and can sustain their traditional electoral strength. Moreover, these countries have seen the most significant rise of the welfare chauvinist populist right.

As Pontusson (2011) argues, the Nordic model's strong encompassing unions, solidaristic wage bargaining and active labour market policies, high investments in public education, high levels of 'information age literacy' and high skill levels at the bottom of the skill hierarchy has 'worked'. It is in fact a model of the 'social investment state' and difficult to emulate. Good levels of economic growth since the mid 1990s, low rates of unemployment, an ongoing expansion of service sector jobs and high levels of female labour force participation have not been accompanied by a strong increase in labour market dualism as in continental Europe, due to the greater flexibility of Scandinavian labour markets, their greater reliability on basic skills, and the important macro-corporatist role played by the state.

But is it possible that a strong social democratic political economy can survive without a strong social democratic party? As Pontusson notes, other left parties as well as centrist or centre-right parties have embraced social democratic policies and weakened the electoral appeal of social democratic parties (2011: 113). Thus, political competition has driven the Swedish Conservative Party (Moderaterna) to change its welfare state preferences, moving towards the (welfare supporting) political centre over time (Lindbom 2008). Meanwhile, the Social Democrats in Denmark and Sweden have moved closer to their conservative parties to prevent a more serious challenge from the latter to the universal welfare state by 'liberalizing without retrenching' (Bergh and Erlingsson 2009) and making pre-emptive reforms to the labour market and other areas of welfare policy (Klitgaard 2007).

There is evidence, therefore, not just of a loss of welfare state ownership on the part of social democratic parties, but of an inability to sustain electoral support. Using the same measure of contemporary success as for the other countries (the percentage of votes in 2000–9 compared to the best average performance in any decade since the 1950s), social democratic parties in the Nordic welfare states register some of the heaviest losses, with declines of 33.3% in Denmark, 35.2% in Norway and a lower 22.6% in Sweden (Moschonas 2011: 63). Electoral decline is reflected in a generalised loss of office. In Denmark, a centre-right government governed from 2001 until 2011 with the support of the right-wing populist Danish People's Party (DF); in Sweden, the Social Democratic Party (SAP) lost the election in 2006 and has been excluded from government since; and in Norway, although the Social Democratic Labour Party is still dominant in government, it can only govern by leading a three-party, Red-Green coalition (Jochem 2012).

A significant challenge comes from a surprisingly strong far-right. Echoing Freeman (1986, 2009), Schwartz (2010: 370–3) attributes an erosion of social democratic solidarity in these countries to the demise of ethnically homogeneous populations. With an immigrant presence of around 12% in Sweden and 10% in Denmark and Norway, the neo-liberal anti-immigration and pro-law-and-order Norwegian Progress Party is the second largest party in the parliament, with a quarter of all seats. In Denmark, the Danish People's Party, a welfare chauvinist party which has attracted many former Social Democratic Party voters, is the third largest party, and its tacit support for centre-right governments in the early to mid 2000s brought significant immigration restrictions (Akkerman 2012). The Sweden Democrats entered parliament in 2010 and are another welfare chauvinist party, combining anti-immigrant sentiments with a strong defence of the social democratic welfare model (Hellström and Nilsson

2010). The welfare chauvinist, anti-migrant True Finns also combine left-wing economic policies with conservative social values, and won over 19% of the vote in the 2011 Finnish parliamentary election (against 4% in 2007). They are the country's largest opposition party and with thirty-nine seats have only four less than the Social Democrats. As Jochem (2012) argues, not only do right-wing populist parties challenge social democratic parties, they also change the dynamics of party competition and restrict the possibilities for coalition building and consensus-based politics and reform.

## Conclusions

This chapter began by asking whether social democratic parties are particularly vulnerable to party system and socio-economic changes. I conclude that they are. As Mair (2003) argues, the political right has less to lose with the demise of political parties as mass parties than the social democratic centre-left, for whom 'distinct social constituencies bounded by clear collective interests' were always more important. Those social constituencies have fractured in European countries and the clear collective interests have lost their coherence as the traditional manual working class has shrunk, and the gap between the employment and welfare policy preferences of lower-skilled and higher-skilled workers and middle-class professionals has widened.

Gravitating to the centre and modernising their electoral appeal has been very costly for social democratic parties, forcing trade-offs between the pursuit of equality and the pursuit of votes and office, especially in those countries where social solidarity was the *condicio sine qua non* of social democratic identity and ideology. As a result, continental and Nordic social democratic parties risk surrendering the pursuit of those goals to radical left- or right-wing parties – and sometimes to both. As Keman (2010) argues, gravitation to the centre on economic, employment and welfare state issues has allowed social democratic parties to retain office-seeking power via coalition participation in PR systems, but their vote-seeking capacities have not thereby been enhanced.

A somewhat paradoxical conclusion from the above analysis is that social democratic parties are less imperilled electorally in countries where welfare states have been weaker and labour markets less regulated – the liberal welfare state countries. The most profound challenges seem to face those social demo-cratic parties that, historically, were builders or co-builders of large, highly decommodifying welfare states, as in the Nordic and continental-conservative countries. This can partly be explained by the fact that in the liberal welfare states, there is also far less to lose in the post-industrial era in welfare state terms, and the socio-economic challenges are less intense – or at least not generated, as in the continental systems, by insider-outsider cleavages. In a liberal market economy, those divisions are less visible and less likely to feed into political conflict. A major contributing factor, of course, is a majoritarian electoral system, which, in the UK, allows little space for the emergence of significant political competitors on the radical left or the radical right or further fragmentation of the party system – a major part of the problem facing social democratic parties in PR systems, whether on the continent or in Scandinavia.

As Picot (2012) has argued, fragmented party systems have contributed in the past to the segmentation of social protection and social rights. Social democratic parties in fragmented party systems today and in the future will find it doubly hard to propose and gain political support for all-encompassing welfare state and labour market reforms – or to recreate the virtuous circle that once linked welfare state construction and redistributive policies with electoral success.

## Notes

1. In Western Europe, the regime categorisation of countries is as follows: liberal (UK and Ireland), social democratic (Denmark, Sweden, Norway and Finland) and continental-conservative or Bismarckian (France, Belgium, Germany, Austria, the Netherlands, Italy and Spain), though the Southern European countries have sometimes been in a separate group.
2. It is difficult to assess the potential for parties pursuing the welfare chauvinist vote, but recent data from Reeskens and van Oorschot (2012) suggests that those who believe that welfare benefits should target the neediest are least sympathetic to welfare provisions for immigrants. They also estimate that 40% of Europeans believe that immigrants should have access to social rights after having worked and paid taxes (which the authors refer to as 'chauvinism in the soft sense'), that 35% would restrict access to those with citizenship only, while only 7% would deny immigrant access to benefits altogether. National context is important, however: those living in more diverse societies are less likely to want restrictions on immigrant access to welfare.
3. In the 2010 General Election, the xenophobic British National Party received only 1.9% of the vote and failed to win any seats.

# CLASS POLITICS AND THE SOCIAL INVESTMENT WELFARE STATE

Colin Crouch

## Introduction

The historical achievement of twentieth-century social democracy was to represent the interests of the working classes of democratic industrial societies within a capitalist economy through a particular combination of social policy, redistributive taxation and business regulation. Social democrats remained suspicious of the inequalities of power and wealth represented by capitalism, but tried to achieve compromises within a capitalist system through these policy instruments. By the end of the century it was becoming increasingly difficult to maintain this stance, as the globalisation of the economy, the decline of the organised industrial working class, and the growing dominance of neo-liberal ideas were shifting the balance of power against those forces on which social democracy depended. Among the various responses made by social democrats to this situation, the most prominent was that associated with the 'Third Way' (in the UK) or, to a lesser extent, the '*neue Mitte*' (in Germany). This advocated no longer regarding capitalism and corporate power as problematic and reshaping social democracy's traditional policy approaches to be more accepting of them. Such a stance involved overlooking several major problems. This chapter will explore certain weaknesses in this approach and will argue that a revised position is possible: the concept of the 'social investment welfare state' promoted by various social policy specialists and practised in some European nation-states, particularly in the Nordic countries that have long represented the core of social democracy. This then has to be combined with greater willingness to use regulation to check the political power of global capital; this can only be achieved if social democrats are willing to act with more international collaboration than has usually been the case in the past.

The abiding importance of social democracy lies in the fact that the making of markets usually creates a need for compensatory policies. Markets achieve efficiency by pursuing those activities from which profits can be maximised and ignoring others. Sometimes those overlooked activities are best left ignored; but they may embody important values or interests that have some claim to be recognised – as in the case of people in developing countries being thrown off their land to make way for profitable investment. Sometimes the marketed activity itself creates damage, the 'externalities' of economic theory, such as pollution, which might need to be addressed. Tackling such problems may involve the establishment of new markets to serve the neglected interests, and sometimes market actors themselves find means of doing this. But this cannot be guaranteed, and the market's 'victims' may seek public policy solutions. The stronger the drive to marketisation, the more important it is to be able to remedy its negative consequences. If societies lose their capacity to do this, such problems can never be addressed, and the only interests served are those that are served by the market alone. Given that ability to use the market is directly dependent on wealth, this means a constant bias towards satisfying the interests of the wealthy.

Even if this basic approach is accepted, however, major problems remain for social democracy. Like most other democratic political forces, it assumes a basis of national citizenship for its activities. This is becoming increasingly unrealistic. Two aspects of this will be tackled here: business power in the global economy, and immigration.

### The 'Third Way' and its weaknesses

Although the Third Way approach has been criticised as inadequately political, it began with a principled critique of straightforward neo-liberalism. According to the latter there is little constructive place for social policy at all. In particular the neo-liberal solution to problems of employment is to act negatively on the supply side, reducing the cost of labour. Exponents of the Third Way argued that this was mistaken, and that certain forms of social policy could play a constructive role in the economy, in particular by improving the quality of labour supply (Giddens 1998). This led in particular to a stress on education and labour market activation policies and to childcare policies that would enable increasing numbers of women to join the labour force. Behind these ideas stood a positive view of expansion of the labour market. In contrast, traditional social democrats (especially at that time in Germany) were clinging to the idea that high levels of employment could be maintained only by reducing labour supply such as by reductions in working hours, maintenance of the 'male breadwinner' idea of employment, or citizens' income (Crouch 1999; Esping-Andersen 1999a, 1999b; Offe 1999). The Third Way arguments made use of the analysis of 'new social risks' that had been emerging from social policy specialists. This started by defining certain 'old' social risks – primarily unemployment, sickness and disability – which were deemed to be of declining relevance by the late twentieth century. Instead, the circumstances of modern life created a set of 'new' risks, prominent among them being those associated with: the entry of large numbers of women into paid work; the ageing of the population; the decline of unskilled industrial manual work; and the expansion of private services employment (Bonoli 2007; Häusermann 2010b; Taylor-Gooby 2004). The 'old' risks had been based on the distinctly class-based deprivations of the old working class. The 'new' risks were not class-related; they were felt to be the distinctive problems of a post-class society.

This general shift was highly attractive to a generation of social democrats aware that the class divisions of industrial society could no longer inform the politics of a new age, and perhaps rather grateful that this meant that they no longer needed to see their political mission as contesting important and powerful socio-economic interests. They also saw how these newly defined risks indicated important possibilities for social policies and therefore public spending that would expand labour force participation. This would be funded through a reduced need for spending on protection against the 'old' risks. On this last point the Third Way tended to share the neo-liberal belief that recipients of 'old risk' benefits should be encouraged to join the labour force through 'workfare' policies, though they would add some positive activation measures. From this followed the emphasis on education as the single most important field for social policy, and a de-emphasis on the classic social democratic goal of using public spending and taxation as instruments of redistribution. According to some Third Way politicians, in affluent societies there was no further need for redistribution. As Tony Blair expressed it in a television interview with the BBC's Jeremy Paxman in April 2005: 'What I am saying is the issue isn't in fact whether the very richest person ends up becoming richer. The issue is whether the poorest person is given the chance that they don't otherwise have.'

As the UK Labour minister Peter Mandelson famously remarked in 1998 when the CEO of Hewlett-Packard told him that he was disinclined to invest in the UK while it had a government that was 'introducing socialism': '[New Labour is] intensely relaxed about people getting filthy rich – as long as they pay their taxes' (quoted in Malik 2012).

Third Way politicians believed in equality of opportunity, not equality of outcome – though this was not the case with the movement's leading thinker, Tony Giddens (1998: 101–4). They did not seem to be aware that this had been the slogan of centre-right politicians ever since World War II. To take a particularly important example, R. A. Butler, introducing the Education Bill 1944 to the British House of Commons, argued that it would provide 'equivalent opportunities to all children over 11' (Hansard 1944). Centre-right politics could never have become a dominant force in mass democracies without committing itself to this principle. The Third Way therefore narrowed the party difference in the social policy field to one of the lengths to which left and right would be willing to go to support that equality. They then narrowed the field even further by disclaiming overall redistributive aims.

Basing labour market and other social policies on the thesis that new social risks had replaced old ones enabled the Third Way to put behind them the problem of class in two respects. They no longer needed to seek a new class base for their parties; this in turn enabled them to try to make peace with the business interests that had been the traditional opponents of social democracy. This was useful, given the increasing power of those interests produced by globalisation and deregulated financial markets. Third Way social democracy therefore emerged as a political force only thinly distinguished from neo-liberalism and without a strategy for dealing with business power.

Meanwhile, the reality of that power was rooted in a paradox. The core of neo-liberal ideology is a belief in the superiority of markets over states in solving problems and achieving goals, and a reassertion, against the traditions of the Keynesian welfare state, of the need for markets and states to be separate from each other. However, many product markets in the modern economy are dominated by large global corporations. These are not fully subordinated to market forces of the kind anticipated by economic theory and as applies to small and medium-sized enterprises (Crouch 2011). They have become the sources of extraordinary concentrations of wealth, partly because globalisation has led to a large world labour surplus; the basic division of revenue between capital and labour, which had shifted towards the latter for most of the twentieth century, is now moving towards the former almost everywhere (Lansley 2011). Extreme concentrations of wealth have accumulated in particular in the financial sector, through what we now know to have been extremely dubious methods of trading made possible by banking deregulation. In a free economy with relaxed rules about political funding, it is very difficult to prevent economic wealth from being converted into political influence. Therefore, the more unequal the division of wealth becomes, and the more large concentrations of wealth accumulate in the hands of those who have strong motives to use that influence, the more the division between states and markets is undermined.

Democracy and the market, far from inhibiting the political power of the rich, as each of them should in their different ways do, both intensify it. Mass democracy requires enormous resources to mobilise opinion; the opinions may be those of the many, but the resources to mobilise them belong mainly to the wealthy few. The market system may depend on the separation of economy and polity, but it can do nothing to prevent the rewards earned in the former from being deployed in the latter – partly in order to secure privileges in the economy in turn. Only political action can erect rules to limit such behaviour, but where neo-liberal ideas have become influential there are inhibitions about using political power in this way. We therefore find the toughest rules about political funding in the countries where neo-liberalism has been most contested by social democracy (i.e. the Nordic countries), and the weakest in the heartland of neo-liberalism, the USA. The fact that political power and economic wealth can become, if not strenuously prevented, mutually convertible currencies was a point completely missed by Third Way social democrats. Seeing wealth only in terms of the products and services it could buy, they were able to maintain their position that inequality did not matter provided the masses were well provided for; wealth as such was seen as a positive-sum game. But power is often (though not always) relative; more power for corporations to influence politics usually means less power for some other interests. This is why the class division of wealth between capital and labour continues to matter.

## The Nordic social investment welfare state

Much in the Third Way agenda resembles the concept of the social investment welfare state, in particular the stress on education, and the need for social policy to encourage people to join the paid workforce rather than enable them to leave it. But those aspects of the Third Way interpretation of such an approach that insisted that the problems of 'old' social risks had been transcended were not essential to the social investment theme. If the new social risks are seen not as supplanting the old risks of class society but as supplementing them, one has the possibility of a rich social policy agenda (Morel et al. 2012; Vandenbroucke and Vleminckx 2011; Schmid 2006, 2008). According to this perspective, unemployment and disability remain conditions that have to be compensated generously, since they are seen as caused at least partly by inadequacies in the system and not just as the results of individual failings. Further, because this compensation raises the reservation wage, less use can be made of the negative sanctions of the neo-liberal labour market to push people into employment. More emphasis therefore has to be placed on positive activation, in particular education and training (see Hilpert, this volume), child care and family-friendly work policies. Further still, if legal protection from dismissal is to be weakened in the interests of making labour markets more flexible, but if the employment relationship is still seen in class terms as one of power, employees will need some other forms of protection from arbitrary and unreasonable action by employers. This may be best provided by strong trade unions. Finally, if increased spending on labour market and family policies cannot be partly funded by savings on policies to meet the 'old' risks, the overall level of public spending will have to be higher than hoped by Third Way strategists.

This 'combined social risks' strategy constitutes the full form of the social investment welfare state. It is most fully developed in the Nordic countries, where it is associated with very high levels of employment as well as strong records of economic innovation and modernisation. Denmark has gone further than the other countries in the neo-liberal direction of replacing employment protection law by a combination of comprehensive positive activation measures, generous unemployment compensation and strong trade unions (Bonoli 2012; Crouch 2013; Emmenegger 2010; Madsen 2007). Finland, Norway and Sweden maintain employment protection law too. As Steinmo and Rothstein explain elsewhere in this volume, the Nordic countries have long been the only ones where social democracy has been pursued in any strong sense. Importantly, they are the countries where the balance of class forces has been least skewed towards business interests; their trade unions are the strongest, their inequalities of income and wealth the lowest (OECD 2011), and their public spending is the highest in the world. It is therefore not surprising that they have avoided the strict neo-liberal paradigm in confronting contemporary economic challenges, unlike the UK or Germany. The success of the Nordic approach is such that, by and large, it survives changes of government.

One finds elements of the Nordic social investment welfare state elsewhere: in Austria, but with less of the family policy agenda; in the Netherlands, but with a higher level of income inequality; in Belgium, but with a less successful economy; in Ireland and Switzerland, but with higher inequality and without the family policy. Germany is less easy to locate on this scale. The German welfare state has recently moved in a neo-liberal direction, with harsh pressures to lower the reservation wage (Streeck 2009). But this co-exists with a strong social partnership model for existing, especially skilled, employees, strong investment in training, and government subsidies to assist the retention of valuable staff during the recession. Emerging from this is a segmented labour force, with one part enjoying an essentially social democratic regime and another (in which immigrants and women are concentrated) a neo-liberal one.

In Central and Eastern Europe there are strong elements of the Nordic model only in Slovenia, the only CEE country already to have achieved overall income levels approaching those of parts of Western Europe. Elsewhere in the region a more unequivocally neo-liberal approach dominates.

The south-west European states (Greece, Italy, Portugal, Spain) remain furthest from the social investment welfare state. Labour market policies continue to be focused on laws that protect the rights of established employees, leaving large numbers in temporary jobs, in self-employment, or in an extensive shadow economy. Unemployment compensation is generally low, positive activation policies very weakly developed, and union representation patchy. These approaches bear the marks of late industrialisation and, in all except Italy, short democratic histories. Employment policies were based on a small industrial working class and an even smaller group of public employees. The former could prove rebellious, often communist; the loyalty of the latter to the state had to be guaranteed. Employment protection could be provided for these categories, leaving out the majority of the working population outside the organised modern sector. Large employers did not object to the potential labour market rigidities of this system, as the state provided them with largely protected markets. The gradual movement of the majority of the working population into the modern sector, followed by the removal of protection in the single European market, has removed the features that made this model viable. But the balance of class forces within these societies has until now prevented them from moving towards either a full neo-liberal system (fears of social turmoil having been too great) or a social investment welfare state (labour movements are too weak, and the welfare state base insufficiently developed). As these countries fall into sovereign debt crisis, the combined weight of the European Union, the European Central Bank and the International Monetary Fund is pushing them to accept the risks of the former approach. France occupies a highly complex position. In some respects its legacy of protected 'national champion' firms and delayed industrialisation have imparted a 'southern' logic to its social policy development. But the strong, modernising state keeps it away from the more negative implications of that.

While the Nordic countries continue to point to the most attractive paths to social democratic renewal, as they have done for decades, they are now beset by two worrying problems that are also of general importance. One of these still concerns the changing balance of class power; the other is the problematic position of the nation-state as the primary shell for social democracy, which has indirect but highly important class implications.

### *The changing class balance and the Nordic models*

The success of Nordic social democracy is such that it has survived the electoral decline of social democratic parties themselves. This decline is, as discussed elsewhere in this volume (see chapters by Milner, and Rothstein and Steinmo), primarily a consequence of the failure of *any* parties today to build secure constituencies. However, it matters most for social democrats because the political power of non-capitalists depends predominantly on elections, while the business interests that form the main constituency of the centre-right have other means of guaranteeing their influence. The success of social democratic policies ensures the continuation of strong welfare states, but the changed configuration of class power is bringing a change to their structure. Increasingly, delivery of the Nordic welfare states is contracted out to private firms (Tritter 2011).

Here, the Nordic countries fit into a general pattern; it looms larger there, because their welfare states are that much larger. We can see the terms of a distinctive and not very attractive twenty-first-century social compromise emerging: strong welfare states can survive, provided they are delivered by private corporations who win contracts from governments in a so-called 'market' where the providers are a small number of large corporations and the customers are government departments. As Mark Freedland (2001) analysed, the public ceases to be either citizen or customer, and becomes just a user. Significantly, at least in the UK, many of the firms active in these fields have past records of experience in such classic areas of government contracting as armaments and road construction. These corporations are now running education, health and other care, and administrative services for public authorities. Their expertise and core business lie in making government contracts, not in the delivery of the services concerned. This is logical, as their customer-supplier relationship is with their public contract partner, not the users.

Since the decline of manufacturing industry in the advanced countries, investors have been seeking profitable opportunities in the provision of services. A problem for them, particularly in Europe, has been that so much mass service activity has been publicly provided, beyond their reach. Full privatisation of these services would not however be the most attractive possibility for them, as demand for education, health, care and policing would decline if users had to finance them for themselves. Services funded by governments for universal provision but contracted out to firms provide an attractive option. A high and consistent level of demand is ensured, and marketing activities are concentrated on a few politicians and officials rather than on a mass public. While the extensive European welfare states are the prime locations for the new compromise, the deal eventually reached for President Obama's health service reforms involved federal government being able to expand its spending, but with private firms taking most of the resulting new business.

Contract deals between governments and large corporations have long been notorious sites of dubious practice, even corruption. It is a paradoxical outcome for social democracy to have ushered in a vast new wave of this activity; even more, for it to be a consequence of neo-liberalism, such contracts being one of Adam Smith's main targets in his attacks on state involvement in the economy. Indeed, actually existing neo-liberalism has blurred the boundary between the economic and the political in a way that social democracy never did. To the extent that social democrats practised Keynesian demand management, they used a distinctly hands-off form of economic governance: government set a few basic indicators to provide a framework within which firms were largely left alone. To the extent that they practised nationalisation (and, strictly speaking, only Austrian and British social democrats, and French socialists briefly in the 1980s, did so), they also restricted their attentions to a small number of sectors (usually those where there was not much competition) and again left the rest of the economy largely alone. A neo-liberal economy shot through with privately delivered public welfare policies presents much more of a public-private fudge.

## Social democracy as nation-bound

The above has tried to demonstrate the viability in the modern economy of a reformulated version of the social democratic welfare state. However, there remains an important problem. The welfare state has developed as an essentially national institution, with national solidarity as the moral base for its appeal for the shared funding of social risk. This is true everywhere, but is seen most strongly in the Nordic cases, where citizenship rights which are based on shared membership of the people's home (the Swedish concept of *folkshem*) are most strongly developed. The stronger a citizenship right, the worse the consequences of being excluded from it. It may also be true that the stronger a set of citizenship rights, the more useful it can be to have some non-citizens who are excluded from it, providing some marginal flexibility.

Thus, although social democracy has always had an internationalist aspiration, it is deeply rooted in the nation-state. When social policy specialists talk of 'universal' welfare states, there is an implicit national boundary around their universe. Whether or not immigrants are included in it is just the most pointed part of a more general confrontation between the neo-liberal global and the social democratic national. The global level acknowledges no social rights, and no citizenship except that of the global corporations who make its rules. Global society is an extreme form of class society. Increasingly the battle between neo-liberalism and social democracy takes place at different geographical levels; but the global can penetrate the national in a way that cannot be reciprocated.

The fact of widespread immigration has important implications for this national basis of the welfare state. At first sight, the employment of large numbers of immigrants in the advanced economies is evidence of a continuing demand for low-skilled labour, as (with important exceptions) these are the levels at which immigrants usually work. Closer inspection, however, often reveals that what immigrants provide is over-qualified labour. Partly because of problems in the recognition of 'foreign' qualifications, partly because of their lack of informal contacts, immigrants coming from poorer to richer societies frequently have to take jobs below their level of education or aptitude. They also often lack at least some social security rights, and are more likely than native workers to be employed precariously, including in the shadow economy. They are the ideal workers for a fully neo-liberal economy.

For that same reason, their position within a social democratic economy is problematic. As Susi Meret and Birte Siim point out elsewhere in this volume, the social inclusiveness of Nordic societies is increasingly finding its limits with large-scale immigration. The policies of the social investment welfare state have increasing difficulty reaching immigrants, and there is increasing public hostility towards them, adding strength to the racist populist movements that have been growing in the UK as well as elsewhere. Compared with many other countries experiencing high levels of immigration, the Nordic record is still good. Social provision for immigrants, as well as native attitudes towards them, remains better than in countries with lower general welfare state provision. As Martín-Artiles et al. (2012) argue, the populations of strong welfare states have less reason to feel the anxiety and uncertainty about their own future that breeds hostility towards immigrants.

The Nordic states are by no means alone in having immigrants concentrated in temporary jobs. However, increasing use is being made of this phenomenon as the other side of the coin of continuing employment security for employees with permanent contracts. Sweden in particular is following this path. It is as though, given the global shift in the terms of the capital-labour relationship, the social democratic welfare state can be preserved only at the cost of a growing margin of excluded persons. If, as in the German case as a result of the youth training system, young people in general do not form an excluded generation (as they do in Spain, for example), the strain is taken by immigrants.

In the long term one approach to these problems would be to move towards construction of a 'social Europe' as at least a way station between these extremes, of an intermediate attempt at constructing a transnational social citizenship. However, as Yves Mény argues elsewhere in this volume, Europe is moving in the very opposite direction. Recent judgements of the European Court, particularly some cases relating to Finland and Sweden, have declared aspects of national industrial relations systems to be contrary to EU competition law (Höpner 2008). Further, although in principle national governments can exempt social services from the reach of European competition law, it is possible for the Court, at the prompting of firms seeking contracted-out public business, to rule that governments have defined the reach of public service too broadly. These provisions fall under the recent extensions of competition law into services of general economic interest (SGEI) and social services of general interest (SSGI) (Barbier 2011). This has happened recently, for example, to social housing in the Netherlands (Sol and Van der Vos 2011) and Czech employment services (Sirovátka 2011). Fritz Scharpf first argued over fifteen years ago that European integration would always be a force for market-making rather than institution-building (Scharpf 1996, 1999, 2001). This was because the former was a process of negative integration, breaking down barriers to trade, on which it was relatively easy to secure consensus; while the latter constituted positive integration, on which there would be several alternatives, making agreement difficult.

It was asserted at the outset that the stronger the drive to marketisation, the more important it is to be able to remedy its negative consequences, and that if societies lose their capacity to do this, the interests of the wealthy will be disproportionately served. If Europeanisation comes to mean uncompromised marketisation, it joins globalisation as a force driving out that capacity to remedy market externalities.

In this context social democracy increasingly finds itself fighting a rear-guard action to retain issues at a national level. The temptation to turn to a sealed-off, protected national community having restricted trade with the outside world becomes strong, as we see in the 2012 response of the Greek left to the neo-liberal solutions being forced on that country to resolve its profound debt crisis. There is no future here. Historically social democrats have not been protectionists. Protection favours producers over consumers, and the producer interests that primarily benefit are those of the owners of protected firms. Ordinary workers suffer as protected domestic firms provide their captive markets with poor products at high prices and with little in the way of innovation. Social democracy has no option but to fight for a more balanced European and, eventually, world regime.

## Conclusions

The challenges confronting social democracy are daunting. Changes in occupational structure have weakened its electoral base. Social democrats confront an adverse shift in the balance of power between capital and labour induced by globalisation. They are increasingly able to retain its greatest achievement, the redistributive welfare state, only by allowing corporate interests to dominate it. Social democratic arguments are stranded at a national level that cannot engage with the main forces in the global economy. However, there are points of vulnerability in the present system on which social democrats can work. Whatever its weaknesses, the Nordic version of the social investment welfare state remains a practical example.

There are also paradoxical consequences of the triumph of neo-liberalism. As noted above, it has produced societies dominated not by markets but by giant corporations. These have acquired political prominence, and therefore visibility and vulnerability. This has been an odd consequence of the neo-liberal critiques of the state as incompetent in comparison with corporations. This led to policies for privatising public service delivery, the adoption of business criteria in how government conducted its own services, and, partly to facilitate this, encouragement of intensive interaction with, and learning from, the private sector by public servants – including the secondment of corporate employees to government departments and the cosy relations between corporations and public officials that result from contracting out public services to favoured firms. Neo-liberalism might have limited major forms of government intervention in the economy, but it opened the path to greatly increased intervention by the economy (that is, firms and highly wealthy corporate individuals) in the polity (Lansley 2011). When this is combined with the intensified corporate lobbying that is another consequence of business power, there is a breach of one of its own fundamental principles, and this becomes the Achilles heel of neo-liberalism. Giant corporations so obviously intervene in politics that it is very difficult for them to continue to claim that they just perform their market role, and that if we do not like the externalities produced by some of their actions, then we must address ourselves to parliament. We know that the corporations will be there too, wielding far mightier resources to ensure that parliament ignores us. As a result, corporations, as well as or even rather than governments, are now likely to be the direct object of campaigns over contentious issues, and some of them have responded proactively by claiming to take the lead in good corporate social responsibility. This then makes them vulnerable to criticism and challenge over the truth of their claims, or over abuses that they have not remedied. A particularly prominent example of this was the experience of BP and its involvement in pollution of the Gulf of Mexico. BP had made strong environmental credentials a major element of its brand identity. The Gulf incident shattered that reputation, creating a crisis within the corporation. The politicisation of the corporation is not just a matter of growing corporate power; it also offers an extension of political arenas.

It has been striking how, since the banking crisis of 2008, there has been a new public awareness in many countries of the growing inequality being produced by the concentration of wealth at the very top, and of abuses of power by banks, media corporations and others. Issues that were simply not on the political agenda even five years ago are now prominent. This may be a temporary phenomenon that will die down once the financial crisis seems 'solved', but it builds on earlier protest movements over the exploitation of Third World labour and damage to the environment (Della Porta 2003; Della Porta and Reiter 2003). Criticisms of global capitalism that a decade ago were restricted to small protest groups are now heard even in the mass media on the centre-right. The elites of contemporary capitalism, being both richer than ever and detached from any particular national polity, have allowed a gulf to appear between them and the middle classes who were historically their allies in a struggle against the propertyless working masses. These masses no longer exist, and a confrontation between a small arrogant elite and the great majority should be attractive territory on which social democrats can fight. All simplifications of complex societies are distortions, but the replacement of the Third Way image of a society where the top 85% were together against a troublesome bottom 15% by the 'We are the 99%' slogan of the Occupy Wall Street movement carries great potential.

The extension of the political arena to include direct conflicts with corporations should not be seen as a failure of social democracy, but as a new phase in its history. Social democrats need to diversify their historic (and ultimately Leninist) strategy of channelling everything through the party. This has become neither necessary nor sufficient. It is not necessary, because working people are no longer socio-political outsiders, with no links to important institutions outside their own movements. It is not sufficient, because parties no longer represent 'movements'. We are currently witnessing post-Fordism finally reaching the political left. While social democratic reformists of the 1990s, such as the UK's New Labour, were quick to see the implications of the end of Fordism for economic policy and for traditional approaches to trade unionism, they did not see its consequences for the traditional model of the political party, to which they clung somewhat, as they enjoyed the centralised power it gave them. They also saw capitalism and large corporations as almost entirely benign. They were thus unprepared for new anti-capitalist social movements and new forms of economic critique. The next generation of social democrats will need to make use of a wider diversity of organisational forms and will need to articulate new criticisms of corporate behaviour. The critical movements of this kind that are currently springing up in many countries have three major advantages over traditional social democratic parties for this purpose. First, not needing to contend for office, they do not need to curry favour with business interests and attract election funding from them. Second, they do not have to worry about taking risks in prosecuting issues that are not yet popular. They are political entrepreneurs, trying out new themes. Some will work and enter the mainstream; others will fall by the wayside. A big party cannot risk having any of the latter, but without risk-taking it becomes incapable of innovation. Finally, many of the new social movements are international, or post-national. This is vitally important in challenging the conservative globalisation argument, that if firms are criticised they will take investment and employment elsewhere. Transnational critical movements can harry corporations across a number of countries. Also, by tracking global corporations rather than national polities, these movements escape the immobilised position of traditional parties, which have had to contend with global footloose corporations while themselves being geographically bound.

The political stance of this new social democracy will need to be very carefully defined. Many of the new social movements are 'anti-capitalist', though they rarely have viable alternative economic models. Social democracy is an ideology that accepts the capitalist economy, and wants that economy to work dynamically and efficiently, but it is critical of many of its social consequences, seeks various checks on these and promotes alternative forms of activity where these are likely to provide superior outcomes. There seems no prospect today of trying to base an advanced economy on anything very different from these assumptions. A social investment welfare state that retains an awareness of the continuing class nature of society – and therefore of the need for various forms of regulation – remains as far as it is both feasible and desirable to move in envisaging alternatives.

# LABOUR, SKILLS AND EDUCATION IN MODERN SOCIO-ECONOMIC DEVELOPMENT: CAN THERE BE A SOCIAL DEMOCRATIC ECONOMIC AND INDUSTRIAL POLICY IN A GLOBALISED ECONOMY?

Ulrich Hilpert and Desmond Hickie

## Introduction

Between 1945 and the 1980s, successful social democratic economic policy was facilitated by Keynesian demand management policies, fostering full employment, increasing employees' incomes, and built on a close relationship between government and trade unions. This was seen most clearly in the Nordic countries and in Germany under Willi Brandt. However, elements could also be seen, for example, in British 'Labourism' and French *dirigisme*. During the last thirty years globalisation has posed profound challenges for the economies of Western Europe in general and for social democratic ideology and economic management in particular. Mass-produced goods are largely manufactured in Newly Industrialising Countries (NICs), and the number of blue-collar jobs is falling in Western Europe. In addition, advanced economic and industrial development is increasingly both regionalising and exacerbating uneven economic development within nation-states. This increases social divisions and undermines social cohesion. Nevertheless, there are still European industries, enterprises and regions which develop very competitively (Hilpert 2003, 2006). They are usually knowledge-intensive, based on high technology and scientific research, and on the manufacture of high-quality products.

These global structural changes were accompanied by a new ideological hegemony of free-market neo-liberal economic policies, sometimes in tandem with conservative social policies. This ideology, 'market fundamentalism' (Block 2011), accepts only a restricted role for the state in economic and industrial policy. The state is charged with creating a benign and stable macro-economy, liberalising labour markets and perhaps intervening where there is identifiable market failure. The state is seen as slow, inefficient and inept. In such a context the old social democratic policy solutions are seen as at best irrelevant and at worst embedding inefficiency and ensuring international economic decline. This new hegemony sapped the confidence of social democrats in their ability to address key economic issues and they often adopted the rhetoric, and even some policies, of the right, perhaps most notably with the Blair government in the UK. Yet neo-liberalism, with its misplaced faith in the self-regulatory capacities of markets, has been confounded by global economic events since 2008. Furthermore, the view that the development of globally competitive and innovative high-technology industries can be left to the market is demonstrably unhistorical even in the USA (Block and Keller 2009; Mazzucato 2011).

Social democrats, therefore, need to ask whether there is still practical value and potential in the design of social democratic industrial policies. Here, one has to take into account what products can still be manufactured competitively in Western European high-wage economies, such as materials technologies, mechanical engineering, pharmaceuticals, environmental technologies, transportation systems and advanced automobiles. These industries are generally the ones which have characterised European economies since 1945. But, while their earlier development was in part based on relatively cheap labour and much simpler products, manufacturing today is based on robotics and highly skilled labour. Technological advance in such industries means that they require highly skilled, well-paid, university-trained personnel (Berry and Glaeser 2005; Williams et al. 2004; Herzog et al. 1986).

Questions arise about whether these industries can still compete in Western Europe in the face of globalisation, and whether a social democratic polity can still deliver well-paid jobs and a high quality of life. Social democratic policies were always, *inter alia*, associated with equality of opportunity, with enhancing the quality of public education, and with improving general living standards. Policies on education, equal employment opportunities and industrial restructuring and innovation must be at the heart of a social democratic philosophical and policy response to globalisation. This does not necessarily require wholly new and distinctive policy instruments exclusive to social democratic parties. Proven and widely accepted policy approaches would be easier to 'sell' to potential social and political partners, although they may not be able to create the persuasive hegemony of ideas that the Keynesian model provided in Western Europe for thirty-five years. A social democratic response to globalisation needs to draw on both new and existing policy instruments, and to reinterpret them to meet the needs of modern citizens. Modern social democrats should make use of successful policy models, not least from the USA (Block and Keller 2009; Mazzucato 2011). Such policies can bring together the interests of advanced manufacturers, modern unions and high-technology workers. Social democratic policies can be oriented towards higher value added, rising incomes, enhancing the quality of jobs and living conditions.

### The success of social democratic policies after World War II and the preparation for globalisation

Social democratic success after World War II was associated with industrialisation based on Fordist production, increasing productivity and, as a consequence, growing markets. The locus for these developments was nation-states, national economies and national economic policy-making. Strong trade unions negotiated rising incomes, benefiting the workforce as a whole, and so providing the demand for mass-produced goods. Competitive Fordist manufacturing and low costs for raw materials and energy provided economic growth. Social democratic governments offered economic management foundations for growth (and hence rising incomes) and redistributive welfare policies. The social democratic aim of improving living conditions for the working class via capitalist growth was attractive and industrial workers generally supported it. Various degrees of tripartism, more in Germany and Scandinavia, less in the UK, were believed to provide a process which was beneficial for capital and labour, and an economically active state provided a politically stable framework for this economic development.

Based on improving productivity, thanks to modern machinery and automation, social democratic ideas were closely allied to positive approaches to scientific and engineering advance, which Harold Wilson in 1964 called 'the white heat of the technological revolution'. Modern unions negotiated successfully for improved working conditions. Increased automation meant that industrial work became physically less exhausting. Alongside these beneficial processes, the importance to competitiveness of knowledge, research and engineering increased from the 1950s, becoming critical from the late 1970s. However, automation simultaneously reduced employment in manufacturing, especially for those with lower skills. The social and economic basis of the social democratic consensus faced erosion, as did its electoral base in an increasingly pluralistic society.

When oil prices rose in the 1970s, followed by those of other raw materials, capital began to flow away from Western industrialised countries. New industrial locations emerged in former Third World countries, manufacturing products for markets in Western industrialised countries based on cheaper labour and lower regulation. Mass production was relocated even in more advanced sectors, such as microelectronics and automobiles. The deregulation of world markets (via GATT and WTO negotiations) and a globalisation of production had a fundamental impact on Western industrialised countries which led to growing unemployment, a displacement of low-skilled industrial labour, a fundamental structural crisis in some sectors and structural change in others.

The industrial crisis emerged in many of those regions which had provided both the industrialisation and the political success of social democratic parties after World War II. Mass-produced, standardised consumer goods, steel, shipbuilding and mining were clearly adversely affected by changes in the international division of labour. The political and economic structures which had sustained these industries – the employment of less-skilled labour, increasing workers' incomes, high levels of unionisation and strong social democratic parties – were clearly undermined by this crisis (Abel and Deitz 2009; Berry and Glaeser 2005; Lawton Smith and Waters 2005; Florida 2002). Regions which had no or few heavy industries or mass manufacturers were able to avoid these profound social and economic problems. Regions and metropolitan areas became more divergent in their socio-economic structures and processes, as well as in their political allegiances. This divergence could be seen in the economic and social contrasts between regions such as the Ruhr and Munich in Germany, North East England and London in the UK, or Nord-Pas-de-Calais and Rhône-Alpes in France. The ascendancy of social democratic ideas and parties appeared to be over, raising the question of whether social democracy could continue to be politically and economically relevant in these new conditions.

### Towards a new social and industrial structure: the role of social democratic policies in creating equal opportunities in modern societies

In the era of social democratic hegemony, social structures changed significantly. Aiming, at least in part, at greater equality and social mobility, universities were enlarged and new universities created, notably in the Ruhr, in Northern England and in the more peripheral regions of most European countries. While this reflected a traditional aim of unions and social democratic parties to provide and foster social mobility, it also addressed the labour requirements of a changing economic structure (Simonen and McCann 2008; Power and Lundmark 2004; Herzog et al. 1986). New industries such as new materials and biotechnology, characterised by highly flexible and specialised manufacturing, changed the structure of the workforce. An increasing number of knowledge workers were and still are needed. Thus, many university graduates in recent generations have entered a career path which is fundamentally different from that experienced by their parents. Those well enough qualified could enjoy greater workplace autonomy and enhanced career opportunities. However, improved opportunities and higher wages also benefited non-graduates as well as qualified blue-collar workers.

Established industrial countries transformed their economies towards knowledge-based industries, and even traditional manufacturing and industrial work became dependent upon aspects of advanced knowledge such as robotics and new materials. As a consequence, science and research became increasingly important, while employment in mass manufacturing decreased. A knowledge-based economy allowed industrialised countries to retain modernised and innovative industries, as well as developing advanced service sectors and innovative start-up enterprises (Williams et al. 2004; Malecki 1989). The average knowledge and skill levels of workers in such industries increased, and much low-skilled or semi-skilled work disappeared. Today in Scandinavia or Germany, fewer than 30% of the workforce is unskilled or semi-skilled, and the proportion of university graduates has increased to 25% among younger age cohorts in the labour force and continues to rise; almost half of these age cohorts graduate from high school after twelve years' full-time education. In addition, the quality of apprenticeships has advanced to a level that is comparable to that of university-trained engineers twenty-five years ago.

Such changes in industrial structure were made possible by new scientific research findings and advanced engineering. The modern knowledge-based economy creates a strong demand for highly skilled knowledge workers, while standardised manufacturing will either be done mainly by robots (in advanced automobile industries) or relocated to NICs with cheap labour and low levels of regulation. Science and engineering underpins both the continuity and the modernisation of Western industrial systems, but it also changes the economic and social structures of these societies. New enterprises are frequently created as spin-offs from university research and public research institutes (as in bio-technology) (Marginson 2006) and increasingly contribute to techno-industrial innovation. In these economies even long-established industries have changed their product focus fundamentally. For example, textile industries may special-ise in industrial textiles for filter systems, and ceramics industries may focus on industrial ceramics for modern engines. Whenever such changes take place, they create new opportunities for spin-off firms based on scientific research or engineering (Berry and Glaeser 2005; Franco and Filson 2000). Today, such modernised industrial sectors in advanced European economies are less dominated by large enterprises; due to outsourcing, small- and medium-sized enterprises now play a much more significant role (Simonen and McCann 2008; Mahroum 2000).

Networks of collaboration among firms and clusters of research-oriented enterprises involve a growing number of high-tech entrepreneurs. Industrial modernisation is characterised by changes in the workforce and a change in society (an increasing number of entrepreneurs), induced by the need for scientific research and its economic exploitation (Mahroum 2000). While tech-nologically advanced industries are based on fundamental structural changes, they also create a demand for new, varied and highly advanced services. Those services may be concerned with product development and commercial research, or be oriented towards small firms' demands for rather specialised financial and legal services such as venture capitalists and patent lawyers. Established banks and insurance companies introduce new services, and in addition specialised service and consulting enterprises are founded. Finally, to meet private lifestyle and accommodation needs, personal and property services have also grown, further contributing to the number of new service businesses and independent professionals.

Over several decades from the 1960s to the 1980s, social democratic education policies (based on universal secondary education and much-expanded university education) helped underpin a gradual structural change towards a knowledge-based economy and new social structures. These new social structures are characterised by a more heterogeneous range of social groups and political interests. The social classes that underpinned earlier social democratic success (notably a strongly unionised working class) have diminished in size and political significance. The modern citizen, who may have climbed the social ladder benefiting from public education, may well retain a certain commitment to ideas about equal opportunities. However, these may identify more with new groups, and newer political causes like equality for sexual minorities, and the environment. In addition, this new and increasingly influential creative class (Florida 2002) is aware of its own economic and social interests, which include public services. While socially liberal, they are not attracted to the collectivist and labourist policies which characterised post-war social democracy.

A regionalisation of social structures was associated with a regionalisation of economy and industry, and new and attractive jobs for the growing number of university-educated groups emerged predominantly in metropolitan areas (Hilpert and Lawton Smith 2012; Florida 2002). Since modern industrial structures require knowledge, research, education and science, this social and attitudinal change took place first in those urbanised regions or metropolitan areas where these advantages were most strongly present. The new structures reflected social and economic changes most strongly affecting well-educated, professional urban dwellers. In these urban areas with strong knowledge-based economies, social democratic allegiance was often weakened, and sometimes replaced by a rainbow coalition of new and pluralistic groups representing high-earning young professionals.

Technologically advanced societies are characterised by large numbers of graduates, the movement of people to conurbations, a declining traditional working class, less manufacturing employment, and by a leading economic role for innovative metropolitan areas, providing about two-thirds of research activity, innovative labour markets for highly skilled personnel from blue-collar workers to top scientists, and a socially liberal environment and lifestyle (Hilpert and Lawton Smith 2012; Hilpert 1992). In the end, knowledge-based economies are not simply transforming societies in general towards a more pluralist social structure. These transformed economies are also strongly regionalised and are creating new forms of metropolitan industrial structure based on knowledge-intensive and high-tech products as well as forms of manufacturing that do not require great physical space or natural resources. The social and economic conditions which sustained social democratic parties in these urban areas have disappeared or shrunk, and social democratic parties have increasingly had to build new political alliances with partners from other political traditions. As the aims of social democracy were largely realised for many citizens, traditional social democracy played a significant part in undermining its own social and political relevance and electoral base. But traditional social democratic aims such as high incomes, secure jobs, low unemployment and equal opportunities remain on the political agenda and voters can be attracted by policies which help to achieve them, reinterpreted for a modern industrial and social environment.

### Can general social prosperity be achieved under globalisation? The continentalisation of innovation

The processes of globalisation were experienced by semi-skilled and unskilled workers as problems of unemployment and falling incomes. The economic policy instruments which had proved so successful previously were now largely ineffective. Keynesian demand management policies, if they led to greater consumer demand, were likely to increase imports rather than increase demand for troubled domestic mass manufacturers. Globalisation, thus, was a troubling process for traditional and mature producers, and continues to be so. As a consequence, industrial labour in Western countries was affected by a constant threat of unemployment and social marginalisation. The social democratic policies, which previously had led to prosperity, appeared to offer no feasible solutions to their problems.

Simultaneously, however, there was a dynamic development in innovative and knowledge-based industries, both creating new industries and refocusing older ones into new niches. Dynamic processes of industrial development occurred and contributed to the restructuring of traditional centres of industrial manufacturing (Hilpert 2003). The demand for unskilled and semi-skilled labour largely disappeared, while in other parts of the economy there was an undersupply of sufficiently skilled labour. Higher levels of education and new competences were needed to create the numerati, literati and entrepreneurs, as identified by Teece (2011: 531). High incomes were based on individual knowledge, skills and opportunities.[1] Public educational systems, strong research-based universities and modernised apprenticeship schemes enabled the development and manufacture of products without challenging competition from low-cost countries.

Innovation and advanced products based on science and research allowed continuing and even increased prosperity for those meeting the knowledge and skills expectations of a modern industrial system. These processes can be identified in OECD countries, particularly the USA and the most technologically advanced West European economies. While there is globalisation and relocation in mass production industries, in innovative, more technologically advanced industries, the established international division of labour has continued. Knowledge-intensive industries have experienced little impact from globalisation, except where products are themselves more mature, as is the case with consumer electronics such as audio systems. Cutting-edge science and research, linked to industries ready to innovate, allows such industries to retain their competitive position (Hilpert 2003, 2006).

The manufacture of high value added products is still based in the United States and Western Europe, and located in places where new scientific and technological knowledge is generated. Even newly developed economies which have established their own research capabilities remain marginal in research collaborations and the international exchange of researchers. They have no significant participation in global research networks; in biotechnology only about 5% of all collaborations involved partners from countries outside the USA or Western Europe (Hilpert 2005). This reinforces a developmental pattern identified in biotechnology and other areas of technology decades earlier (Hilpert 1992). A detailed analysis indicates a continentally focused pattern of collaboration and knowledge exchange in research. Collaboration data for researchers in biotechnology indicates that about 75% of all collaborations were either exclusively North American or exclusively Western European; another 20% of biotechnology collaborations were made across the Atlantic Ocean (Hilpert 2005).

Although US research opportunities attract most 'star scientists', they are not the centre of all research networks (Trippl 2012). Europe retains its relative importance in science and technology, based in those countries with strong research systems. National competences and national policies for research and techno-industrial innovation together create a distinctive European research structure. Here international collaborative linkages form elements in continental research networks. Investment in science and education develops the labour force to support such processes and provides the basis for innovative research structures. So leading-edge innovatory industries are characterised by continuity rather than by any globalised relocation process.

As explained earlier, such continental processes are concentrated at a discrete number of regions and locations. Opportunities for innovative industrial development must be underpinned by the dynamism of new research and research-based new enterprises. Outstanding universities, research institutes, academic labour and the public funding of scientific research provide the basis for innovative development, but these resources are unevenly distributed. Cutting-edge research provides the basis for economic growth. Researchers seek to work and scientific networks are built at such locations because they allow for the exchange of knowledge, personnel and research findings (Trippl 2012; Williams et al. 2004; Mahroum 1999, 2000). The more attractive and competent research teams become, the more successfully they will compete for funding. An accumulation of funding and human capital is identifiable at these favoured locations alongside a concentration of research capabilities, new and innovative enterprises and expanding labour markets offering jobs for knowledge workers, all built upon a foundation of outstanding scientific research (Hilpert and Lawton Smith 2012; Singh and Briem 2012). 'Islands of innovation' are formed which differ fundamentally from other regions in their processes of socio-economic development (Hilpert 1992). There are about a dozen of these in the USA and – due to varied national policy frameworks – about fifteen to twenty in Europe.

Although they may differ quite significantly in size, it is interesting that on both continents, such 'islands of innovation' concentrate about two-thirds of the necessary national resources, and can be demonstrated to have done so over a period of thirty years. They seem likely to do so for the foreseeable future. Public funding of both scientific research and university education in general creates enduring effects in terms of industrial modernisation and prosperity. It is strongly concentrated and generated at these 'islands of innovation'. The critical role of public policies and funding has not been readily recognised and neo-liberal economists and politicians unquestioningly and unhistorically have attributed economic success to free markets and private enterprise (Mazzucato 2011). Politically, this was a message understandably adopted by some enterprises, and it proved easy to sell to many of their employees, who were often not unionised and who saw their futures as determined more by their individual efforts than by collective social action.

Although the European and North American continents show divergent patterns of innovation, they clearly demonstrate the fundamental role of government and university-trained labour in high-technology-based economic development (Hilpert 1991; Block and Keller 2009). Policies that support both wide participation in university education and a concentration of scientific personnel based on strong research funding are important for socio-economic development in ways that benefit the broader society. As demonstrated in the innovative restructuring of industries, individual advantage and social participation in prosperity can be achieved once the relationship between individual opportunities and societal support for education and training is harmonised. Globalisation and continentalisation change the way in which prosperity might be distributed, but education and well-trained labour allow a broad participation in growing prosperity.

### Where modern development takes place: metropolitan techno-industrial innovation and the opportunities of structural change

The success of 'islands of innovation' contributes to uneven regional development which may be disadvantageous for people who do not live in such favoured metropolitan areas, but in places which lack the potential to become engines of innovative, socio-economic development. In addition, techno-industrial innovation may reduce the number of unskilled and semi-skilled jobs because of the increasing use of robotics and so does not provide for wider prosperity among those with less human capital. There are rich cities, like New York or London, which are well known as international centres of finance and property services, but are also characterised by particularly wide disparities in incomes. Although these metropolises are also important centres of science and research, economically they are particularly dependent on finance and property services, making them rather different to locations more specialised in advanced manufacturing and high-technology products. Metropolitan areas characterised by high-tech industries and services generally have higher median and average wages or per capita incomes than those characterised by lower levels of technology and less knowledge-intensive services (Hilpert and Nagler 2011). In 'islands of innovation', average incomes per capita and median incomes are the highest for all types of metropolitan area. In these favoured metropolitan areas, networks link both large and small high-technology businesses with research-intensive universities and government research laboratories, focusing on the development and application of particular advanced technologies, such as the case of IT along Route 128 in the USA. Here, one often also finds advanced medium-technology industries, high-tech services, and finance and property services which are required to serve the needs of prosperous businesses and individuals. Hence a prosperous local economy based on high-technology skills is created.

The relationship between advanced industries and scientific research provides attractive jobs for highly skilled and university-trained labour. Knowledge workers live where they can find jobs. So, metropolitan areas with their research universities, innovative enterprises and advanced services attract graduates and postgraduates (Singh and Briem 2012; Florida 2002), including from abroad (Dickinson et al. 2008; Regets 2007; Khadria 2001). Once there, they can find opportunities to change jobs and to continue a career without leaving the area. University-trained labour is attracted to metropolitan locations in general (Singh and Briem 2012) and even more strongly to 'islands of innovation'.

While globalisation had a critical negative impact on mature industries and hence on employment, innovative metropolitan areas can take advantage of their existing skills base, institutions and opportunities by focusing on new products based on science and technology. The existing knowledge of employees and the ongoing generation of new knowledge through scientific research help to maintain and strengthen their competitiveness over many decades. Highly advanced industrial manufacturing and new technological opportunities make these metropolitan areas internationally competitive and enable them to transform their role within the global economy. Thus, they participate in new technologies while retaining and modernising their existing industries. Examples include aircraft in Bristol and Toulouse, electronics in Munich and Boston and mechanical engineering in Stuttgart. Public policies for higher education and science focus on these favoured locations, though not necessarily overtly, and a networked innovative labour market is formed both within and between technologically related 'islands of innovation', providing for the essential exchange of knowledge and personnel (Hilpert and Lawton Smith 2012).

As metropolitan areas absorb most of this labour and educate most graduates (Ackers 2005), more peripheral areas cannot establish the necessary research and educational structures to emerge as innovative centres nor build highly innovative industrial structures. Nevertheless, there are enterprises which merge traditional competences and experience with a highly skilled workforce to create opportunities for new technologies, new products and new materials. They frequently form clusters in innovative areas (Bercovitz and Feldman 2006) and act as unique combinations of competences based on a group of collaborative enterprises. Small production runs help them to find their place in international niche markets. While mass production has been transferred to low-cost locations, such specialised, high-competence clusters cannot be moved easily in this way because they rely on the architecture of regional clusters and a highly specialised labour force. Intense collaboration characterises the firms working in these niches. Such clusters of advanced manufacturing, applying new technologies, depend strongly upon the competences located within the region. These firms develop new products and provide a contrast to the pattern of collaboration among science-based locations. Thus, firms located in such places achieve about 75% of their collaborations (Jakszentis and Hilpert 2007) within the same region or cluster, creating a specialist niche that other regions struggle to replicate. Their successful integration into the global economy helps reinforce collaborative behaviours and generates employment and prosperity even outside major metropolitan areas, as demonstrated by precision engineering and optical instruments in Baden-Württemberg, Thuringia, Brandenburg and Saxony.

The attraction of innovative metropolitan areas and their particular mode of development on the one hand, and competence-based opportunities in more peripheral regions on the other, indicates the divergent paths of development that exist for different regions and locations. A single policy cannot adequately support such divergent developments. Rather the unique qualities of different situations have to be identified, in order to devise sufficiently focused development policies. Experiences in transforming mature industries to generate dynamic modern processes of development help to identify the competences and potentials which exist in the labour force and in enterprises, for example in specialised shipbuilding and special steels. However, such opportunities are not available to all former industrialised regions, such as those based on mining, for example, in South Wales, which may require more profound structural change.

New industries in innovative metropolitan areas demonstrate the close relationship between skills, education and socio-economic development. Equally, competence-based development can create prosperity in more peripheral regions and revive some mature industries. These divergent paths both depend upon modernised industrial structures, which are much more flexible and adaptive to new knowledge, technologies and scientific findings. Networked smaller businesses and specialised localities can also serve niche markets competitively. Their competitiveness can depend upon knowledge that does not exist in every enterprise, but may be part of the human capital of particular knowledge workers. High-tech services, for example, specialise in particular service niches and so can provide state-of-the-art services. New research-based or competence-based enterprises may also demand specialised financial and property services. It is the architecture of services and manufacturing, flexibility and specialisation, which generates high-quality products and competitive processes of economic development, providing a market for such high-competence-based services and a labour market for knowledge workers in this area.

Continuing processes of innovation and structural modernisation require enhanced human capital among both blue-collar workers and graduates. Manufacturing still demands highly skilled workers, and the more innovative products become, the greater is the need for university-trained labour to play a key role in developing new products and manufacturing processes. Structural change towards the development of high-tech industries creates a demand for well-paid jobs throughout the economy. As clearly demonstrated within 'islands of innovation', average incomes are high and are enjoyed by a large percentage of the population (Hilpert and Nagler 2011). Although some top managers and top engineers or scientists may earn extraordinarily high rewards, the average knowledge worker and the average blue-collar worker achieve higher incomes as well, as they enhance their skills. A society which educates and trains its people so that they can develop the high levels of human capital necessary to participate globally in such high-technology markets both enables effective economic development and allows prosperity to be shared widely amongst a well-educated, globally competitive labour force.

In Western industrialised countries, complex economies have emerged which rely upon scientific research and innovative metropolitan areas. Here, techno-scientific progress is generated which promotes new industrial development and new research-based firms, as well as enabling strategic renewal in geographically peripheral but highly competent enterprises. This contributes to socio-economic structures which are no longer characterised by a single enterprise or industry, nor only by a narrow range of competences developed to produce a narrow range of mass-produced goods. Mass production cannot meet the whole of demand. Consumers' needs are increasingly heterogeneous, in turn requiring heterogeneous and flexible industrial structures and labour markets for the highly skilled. Hence they can generate high incomes, a broad participation in prosperity and close linkages with high-quality services. While globalisation is accompanied by a radical reduction in mass production in Western industrialised countries, it does not necessarily mean that attractive employment opportunities and prosperity are unattainable.

## Social democratic opportunities in changing economic and social structures: skilled labour, scientific research and education

While globalisation was widely associated with financial capital, there are alternative forms of development and policies. As indicated by 'islands of innovation', such alternatives can be even more successful at achieving widespread prosperity than the neo-liberal model. They can generate mutually beneficial compromises between different economic interests to achieve increasing economic growth and prosperity. Western industrialised countries have developed more complex economies and highly differentiated societies. Class-based social structures with conflicting interests cannot be identified as straightforwardly as after World War II. Societies have become more open to social and career advancement for those who have the necessary human and social capital. This does not, of course, mean that opportunities to acquire such human and social capital are equitably distributed in society. Indeed, there is ample evidence to the contrary (Wilkinson and Pickett 2009).

Technologically advanced industries generate high value added and they do so on the basis of highly skilled labour. The labour force in Europe and the USA has changed fundamentally. The number of university graduates has grown to meet the changing demand for labour. The more economically and technologically advanced the countries or metropolitan areas and their industries are, the better educated are their populations. Open societies and national economies that participate in the global exchange of goods can benefit and continue to develop economically and socially, provided they manage to generate and use new knowledge, technologies and opportunities.

So, it is labour and the human capital that it embodies which permits such economically advantageous processes, and it is education which provides the labour force that is fundamental for such modern processes of economic development (Blair 2011). Building 'islands of innovation' and attracting leading-edge research activities is a critical element of such a strategy. New knowledge and the synergy based on collaboration, involving both private businesses and publicly funded research laboratories, enable the development of knowledge-intensive industries creating new, high value added products and paying high wages. Local labour markets in 'islands of innovation' and innovative metropolitan areas foster local knowledge dissemination, tailored to the needs of the local economy. Hence, a policy focus on the development of a well-educated and highly skilled labour force should be grasped with enthusiasm by social democrats. It reflects their core values, because it requires that educational opportunities be developed for the labour force as a whole (rather than focused on a narrow social elite); it facilitates greater equality of opportunities; and it allows prosperity to be spread more broadly. Furthermore, it draws on policy fields and approaches with which social democrats feel comfortable, because they do not have the neo-liberal ideological 'hang ups' that would inhibit them from making the necessary public investments in education and scientific research, and from showing willingness to intervene positively in fostering, even creating, the necessary public-private networks of institutions that underpin the development of high technologies and industries.

While in scientific research and new technologies international collaboration is considered increasingly important, it still has its limitations. The increasingly free exchange of knowledge and ideas in science indicates that national circumstances are less constraining than previously. Not least, the European Union fosters transnational research projects. Nevertheless, a tradition in research and continuity in collaborative activities indicate that high-value scientific and technological networks are geographically restricted. About three-quarters of inter-organisational research collaborations are either in Europe or in the USA, and are conducted with partners from the same continent. Thus, Europe can compete in global markets with locally designed knowledge-intensive products whose competitiveness is critically dependent upon a highly educated workforce. The continentalisation of innovation processes, seen in inter-organisational collaboration and in recruitment patterns, can contribute to the competitiveness of the European economy and participating national economies (Hilpert and Lawton Smith 2012; Hilpert 2005). Although the USA is highly competitive in most areas of scientific research and new technologies, European countries and their 'islands of innovation' can still participate effectively in the transatlantic scientific community and can take advantage of the new knowledge generated. But there are divergent paths of development on each continent. Continentalisation demonstrates a distinctively European pattern of development which engages European policies, national strategies and European 'islands of innovation'. In this European arena, social democratic educational, industrial, science and technology policies which develop the skills and competitiveness of the workforce as a whole and which use government research budgets and purchasing to generate new knowledge and technologies can underpin and enhance this competitiveness, in particular where private-sector investment is not forthcoming (Mazzucato 2011).

The social democratic idea of an open society which provides opportunities for all social classes and for individuals to use their personal capabilities while contributing to a prosperous and more egalitarian society fits well with the requirements of innovative industries managing globalisation. High-value products demand highly skilled labour in manufacturing; techno-industrial innovation demands academically well-educated labour; innovative industries and high-quality services do likewise. Based on high skills and education, labour must play a critical part in delivering economic prosperity and social welfare in modern societies. Hence there is space for social democratic education, science and technology policies, but they must reflect the variety and flexibility demonstrated by innovative regions, high-technology workers and businesses faced with global competition.

## Note

1. When the dot-com bubble burst, those knowledge workers experienced their skills being devaluated and no longer providing high incomes. They suffered unemployment and learned perforce the advantages of unionisation and social democratic ideas of labour market regulation.

# FROM SINGLE MARKET TO SOCIAL MARKET ECONOMY: IS THERE ROOM FOR SOLIDARITY?

Yves Mény

## Introduction

Each political season calls for new discourses and novel rhetoric. The Europe of Monnet was the Europe of peace and economic growth. The continued transformation of the European project over the past fifty years has required new narratives. The Lisbon Treaty rallied to the post-1945 German motto of committing Europe to 'the social market economy'. It was a useful reminder of the ongoing challenge that advanced capitalist economies have had to face over the past 150 years: how to reconcile market iron rules with the imperatives of (social) democracy. Over the past century this historical compromise has taken on national traits and characteristics. Causes and objectives are similar across borders; agendas, timing and solutions are not, and have a distinctly national flavour. The issues that Europe is facing today are not so distinct from these past challenges; however, they are occurring in a very different context.

There is indeed a big difference: welfare state systems were constructed within distinct polities, run by national governments emanating most of the time from embryonic political parties. Governing elites were in control of economic, monetary, fiscal and budgetary policies. This is not true anymore within the European Union, in particular for those countries belonging to the eurozone. A radical division of powers between the supranational institutions and national governments deprives the former of most competences over welfare policies, while the latter has limited powers in the field of economic regulation (and, for the eurozone countries, no monetary powers). The phrase used to characterise the Soviet Union satellites has been brought back into use: eurozone countries have been described as 'states with limited sovereignty'. The traditional compromise between market and social forces embodied in the welfare systems is not impossible, but its feasibility has been put into question as in many countries it relies upon the funding of present welfare commitments through public debt. The present crisis has shown that the party is over.

National states have always been limited in their policies by internal and external constraints, but globalisation has considerably reinforced these limitations over the past few decades. EU institutions and rules have further accentuated this evolution in Europe. However, Brussels cannot intervene in many policy areas which remain the exclusive domain of states. It has a limited capacity to react swiftly to unforeseen situations due to the requirement to build consensus between (now) twenty-eight different governments. It has a narrow range of policy instruments available and a limited capacity to distribute or redistribute resources in order to offset the negative consequences of its own policies or external shocks. The Union finds itself a victim of the combination of its own 'joint decision-making trap' (Scharpf 1988) and the increasing inflexibility of its rules (De Witte 2009).

These policy difficulties are further aggravated by the gradual elimination of traditional politics in the functioning of European institutions. It has become a functional instrument that the national political masters need. In the European Council or in the Council of Ministers, political affiliation plays second fiddle to crude national interests or shifting alliances between the major players. In the European Parliament, compromises and consensus are the main decision-making instruments and the Commission has become an ever more complex bureaucracy whose political wings have been cut off (Mény 2007). Paradoxically, and somewhat by accident, one of the places where major policy choices are currently made is the European Court of Justice. Their rulings trigger political debates, but only *after* the fact, when there is no more room for input by the public. In Lamping's (2010) words, it 'functions as a substitute or surrogate for politics'.

When the king is naked, the only option left is political rhetoric. Words become the substitute for policy or at best the instruments for giving some sense of direction to political (in)action. This is particularly true when the gap between desirability and capability is or seems insurmountable. Welfare state policies and the invocation of European solidarity are a case in point. The idealism of some welfare policies should not hide the crude reality: there is as much self-interest as solidarity in this process. Bismarck himself was no philanthropist. The national welfare states have developed in parallel with the process of industrialisation as much as in relation to the influence of leftist or social democratic parties. These parties have been instrumental in promoting welfare programmes, in pushing, together with trade unions, for reform and in implementing social policies when they have been in power. But it is also striking how much conservative parties (sometimes with different targets and priorities) have also contributed to the building up of welfare policies, notably in those countries where the Church has a strong influence (Esping-Andersen 1990).

As underlined by Maurizio Ferrera (2009), welfare states in Europe are characterised by being synonymous with national boundaries, or, to put it according to Abram de Swaan (1994), 'Welfare States are national states'. Each political system had put in place a vast array of social policies in order to cover most social risks, to compensate for market-driven inequalities and to fight poverty. Social policies encompass every aspect of life 'from the cradle to the grave' to such an extent that welfare was and still is considered as an indissoluble part of contemporary democracy. Capitalist states, in order to consolidate their legitimacy among the working class and trade unions, have had to accept that democracies are identified not only with politics and rights but also with social justice and redistribution (Mény 2003). It is telling that both the French trade unions in the 1950s and the British ones in the 1970s were suspicious of the European common market as a potential Trojan horse contributing to the weakening and dismantlement of their *droits acquis*. They were probably right.

Here is the challenge. Since 1958, Europe has been in charge of economic regulation in lieu of nation-states. It has taken up the historical mission to eliminate obstacles to trade. It was expected that, thanks to the free circulation of goods and services, competition would be strengthened, and by way of consequence European competitiveness on international markets would increase as well. Overall this scheme has worked well but the implications for the social, societal and political fabric were underestimated or unforeseen. Indeed, for the first time in the development of democratic states, traditional areas of intervention were considered out of their reach in legal as well as political terms. Even more serious, the nation-states were left to deal with the expected or unexpected consequences of this new form of power-sharing.

A new division of labour (which has nothing to do with the subsidiarity principle) was put in place. The common market and later on the European Union took on the deregulation and reregulation of markets. The member states kept the management of social policies which were like inverted images of the market failures or deficiencies. Initially this division did not create too many problems. The first reason was the imperfect and incomplete character of the common market. There were many loopholes, exceptions and incomplete implementation, so that collateral damages were still bearable; not to mention the fact that in the early days, competition was between countries similar in terms of development, unlike today with the added impact of globalisation and enlargement. The second reason for the relative acceptance of this new state of affairs was the economic growth which accompanied the construction of the common market, the so-called *Trente Glorieuses*. The third was that in the sectors identified as the main potential victims of this ongoing 'great transformation', generous financial compensation was put in place: coal, steel and agriculture benefited (and still benefits, in the case of agriculture) from very generous social packages (Mény 1987). Transition was not without pain, but was made easier thanks to a full range of social sweeteners.

The issue has become much more tricky over the past twenty-five years for several interlocking reasons. First, the Single European Act gave a formidable impulse to the completion of a unified market. The objective of a common market came to fruition with all related consequences, some positive, some painfully felt and resented by specific sectors, regions or people. Secondly, the European Community and later on the Union became more heterogeneous in economic terms, development, competitiveness and ability to access international markets. By way of consequence the social impact was also differentiated according to the capacity of individual states to cope with the new rules of the game. Thirdly, the 'escape routes' that some member states were initially able to exploit were less and less accessible: sectoral or temporary measures exempting some from the full application of rules faded away, mutual checks and controls made cheating and non-implementation more difficult, and rulings of the European Court of Justice (or extensive interpretation of the Treaties) also reduced the member states' capacities to avoid pain through various forms of exit strategy.

The problems increased in severity with the growing differentiation within the Union not only of economic wealth but also of values. The respective role of markets and states, the nature of welfare policies, the regulatory functions of public authorities and the role given to free trade were divisive issues under the rhetorical cover-up of an 'ever closer Union'. As stated in the title of a French book, it was becoming obvious that there was only 'a single bed for two dreams' (at least) (Fontaine 1981).

The illusion that economic growth would be enough to compensate for the social tensions introduced by the European integration process has dissolved in spite of the recurrent rosy forecasts proposed by the Commission for the long term. The Lisbon Agenda has been a mixed success (or failure), with the 'most advanced knowledge society in the world by 2010' still a programme to be fulfilled and the *lendemains qui chantent* promised by the Monetary Union replaced by today's hard times and Euro-crisis. Many people are not convinced anymore that Europe can be the solution, and an increasing number believe that it is the problem and that European integration jeopardises their social *acquis*, the protective umbrella provided by their respective national welfare states. The division of labour between Union and states is now working at its full potential, and exposing the tensions and contradictions that it contains.

The founding fathers of the European dream were aware of such potential implications but by choosing a step-by-step strategy they left the contract incomplete. They paid lip-service to the solidarity principle but refused to give substance to it. In spite of the attempts by the Commission and some member states to fill in the definition, solidarity has not yet gained much weight. The lack of agreement about the fulfilment of positive integration has allowed the

Court of Justice to step in, but has underlined the limits of 'integration through law' (Vauchez 2008) when core democratic values are implicated. So is it possible to reunify the economic and social regulations which have been split between the European and national authorities under one European umbrella? In other words can we continue the hollowing out of national states, making democracies empty boxes and the European institutions even more 'undemocratic and unaccountable'? Or, if this is unfeasible, what kind of mechanisms could correct the invisible but dramatic redistribution that has taken place through EU regulation, and its visible and sensitive social implications at national levels? How can we avoid the perception that necessary adjustments and reforms are a race to the bottom?

### Solidarity: dead-end or new avenue?

Solidarity is an ambiguous concept. It resonates in most European countries and in particular where the Catholic Church and the Christian Democrats have been powerful or where socialist or social democratic ideology exerted its influence. It might sometimes be a rather empty reference to the social contract linking individuals within a polity; it remains however an appealing and powerful argument in political debate. It justifies redistributive policies, but it may also be negatively used, for instance by nationalist or populist parties in order to reject access of non-members (foreigners) to the benefits of the welfare system. However, solidarity – which supposes a minimum of social bonds beyond the basic unit of the family or village – is more a kind of programmatic ideal than a substantive reality. Like the principles of subsidiarity or federal loyalty, it needs rules and resources to become part of the policy process. For instance, Rhodes and Mény state:

> The notions of 'social contract' and 'solidarity', which are pervasive in the welfare state discourse of continental Europe, sound strange – and even alien and threatening – to some. It also explains why the British – regardless of political complexion – find it so difficult to accept 'continental European' notions such as the 'social dimension' of the European Union and its 'Social Charter'. (1998)

As noted ironically by Philip Stephens in the *Financial Times* (2012), 'some words are the property of continental Europeans. You do not hear many Brits or Americans talking about "solidarity". The expression belongs to the soggy (to Anglo-Saxon minds) consensualism of social market capitalism and to prophets of European unity.' Its multi-faceted meanings have been recently explored both by Kalypso Nicolaïdis (Nicolaïdis and Viehoff 2012) with a sophisticated theoretical perspective and in a more policy-oriented approach by the Paris-based think-tank Notre Europe (Fernandes and Rubio 2012). This latter study makes a distinction between the simple transactional arrangements which are a pragmatic, insurance-like distribution of costs and benefits, and a less selfish approach consisting in redistributing wealth among people, regions or nations in the name of social or cultural pre-existing (or yet to be created) bonds.

Solidarity was mentioned at the very beginning of the European integration process. The Coal and Steel Community Treaty evoked the concept for the first time in its Preamble. One could argue indeed that such a vague reference is part of rhetorical euro-speak in its early phase and that the idea is of little relevance, and there is some truth in that argument. In proposing the Single Act, Jacques Delors had the ambition of establishing parallel social goals but failed to convince Margaret Thatcher, and had to content himself with the creation of the Structural Funds. Together with the pre-accession financial measures and the Solidarity Fund created in order to alleviate the *délocalisation* issue, these various instruments are presented as a testimony of collective solidarity on the part of Europe. But these forms of collective solidarity are not perceived as such by most of the citizens, as their benefits are either diffused (the financing of a road or a bridge) or too concentrated (more for economic actors than for the poor). It can even trigger hostility or criticism among the taxpayers who are supposed to express solidarity but are reluctant to pay for their neighbours (the Greek debt issue has been a clear illustration of the limits of the solidarity principle within the EU). In principle, one could also add the resources provided to farmers, but as it has been shown that the main beneficiaries have been the wealthiest landowners, the argument is dubious. There is still very little which can contribute to the construction of a shared sense of 'togetherness' among Europeans.

However, two elements can suggest the opposite. The first is linked to the rather generous provisions foreseen for coal and steel workers in case of industrial restructuring or redundancies. At least in the initial European treaty, the rhetoric was not just wishful thinking; the signatories put their money where their mouths were. A second argument, applicable from the origins of European integration up to the present day, is that the importance of wording should never be underestimated. It is part of the diplomatic tradition as well as of the lawyers' reasoning to fully exploit all potentials, even from a very modest starting point, provided that there is a minimal reference in the text. Words can remain inert and unused for years, and then suddenly become the basis of an intellectual and legal construction of major importance. But solidarity has remained undisturbed for many years in the treaties.

This lack of symbolic or effective solidarity was particularly felt by those wishing to push for a more integrated and political Europe (the Federalists) and by the critics of the neo-liberal policies (parts of the Left, the Greens and the radical Left). They managed to push for the adoption of the Charter of Fundamental Social Rights in 1989, in spite of the hostility of the British Conservative government which decided to opt out and then to include a chapter on social rights in the 2000 Charter of Fundamental Rights, by now annexed to the Lisbon Treaty (European Union 2007, title IV, art. 27–38).

The writers of the Lisbon Treaty made an abundant use of the word 'solidarity', following the path opened by the 2001 Laeken Declaration. Solidarity is, for instance, mentioned in the Preamble, then in articles 2 and 3 (al. 3 and 5, European Union 2007), but it is striking that the word has received different meanings in different contexts (social rights, international relations, defence). This multiple personality is further accentuated by the list of areas or policies placed under the solidarity umbrella in the Charter of Fundamental Rights of the European Union. The eleven articles brought together under Title IV cover a rather eclectic collection of areas, some related to workers' rights (working conditions, collective bargaining, child labour), others to family life, healthcare, environmental and consumer protection and finally two wide-ranging articles referring to social security and social assistance and access to services of general economic interest. Even if incomplete, the list could have an enormous impact if these rights were not limited in their application to the European Union policies only.

However, some states, and in particular the Czech Republic, Poland and the United Kingdom, expressed some concern at the creeping expansion of Union law and principles into national legislation. Britain and Poland, in a distinct protocol, insisted that the Charter would not extend the ability of the Court of Justice to find that their laws, regulations or practices were inconsistent with the fundamental rights reaffirmed by the Union and that these provisions would be applicable only to the extent these principles are recognised by the laws and practices of these two countries. These protocols and declarations are less interesting for their content than for the fears they express. Great Britain in particular was afraid of the potential development of a full-bodied European social policy, and in particular through the Court's back door. In the normal legislative process it is easy to control and fight potential initiatives of the Commission, but this is not the case with the Court (Scharpf 1996). These countries identified the risk and have tried to build up Chinese walls to ensure that European principles will be applicable only to European policies.

But to be realistic, these political 'Maginot lines' are fragile in the face of judicial activism. The contamination of national law by EU law through case law is unstoppable. Judges are masterminds in building creative constructions and unexpected policy developments on the basis of a few principles enunciated by political authorities or even 'created' through formal deductive analysis from legal principles (Maduro 1998). This kind of judicial activism can be stopped more easily at the national level by putting courts under pressure from political forces, as has happened on several occasions in the United States. But the problem is not so easy to tackle at the European level.

## Solidarity: window-dressing and policy tensions

The debates on the Constitution on the occasion of the French and Dutch referendums were rather confused, contradictory and very much focused on national issues. However, in particular in France, the social implications of the new treaty were at the centre of a divisive discussion. Public opinion and even the political parties (in particular the Socialist Party) were deeply split. The argument was further inflamed by the circulation of the draft directive on the provision of services (the Bolkestein directive) which convinced opponents that the Constitution, if adopted, would further weaken national welfare systems. The European institutions and in particular the Commission were accused not only of neglecting the social dimension of the European construction but of dismantling the national *acquis*. Faced with the need to win back public opinion while the process of ratification was going on across Europe, the Commission got the message and elaborated the so-called 'Citizens' Agenda' (European Commission 2006). The traditional political rationale for Europe (peace and prosperity) was enriched by a new addition: 'solidarity'. Following the usual processes of consultation involving concerned stakeholders, the Commission published a Communication in 2007 proposing a grandiloquent 'Social Vision' (European Commission 2007) organised around three major pillars: opportunities, access and solidarity. Catherine Barnard has underlined the strong influence exerted by 'Third Way' thinking on this document, notably in its aim for 'a genuine synthesis between the State and the market'. She comments:

> It is important not to exaggerate the function of solidarity in the 2007 communication. Although 'solidarity' has joined 'opportunities' and 'access' as defining features of the new social vision, it is striking just how little the word itself is mentioned . . . This gives the sense that solidarity was too politically sensitive or – worse – was simply added as a make-weight. (Barnard 2010: 88)

It is indeed tricky for the European institutions to address the issue within the present legal and political framework. As noted by Ferrera:

> The vast majority of ordinary citizens and a good number of policy-makers think that the growing friction between the welfare state and the EU has or could have an easy solution: the two institutions should be put on 'separate tracks', as they were in the first couple of decades after the Rome Treaty. (2009: 223)

The Commission is well aware that economic regulation at EU level or the liberalisation of trade have a deep influence on national policies (and capability) but has very little legal and financial means to 'rescue the (welfare) nation states' while member states are sometimes unwilling or most of the time unable to redress this state of affairs without affecting their competitiveness. Since the states are squeezed between their public opinions and the harsh constraints imposed by European integration (and globalisation), conflicts and tensions are partially dealt with through legal means rather than by political instruments. A more hidden and insidious way out has been the financing of generous social programmes by increasing the public debt and transferring the hot potato to future generations.

One of the main avenues to deal with these issues has been the judicial one (Stone Sweet 2004), a crucial indicator of the tensions and contradictions between the logic of markets and the logic of state intervention. As underlined by Wolfram Lamping,

> A lack of consensus and political will among member governments, non-decisions at EU level, a clear tendency amongst governments to ignore the (intended or unintended) effects of the single market on national welfare states, and ambiguous and vague treaty provisions very often have brought the ECJ onto the social policy agenda. (2010: 66)

There are, however, limits to the judicial capacity (and legitimacy) to set up policies in lieu of democratic governments.

It is difficult to decide if the ECJ can be labelled as a free-market oriented judge or a Court preoccupied by safeguarding social protection in Europe. Case law can be interpreted in both directions, depending on the domain and time period. The limits (and drawbacks) of the Court's action have been well identified by Scharpf:

> Given its rights-based interpretation of Treaty obligations, the only remedy the Court can offer to the complaints of private litigants is to disallow national regulations that impede factor mobility or that violate standards of non-discrimination. Hence the immediate effect of such decisions is to deregulate existing national regimes. What the Court cannot do is establish a common European regime that would respond to some of the values and policy purposes which, as a consequence of its decision, can no longer be realised at the national level. If reregulation is to be considered desirable, it could only be pursued through political legislation at the European level. And given the high consensus requirements of European legislation and ubiquitous conflicts of interest among extremely heterogeneous member states, one would indeed expect a strong asymmetry between judicially imposed negative integration and legislative positive integration. (2009: 233)

Being constrained to navigate between conflicting values and norms, the judges through their rulings can contribute towards triggering a political debate and forcing policy-makers to step in. But Scharpf's view on the role of the ECJ in balancing the conflicting values of market integration and welfare protection has changed over time. In the late nineties, Scharpf (1997) still expressed the wish that the ECJ should be able to play an active role in the field of social policies similar to the one it had in the protection of economic freedoms. By 2010, he had lost this illusion and made a plea to set up political mechanisms allowing member states to object when European law 'is felt to impose unacceptably tight constraints on politically highly salient national concerns' (Scharpf 2010: 386).

Scharpf's powerful argument is well known: the asymmetric institutional configuration impedes the legislative process from setting up positive integration policies while the (negative) 'integration through law' moves forward thanks to 'the seemingly inexorable evolution of judicial doctrines protecting and extending the Treaty-based rights of private individuals and firms' (Scharpf 2010: 35). In spite of the reference (for the first time) to the social market economy in article 3.3 of the Lisbon Treaty, the conclusion of his analysis is already indicated by the title of his essay 'Why the EU Cannot Be a Social Market Economy'.

## Is there a way out of the impasse?

To use Maurizio Ferrera's words, 'is the clash avoidable?' (2009: 35). We are heading for a confrontation between the European integration process and the survival of welfare states as we know them, at least on the Continent. Time is passing, contradictions are growing and, more important, these contradictions are becoming better understood by the public. More and more, Europe is not perceived as the benevolent umbrella and as an instrument of economic growth but quite the reverse: the Trojan horse of globalisation and its evils. The increasing indifference in best cases or hostility in the worst scenarios varies considerably between social categories and countries. Some consider that the EU is, by now, an obstacle rather than an advantage in dealing with globalisation, others criticise the dominant neo-liberal approach in Brussels, while some are irritated by the complexity of its regulation or its bureaucratic approach in dealing with and managing policies. Nationalists are unhappy with EU interventions; federalists are upset by the absence of political perspective, by the inter-governmentalist approach and by the lack of a political *finalité*. These tensions are mounting year on year as shown by the difficulty in getting major changes approved by referendum, by the growth of anti-European groups and political parties in even the most 'pro-Europe' countries, and by social movements protesting against European policies and/or their national implications.

The fact that the European construction was an elite-driven process was not particularly important to the public at large when the negative consequences were not felt by individuals in their daily lives and when the economy was going well. Today the EU is in a difficult position vis-à-vis public opinion given the existing division of labour. The EU's claim that its main role is economic and that it is not in charge of social policies at the national level does not alleviate the blame, since growth has not continued in most European countries and social problems are seen as the consequences of EU policies and choices. The unfolding of European financial and monetary crises since the summer of 2011 has further exacerbated tensions. At first sight, there has been some solidarity-in-action; the eurozone countries have contributed to the bail-out of Greece (in spite of the spirit and letter of the Treaties). But public opinion has not been fooled by the apparent generosity of member states; under the cover of solidarity, the member states were acting in defence of their own interests in order to avoid contamination or to rescue their banks and lending institutions. Even when Europe came to the rescue of nearly defaulting states, the bitterness of the medicine increased further anti-European feelings. Far from being perceived as an expression of solidarity, EU intervention is resented by the recipient populations. European solidarity has been more financial than political. In most Southern European countries, banks and financial institutions have been rescued to avoid devastating economic (and social) consequences, while drastic budgetary cuts and welfare reforms have confirmed public opinions in their increasingly negative perception of the EU. In spite of the billions that European governments have injected into many member states, citizens do not perceive these actions as 'solidarity' but rather as unfairly rigid discipline imposed from outside. Two questions come to the fore. The first is: can Europe do something about these negative perceptions? And, if the answer to this question is negative, what are the prospects for the EU?

The responses to the first question are found in three different directions. One can imagine that the EU provides an overall European welfare system over and above national ones; another option is to create buffers against the potential attacks against national welfare nets by strengthening a set of common rights; the third option is to try to work out compromises which will not be perfect but could alleviate the tension.

The first option is ambitious, but so ambitious that very few believe in its feasibility. There are political/psychological obstacles to start with. All surveys show that citizens in Europe are very much attached to their own welfare system even when they are critical of it. There is no pressing popular demand for an EU option. In practical terms, in spite of their commonalities, welfare states are quite different as they embody both the social preferences of unions, parties and citizens and the stratification of national choices. Trying to harmonise systems Europe-wide would be an impossible task, in particular in the present conditions of decision-making. Finally, even if the Herculean scale of the task did not dishearten courageous reformers, the costs of such an enterprise would probably kill it from the start (without even mentioning the political problems of redistribution that this would entail). The present EU budget would have to be increased to an extent unacceptable to national governments. Finally, levels of wealth and poverty and the aspirations of people across Europe are so diverse that there are more chances to multiply discontent across the EU than to satisfy anyone.

Another pan-European option could be to give substance to European citizens' rights. This option is the one developed on a case-by-case basis by the European Court of Justice. This case law allowed the Court to give muscle to marginal and specific regulations (or even soft law) over time by transforming them into 'values' or 'principles' that were later recognised in the Charter on Fundamental Rights and finally the Lisbon Treaty. Little by little, a set of common principles has been applied across Europe and pushes for harmonisation. However, this limited unification has limits. In theory it applies only to European policies, even if this argument is de facto rather weak, as mentioned earlier. Secondly, the Court's work is necessarily a patchwork as it is dependent on the requests of the plaintiffs. Thirdly – and this is by far the most problematic issue – the Court has usually to assess the social rights vis-à-vis, for instance, the four freedoms which are at the core of EU missions. This delicate balancing work is already difficult by itself, but is made even more complex when the Court's rulings have to be applied in different political, cultural and social settings. The reception of recent cases in French public opinion shows the difficulty: in applying the principle of equality between women and men, the Court should have received only applause. In fact, as it meant the elimination of the prohibition of night work for women and the increase of insurance premiums (women drivers had lower premiums as statistically they were less prone to serious accidents and injuries), the response to these judicial decisions has been mixed to say the least. Everybody agreed fully with the principle but much less with its consequences. As Lamping has rightly argued, 'the aspect of deepening the social policy dimension of European integration, i.e. to establish and institutionalise "social solidarity" among European citizens, cannot be addressed through the legal lens alone. Under such circumstances it is more than doubtful that law will be able to perform the tasks associated with it in Member States' (2010: 68).

The most radical critique of the supranational option has been expressed by Gianfranco Majone, who denounces the 'mirage of social Europe':

> A supranational welfare state decoupled from a common political project would indeed be a bureaucratic nightmare – and given popular resistance to large-scale transnational redistribution, an authoritarian nightmare as well. The level of centralized harmonization of social standards required by a 'federation of welfare states' would have been politically difficult to enforce even in the old EU; in the enlarged Union it is simply politically infeasible. (2009: 310)

One can also call for political solutions but from the opposite direction. While a fully functioning European welfare state is an impossible or distant objective, in the meantime the unfolding of EU structural construction is destroying the foundations of the national welfare systems. They are constitutive elements of the social fabric and today's democratic creed. The Germans have been particularly vocal in their critique of these EU developments. The German Court in its ruling over the Lisbon Treaty indicated its willingness to exercise its *ultra vires* controls in any case where the EU would negatively affect the constitutional identity of the country, an understandable move in political terms but a recipe for legal mess if every supreme court adopted the same national approach.

Scharpf evokes but rejects a more proactive strategy, based on political mobilisation of the stakeholders (parties, unions, academics, journalists, lobbyists). His rejection is based on the difficulty of mobilising people across Europe and, given the decision-making process of EU institutions, the impossibility of overcoming the opposition of those countries favouring a neo-liberal approach. When looking at the state of politics in Europe, his pessimism about the potential for collective action seems to me excessive. In many countries, such is the dissatisfaction with the present economic and social situation (Mény and Surel 2002; Leconte 2010) that many scenarios are possible, including the growing impact of protest parties and mass mobilisation (it is striking that social democratic parties, up to now, have made little gain in the context of social malaise). The protests do not need to be pan-European or to advance specific claims. Uprisings do not need programmes; they need a trigger factor and mass mobilisation. The financial crisis seems to have unveiled its main effects. The social crisis in many European countries has still to come, and one wonders how much capacity states like Greece, Portugal or Spain have to face the social crisis that will affect them.

A third, more modest or realistic option is suggested by Maurizio Ferrera, who tries to identify a compromise between the (declining) supremacy of the national welfare states and the need for a (not yet in place) European welfare system. He proposes what he calls 'a strategy of reconciliation and nesting', meaning the 'anchoring of the narrower institution (in our case the national welfare state) within the fabric of the wider institution (the EU)' (2009: 223). This solution would imply mutual concessions: the national welfare states should be protected against undue challenges but would accept the need to make concessions and adapt, and the new European welfare system would have to develop its transnational, cross-regional as well as supranational character. The proposal is attractive as it is largely based on existing features which could develop in an organic way or, if feasible, in a more radical fashion, for instance by putting in place new redistributive schemes based on European citizenship 'without the filter of national institutions and politics'.

Ferrera's proposals are probably the most systematic attempt to combine political realism with potentially ambitious developments in the future. From this point of view, he is very much in line with the ongoing strategy of the European institutions and, in particular, the Commission. For instance, the concept of solidarity referred to in the treaties and with ever increasing frequency in Commission documents is for the time being void of real content. Substantive flesh could be put on the bones if the Commission, the Council and the Parliament were able to put sufficient political energy in this currently empty box.

To tell the truth, I do not see for the time being the political and economic preconditions for such a big leap. All conditions seem adverse. The lack of consensus among member states looms larger than ever, in particular over economic and social policies. A quasi-federal embryonic welfare system would imply a serious harmonisation of tax systems that many countries are not ready to accept, an idea of European citizenship which is not just the extension of national citizenships (which raises the status of immigrants), and ambitious resources which will not be present for many more years.

This rather bleak perspective might however be transformed by two factors, one social, the other political. Social issues are back on the agenda in many countries and it is only the beginning of tensions which might last for years. The permissive consensus about rising inequalities was made possible thanks to economic growth and/or transfers financed by private or public debt. The funding of ambitious national welfare systems by taxing labour is and will be more and more unsustainable. In parallel, unemployment and immigration will remain hot issues that national systems, within the context of globalisation, have been unable to properly tackle. European governments, in spite of their divisions and overall reluctance, might be faced with a social crisis comparable in magnitude to the present economic crisis. One has seen for instance how, under the pressure of an imminent catastrophe, the Union has provided proof of 'solidarity' precisely in the only domain where the treaty was prohibiting it: the rescue of a defaulting state. A similar emergency could occur in the social domain and call for a radical U-turn as well.

But another scenario could prevail. Europe could attempt to survive with low growth, a huge debt and very few innovations in social policies. A European welfare state would continue to be a dream for some and a nightmare for others, while national systems would continue to be eroded by the twin challenges of Europeanisation and globalisation. This stalled situation could go on for some years. However, I do not believe that the division of labour between economic regulation (the domain of the EU) and social welfare (reserved to the state) is tenable in the long run. It is a lose-lose game: national governments, to use Peter Mair's words, are responsible but not responsive. They do not fully control the economic/social puzzle, while the EU is perceived as the bad guy who cannot alleviate the negative consequences of economic transformation. In both cases, the legitimacy of those who govern is weakened, in particular the European institutions whose base was already very fragile. The situation might become unsustainable and a vicious circle would be complete: Habermas's dream (Habermas et al. 2000) of a European welfare state as a necessary component of a European democracy cannot develop the democratic conditions if redistributive policies are not there. At the same time a true European democracy cannot exist – as it is conceived by today standards – without social policies. How long can this contradiction last?

# SOCIAL DEMOCRACY AND SECURITY

Neil Walker

## Introduction: the duality of social democracy

The main aim of this chapter is to account for and assess the dilemmas and difficulties a social democratic approach to crime and security faces in the context of the modern state. It examines the historical approach to these difficulties and identifies some of the new challenges to have emerged over the past thirty years or so. The chapter concludes by assessing the prospects of a new wave of social democratic policy on crime and security in the face of the combination of new and old challenges.

Historically the attitude of social democrats to crime and insecurity has displayed a tension that mirrors the deeper one within the social democratic project itself (Hattersley and Hickson 2011). Social democracy, put simply, has been historically located within the fluctuating terms of convergence and divergence between two narratives of modification of the classical socialist project – the modification of the classical means of socialist transformation and the modification of its classical ends. On the one hand, the social democratic narrative, while not ruling out a comprehensively egalitarian vision as an ultimate goal, has been concerned to map out an alternative parliamentary and constitutional pathway, one that rejects violent and extra-constitutional struggle and favours evolution over revolution. On the other hand, the social democratic narrative has also been about specifying and meeting realisable and self-standing objectives short of full social ownership. It has sought to accommodate enough of the redistributive impulses of socialism within a market-based economy so as to fashion a sustainable equilibrium between a market-based economic order and a wider vision of social and political equality.

Social democracy has a key stress and associated ambivalence built into its historic dynamic – as do the political parties or party blocs who have worn its banner. We can sharpen our appreciation of this by identifying what social democracy is *not*. It is not, on the one side, the 'Eurocommunism' of post-war Europe, whose communist parties insisted on the ultimate goal of full social ownership of the means of production and upon subordinating all contemporary policy to that end, while opting for a democratic waiting game as the contradictions of capitalism approached their 'inevitable' crisis point. And, on the other side, social democracy is not the Blairite 'Third Way' of the left reception of neo-liberalism in the 1990s. This embraced marketisation and consumerism with an emphasis on general affluence and modest tax and welfare redistribution, and just as emphatically distanced itself from social ownership or a strong programme of economic equality (Giddens 1998).

Unlike either of these positions with their respective certainties either of an ultimate vision of socialist perfection or of its decisive renunciation, social democracy has always tended to hold means and ends in tension. It has done so by operating, at least implicitly, in accordance with two distinct temporal logics. First it is concerned with social welfare citizenship as 'real-time' incremental social improvement built on the welfare state and the mixed economy. This has involved a graduated programme of social inclusion correcting or mitigating the worst excesses of market-based inequalities and providing the working class with a stable and extending stake in the political system. Secondly, it has been a staging post for a more open-ended and longer-term projection of class-based social empowerment and economic democracy. The real-time project has tended to operate within the variable shadow of the long-term project. To the extent that the real-time project proceeds towards the gradual material improvement and social inclusion of the working class, as in T. H. Marshall's famous depiction of the incremental growth of citizenship in legal, political and social terms (Marshall 1950), then the long-term 'utopian' project may become both otiose and implausible. In these circumstances, the shadow recedes. To the extent, however, that the real-time project is seen to lack achievement or to lose momentum, then the shadow encroaches, and elements of a fuller project of long-term socialism provide a more palpable condition of current politics.

## The duality of social democracy's security politics

How is this duality of incremental reform and distant utopia reflected in the development of social democratic attitudes to crime and insecurity? Arguably, the problem of crime and security, because it speaks directly to the preservation of the existing social order, provides an acute case of the gap between ends and means in social democratic thinking and the difficulties associated with reconciling the policies and dispositions. Crime and security have been historically understood and treated from the social democratic left as symptomatic of a deeper social and economic malaise, as well as the hegemonic class-based political strategies developed to manage it. On the other hand, criminal justice policy supplies a viable target of incremental social reform, and so a suitable object for the ameliorative and integrative strategies of a progressive social citizenship. Let us look at these two orientations in turn, and at the conflicts between and within them.

Throughout the history of social democracy, the basic capacity of the state as the monopolist of legitimate force has been viewed with some ambivalence by the social democratic left, notwithstanding its commitment to the pursuit of its objectives through the democratisation and utilisation of the structures of the state (Loader and Walker 2007: Ch. 3). A variable but recurrent critical theme of the left, especially when out of power, has been that the primary function of the criminal justice apparatus is to ensure the maintenance of the 'specific order' (Marenin 1982) of the capitalist state. That function is achieved mainly through repressing crimes against person, property and public order that result from the brutalising, alienating or radicalising effects of inequality. The criminal justice apparatus contributes to the fashioning of an ideological climate in which such deviant behaviour is pathologised, and so marginalised and depoliticised, framed as individual aberration or excess rather than as symptom or reaction to systemic exploitation.

This diagnosis of the securitising tendencies of the capitalist state contains a kernel of truth. The criminal justice apparatus – the police, the security services, the prison and correction system – has included amongst its key functional 'effects' the securing of the existing political and constitutional order, and, by that means, the underlying socio-economic formation served by that order. This structural disposition is reflected and reinforced at the cultural level through an active form of 'partisanship' (Loader and Walker 2007: Ch. 3) within and around the security apparatus in favour of that conservative project. Alongside this, the conservative establishment tends to be suspicious of the ambivalence of the political left, viewing it at best as a reluctant supporter, and at worst as a destabilising threat to the security of the state.

The opposing orientations of the political left and the champions of the security apparatus of the state tend to become oppositional. They are mutually justifying and reinforcing in ways that leave a legacy in Western states. The divisions are apparent in times of acute political or economic crisis, and provide reputational backdrop to daily party political orientation and competition. This has sometimes served to compromise the electoral popularity on which social democracy depends. The politics of 'law and order', in which the seriousness of the threat posed by crime to the existing social and political fabric is a pressing theme, is not only divisive across the political spectrum, but traditionally favours parties of the status quo over those focused on social transformation. This is because criticism of the conservative security bias of the state, or failure to provide wholehearted endorsement, can leave the left exposed. It is open to charges of naivety and recklessness in the face of the imperatives of an orderly society, and of political insincerity or hypocrisy – a failure to guarantee the security and integrity of the constitutional system which protects them and through which they undertake to act.

This critical tendency, and its associated oppositional politics, is not the whole of the social democratic story on crime. As with the transformative vision of social democracy, the shadow cast by this longer perspective fluctuates depending on the success of a more immediate strategy. For there is an alternative and occasionally dominant historical narrative in which the social democratic left has seized or shared the political high ground of criminal justice policy and succeeded in setting or influencing the terms of mainstream policy debate. This is encapsulated in notions such as 'penal welfarism' (Garland 1985, 2001) and 'policing by consent' (Reiner 2010).

Penal welfarism, whose golden age and location was Western democracies in the three decades following 1945, has its origins in the late nineteenth century, and has three core propositions. The first is that the combination of a robust and inclusive system of social welfare together with high levels of employment would gradually reduce the frequency of crime; the second, that the state is responsible for the care and, where possible, the rehabilitation of offenders, as well as their punishment and control; and the third, that in dealing with offenders and others who encounter the criminal justice apparatus the state should respect their basic status and desire for (re)integration as citizens, guaranteeing them due process and proportionate treatment by disinterested and knowledgeable professionals. Penal welfarism, then, embodies a belief in the socially engineered improvability of human beings, as well as faith in the ability and good intentions of experts. Offenders are viewed as unfortunate rather than evil, as corrigible products of the system rather than units of wrongdoing. Under the sign of penal welfarism criminal justice institutions and practices became less the domain of the symbolic majesty of the state or the stigmatisation and repression of a security-threatening underclass, as in the earlier phase of modern state formation, and instead became oriented towards liberal legalism, bureaucratic discipline and benevolent professionalism.

At the policing front line of criminal justice policy, moreover, we encounter a similar variation in the political attitudes of the left and in the institutions and practices they seek to address and influence. The politics of accommodation here are somewhat differently configured. Where the rest of penal policy tends to be centralised, some policing policy and practice in Western states continues to reflect its origins in pre-state forms of feudal or municipal authority and so remains at the level of the local state (Bayley 1990: Ch. 3). There is, therefore, greater regional and sub-functional variation as regards the success or failure of the social democratic approach in the policing field, but the basic logic of accommodation follows that of the other criminal justice institutions. The philosophy of policing by consent and strategies such as 'winning by appearing to lose' (Reiner 2000) through avoiding confrontational flash-points

speak to a shift in operational strategy. There is movement away from a policing style which, with the use of paramilitary discipline, tactics and symbolism,
was directed towards the suppression of the class-based threat to an orderly
society from individual crimes against property, persons and the state, and
from collective offences of public order and violence in industrial and political
contexts. Instead, an approach that is more integrative ('community policing')
and less conflict-oriented ('problem-oriented policing') is favoured, and the
possession and deployment of decisive underlying force is played down (Tilly
2008).

In both penal welfarism and policing by consent we see the pragmatism
and the idealism of an incremental model of social democracy. Pragmatically,
there is recognition, supplying the foundation for consensus building and
policy convergence across the ideological spectrum, that the criminal justice
apparatus of the state is never just about the maintenance of 'specific order'
but is also about the preservation of 'general order' (Marenin 1982). Those in
a position of social and economic ascendancy benefit from the maintenance
or restoration of order within the socio-political system that guarantees such
ascendancy; so too, to a lesser degree, do the underprivileged. Much crime
in deeply unequal societies is perpetrated by the disadvantaged against the
disadvantaged. Therefore, working-class victims of crime, like victims occupy-
ing a superior class position, gain from a decrease in crime, while working-
class offenders gain from more restorative regimes of treatment. In more
idealistic, longer-term and left-specific terms, moreover, this compensatory
approach may be a platform for a broader transformation of society in which
class-coded differences in the attention of the criminal justice system become
marginal or disappear.

We should not underestimate the difficulties of maintaining this alternative
gradualist social democratic approach to crime and security. It rests on two
diagnostic premises: a material premise, which associates high levels of crime
with social and economic deprivation, and a cultural premise, which associates deviant and security-threatening behaviour with social exclusion. Those
excluded from the expectations and rewards of an affluent society and the informal social controls associated with an integrated and single-status society will
respond by acting in ways that challenge the security of others. The arguments
of economic deprivation and socio-cultural exclusion may complement and
reinforce each other. Economic disadvantage can lead to social exclusion, and
social exclusion, by depriving the excluded of the requisite cultural competence
and material opportunities, can exacerbate economic disadvantage.

Precisely because of the close intertwining of material and cultural premises,
however, any course of social democratic treatment suffers because it is unable
to attend equally to both. On the one hand, a stress on social inclusion may
lead to a strong emphasis on the role of criminal justice institutions as social
integration and reintegration mechanisms – on prisons and other sanctioning

institutions as rehabilitative devices, and on civic involvement in policing. Yet these may be relatively ineffective, and perhaps oppressive and dignity-eroding without treatment of root economic factors. This is the weakness of the gradualist and meliorist approach. To the extent that it finds cultural factors more malleable than material inequality, it remains vulnerable to a pattern of diminished returns, to a frustrated or jaded idealism, to forms of treatment that are intrusive rather than liberating, to public disillusionment and to criticism from the political right for being 'soft' on crime. To the extent that these weaknesses encourage an opposite emphasis upon material factors and the deep pathology of inequality, this threatens to return the left to its more critical posture, with front-line social control mechanisms (such as police and prisons) dismissed or downgraded as cosmetic, as dealing with symptoms not causes.

As in the social democratic project *tout court*, these tensions can never be fully stabilised. Penal welfarism and associated forms of integration rest in uneasy proximity to left scepticism about the security arm of the state. Parties of the right are the more natural sponsors of a conservative politics of law and order. Caught between underlying reservations about the security functions of the state and the variable efficacy of a less punitive approach to criminal justice policy, parties of the social democratic left inhabit a climate of electoral politics in which they are doubly vulnerable. Being insufficiently committed to the 'bottom line' of security or 'too understanding' of the problem of individual or group deviance can be exploited by conservative political forces.

## The challenge of neo-liberalism and authoritarian populism

In recent years these tensions have been exacerbated by the rise of a new 'culture of crime control' (Garland 2001). For Garland and those arguing similarly, a combination of material and social factors has led to the decline of penal welfarism and the rise of a new approach to crime and its treatment. This is one which involves the return to an older approach, but which also embraces novel elements. Since the 1970s the effects of global economic recession, especially the contraction of manufacturing industry and the growth of un- and under-employment, along with the neo-liberal policies emphasising private over public provision, liberalised trade, capital mobility, the reduction of fiscal deficits and low marginal tax rates, served to exacerbate material and status inequalities. These developments challenged the basic fabric of social welfarism. With the United States and the United Kingdom in the vanguard, but spreading to other Western democracies, this economic sea-change encouraged a political culture of 'authoritarian populism' (Hall et al. 1978) where greater attention to crime and its pathologies feeds off a public mood of intolerance to crime and deviance (Kershaw et al. 2008; Kearns and Bannister 2009). In today's 'risk society' (Beck 1992), the combination of new dangers and forms of precariousness and an attendant increase in modes of anxiety has led to a spiralling of insecurity. New risks are highlighted and new anxieties fostered. These include the self-reinforcing anxieties associated with the decline of secure forms of public space – the spread of 'gated communities', secured shopping malls and mass CCTV – and the retreat from public contact and the erosion of associated social capital, as in the domestication and virtualisation of social networks (Newburn 2001).

There are a number of distinguishing features of the new culture of control. First, there is the increasing political preoccupation with crime, often portrayed as the major threat facing society and individuals. Where crime under the banner of penal welfarism was often successfully depoliticised, it has now been repoliticised, and shapes the political imagination in areas beyond its traditional purview. This repoliticisation has not taken place as envisaged by the radical social democratic left, namely, as a symptom of an unacceptably class-divided society. Rather, as in Jonathan Simon's evocative phrase, we witness ever denser patterns of 'governing through crime' (Simon 2007). Crime control is seen as a key priority of social policy, both in the many security institutions of the state and the encouragement of private security provision, and as a form of social control in areas such as schools, the workplace and family relations (Husak 2008).

Second, crime is increasingly recoded as an individual rather than a social responsibility. Support for the rehabilitative ideal recedes and offenders are seen less as in need of care and support and more as (ir)responsible and undeserving – as risks to be controlled, managed and minimised. This is the product of two quite different but symbiotic themes in the new culture of crime control. In Garland's evocative formulation, a 'criminology of the other' operates in tandem with a 'criminology of the self' (Garland 2001: 137). The former concerns a self-reinforcing pattern of mobilisation and response to a new 'outrage dynamic within which governments feel constrained to "act out" more and more hysterically in response to the most serious crimes' (Lacey 2008: 23). Within this dynamic, the perpetrators of serious crimes are framed as the objects of denunciation and demonisation rather than of sympathetic, sociologically aware understanding. The criminology of the self, on the other hand, has to do with the 'normalisation' and actuarial management of everyday crime and criminal threat. A whole set of strategies are deployed within a new economy of crime control. The use of fines and community supervision (such as 'control orders' and electronic tagging) as an alternative to imprisonment, the contracting out of policing, the encouragement of Neighbourhood Watch and other forms of 'active citizenship', and the deployment of technology and architecture to 'design out' the threat of crime reflect a desire to economise on monitoring, trial and punishment, and an associated indifference to 'deep' criminal motives. In consequence, they offer further distraction from the social etiology of crime.

Third, as part of the emphasis on individuals rather than the collective whole, and on symptoms rather than causes, there is new emphasis on victims and potential victims rather than offenders. The needs and preferences of victims, rather than being subsumed under the public interest in 'general order', are allocated specific individual or collective identity and value, and set against the interest of the offender in the treatment of crime. In turn, victims begin to mobilise in a politically effective manner, and criminal justice policy and practice become more about the negotiation of the interests of particular constituencies than the search for an inclusive public good (Garland 2001: 11–12).

Fourth, it has become accepted in public policy communities that a high-crime society is the norm rather than the exception. Public expectations adjust accordingly. We experience the visible symbols and costs of such a society, through pervasive surveillance, mass incarceration or home security, as well as an increasingly crime-centred political discourse. Regardless of objective levels of criminality – which in some categories have indicated a recent decline (Kershaw et al. 2008) – we come to live with the idea of a high-crime society. It becomes part of the familiar and often unnoticed backdrop to our lives, and this alters social and political calculations of inevitability and accept-ability. The benchmark of acceptable public policy is no more the eradication or severe reduction of crime, but simply its containment. Criminal justice thinking becomes suffused with a new pragmatism – a narrow preoccupation with 'least bad' options that increasingly fails to plan for long-term progress (Garland 2001; Lacey 2008). Policing and punishment are justified as manag-ing an ineradicable aspect of the human condition, simply 'keeping the lid on' through highly expressive forms of deterrence, prevention and incapacitation.

Fifth, the state, though it remains central to the symbolic delivery of punish-ment and to the 'steering' of criminal justice policy, becomes decentred from the instrumental task of crime control. Much security, technological or personal, becomes a matter of private purchase, a 'club good' or an individual commod-ity for those who can afford it and who prioritise it, rather than a matter of public provision (Jones and Newburn 1998). On the other hand, some crime control policy and, increasingly, even operational matters move to the trans-national level. This is true of Interpol, the International Criminal Court or the various Council of Europe anti-crime conventions, and is most emphatically so in the EU 'Area of Freedom, Security and Justice'. Since the Maastricht Treaty twenty years ago, there has been an increasing relocation of policing (Europol), prosecutorial (Eurojust) and substantive criminal policy (e.g. the widespread harmonisation of offence definitions) to the supranational level. This mirrors the shift of the political centre of gravity to that level, with new supranational policies generating new types of crime such as euro counterfeiting and public order offences directed against specifically EU or other transnational institu-tions in protests over regional or global policy. In part it speaks to a new scale and space of criminal activity operating in the new general transnational cir-cuits of mobility and influence (the emphasis on transnational terrorism and organised crime). It also speaks to a growing net-widening preoccupation with the control and management of crime and insecurity, wherever and however it may manifest itself (Walker 2008). The growth of the private and the supranational reflect the anti-collectivist and inherently state-sceptical tendency of an underlying economic liberalism, a philosophy which remains less sceptical of supranational 'public' intervention in the security area. These trends highlight the inadequacy of any single institutional centre of regulation in such an unbounded but pervasively control-centred culture as that encouraged by new economic liberalism.

Sixth, the growing culture of crime control merges into a more general process of 'securitisation' (Huysmans 2006; Zedner 2009) with a momentum that increases with events such as 9/11 and the Madrid and London terrorist bombings, which are intended and framed as general societal threats. Securitisation involves a growing tendency to code the 'crime problem' as one of 'controls' and to extend the jurisdiction of crime into ever more corners of civic life. It also stretches the category of relevant objects of control to cover a much wider range of threats to the long-term security or resilience of our 'way of life'. Mass immigration, asylum seeking, terrorism, the intra-state or cross-border 'new wars' of national ethnic identity (Kaldor 2006) and environmental damage have become more publicly visible in Western societies in recent years (Loader and Walker 2007: Ch. 1). They have come to be viewed as part of the same 'security continuum' (Bigo 2002) – the one and indivisible existential threat. Furthermore, a culture of securitisation extends the range and sense of interconnectedness of the relevant threats, as well as deepening our sense of their political salience. To present something as a security threat – for example, in the realm of terrorism or environmental damage – is to remove it from the normal political discourse, and to treat it as a matter of urgent and non-negotiable priority. Many of the threats on the new security continuum have a transnational source and scale of response, so underlining the state-decentring trend noted above.

## The challenges ahead

The new culture of crime control and securitisation offers a new challenge for social democratic security policy. It is simultaneously structural, ideological and locational, and has to be confronted at all three levels simultaneously. Let us conclude by outlining the three challenges, and by indicating how social democratic thought might respond.

### *The structural challenge*

In structural terms, the economic backdrop to the new culture of crime control is one in which the global extension of free markets takes priority over the traditional social democratic levers for producing material welfare and reintegrative criminal justice policy within local communities – including high levels of redistributive taxes and non-market-based public services. It is difficult to imagine a significant replacement of the crime control frame with a social democratic alternative – one which re-attends to the twin strategy of modifying economic inequality and repairing social exclusion – without some reordering of this economic backdrop. To this challenge, however, two responses can be made.

First, we should not overestimate the extent to which the new culture of crime control has eclipsed the social democratic model represented by penal welfarism and consent-based policing strategies. There is a tendency in some criminological literature to overgeneralise from the experience of the United States and, to a lesser extent, the United Kingdom, Australia and New Zealand, where the culture of control has reached significant expression (Lacey 2008: Ch. 1). However, in Japan, or Scandinavian countries, or the corporatist countries of North-Western Europe, the picture is more mixed. No state in the modern world has escaped the convergent economic logic of a doctrine which resists national or regional political boundaries in the name of global free markets. Nowhere has remained impervious to the macro-political consequences of questioning the basic ethos of public provision or to the sectoral policy consequences of incorporating market logic into criminal justice provision. Furthermore, the electoral consequences of the rise of neo-liberalism are widespread, with a significant long-term ebbing of support for social democratic parties who have trimmed their ambitions towards the liberal economic orthodoxy.

On the other hand, in many countries, the habits and structures of social democracy have remained institutionally embedded and culturally resilient despite the change in the macro-economic and macro-political climate. In particular, those countries that have developed and retained 'co-ordinated market economies' (Hall and Soskice 2001; Lacey 2008) rather than the liberal alternative have been both more willing and more able to sustain relatively moderate criminal justice policy with a robust institutional capacity for integration. Coordinated market economies are those that favour significant social and political capital through sustained cooperation and compromise between different class interests and social constituencies by means of stable structures of investment in education and training, generous welfare benefits, long-term employment relationships and widespread respect for professional expertise. To take one indicator of the continuing contrasts in tolerance in penal policy which this coordinated approach facilitates: in 2006 the incarceration rate in the United States was 737 per 100,000 and in England and Wales an EU-high of 148; in Germany it was 95, in France 84 and in the Scandinavian bloc on average under 70 (Lacey 2008: 60).

Second, if we concede the trend towards neo-liberalism and its link with the culture of control, the current global financial crisis becomes an unstable factor. It provides ammunition for reducing much of the edifice of social democracy – a warning against sustaining public expenditure in the face of accumulated debt, and, to the extent that it comes to be understood as a systemic rather than a contingent outcome of the policies underpinning the Washington consensus, a cautionary tale against the continuing free rein of neo-liberalism. The crisis of public debt highlights the costs of the culture of crime control. The economic costs of mass incarceration are enormous, dwarfing other sectors of criminal justice treatment and of social policy more generally. For example, in the USA, spending by states on prisons has risen six times the rate of spending on higher education over the past two decades (Zakaria 2012). There is no respectable research which shows that these costs are outweighed by the economic benefits of depriving offenders of the opportunity to re-offend (Lacey 2008: 185–96). The case in defence of a large prison population can only be made on grounds emotional and moral, which may be a luxury under straitened economic circumstances, a point that even the UK Conservative Justice Secretary, Kenneth Clarke (2011), repeatedly and candidly conceded.

## The ideological challenge

The ideological tensions inherent in a social democratic criminal justice policy are exacerbated under circumstances of fiscal restraint when the difficulties of treating the material causes of crime are compounded. Yet there are also ideological tensions within the new culture of crime control. It, rather than the utopian alternative of the democratic road to full socialism, has become the key comparative touchstone for contemporary social democratic criminal justice policy. It is by exposing these tensions rather than reconciling its vision with a socialist 'paradise lost or postponed' that social democratic alternatives will become viable again.

In the first place, the culture of crime control, eschewing deeper solutions, depends on managing and containing the problem. However, such a policy, incorporating mass incarceration and high levels of policing, involves strong and expensive state security apparatus – a strategy which is placed under particular pressure in a time of fiscal crisis. Today the USA has two million people in prison, while in Britain and other European countries the prison population has also grown at an unprecedented rate. Moreover, this problem is exacerbated by the distinctive 'ratchet effect' built into the politics of securitisation and crime control. The emphasis on crime and control creates a social atmosphere of unease and an 'arms race' (Lacey 2008: 173) between the political parties in search of more comprehensive forms of security, which reinforces and feeds anxieties. It is striking that during the New Labour government of 1997–2007, with its strong rhetorical endorsement of a 'tough on crime' approach, more new criminal justice statutes were passed than in the previous hundred years (fifty-three to forty-three). The widening remit of securitisation and the casting of the security net beyond crime to questions of immigration and religious fundamentalism also amplify a culture of unease.

The attitudes that underpin the new politics of control do not simply feed on their own anxieties, but also lead to practices conducive to loosening the bonds of solidarity out of which we build 'desecuritised' relations of trust and mutual confidence. Private security, gated communities, the emergence of the surveillance-based 'tracking society' and equating the cultural difference of immigrant communities with a security threat all reflect and encourage the kind of defensive forms of possessive individualism and group prejudice that undermine the bonds of confident citizenship of a common community which help to reduce levels of fear of crime and insecurity. The culture of crime control is arguably spinning out of control, and provides a context for a revision and renewal of the older strategies of penal welfarism. In particular, they are more cost-effective, less prone to feed the expansion of the problem they seek to address, and less inclined to erode the basis of common civility and solidarity from which arises the sense of common confident civil membership necessary to live comfortably with manageable levels of risk (Loader and Walker 2007: Ch. 6).

Even in political cultures where a more coordinated political economy has been less successful at preserving integrative solutions and a more authoritarian 'law and order' political discourse is most prevalent, such as the United Kingdom, this alternative scenario is not merely hypothetical. No criminal justice is monolithic. Pockets of resistance remain, and new ideas emerge or migrate from other policy fields or other political cultures that are reducible neither to the 'new' neo-liberal nor to the 'old' social democratic logic. In the British context, these include the pursuit of a transnationally stimulated interest in restorative justice, the development of a trans-policy-sector rights culture generating substantial new due process protections for persons in court or in custody, as well as privacy and dignity rights for prisoners and the emergence, again cross-sectoral, of a less deferential posture towards police and other criminal justice professionals. All provide cause to move 'beyond lamentation' (Loader and Sparks 2012) for a lost world of left certainties so as to fashion a new social democratic criminal justice policy more sensitive to contemporary conditions and more attuned to comparative advantage over the right alternative.

### The locational challenge

Finally, there is the question of shifting location. In the new politics of crime control the state is no longer the obvious centre of criminal justice policy. Private sites, an expanding range of municipal sites and, increasingly, transnational sites now join the state as key policy-generative domains. This provides two challenges to any reassertion of social democratic priorities.

First, there is a steering problem. Political authority over the criminal justice agenda is now so dispersed that even if a social democratic agenda is adopted at the state level it is likely to be frustrated or diluted at other policy sites. Private-sector security solutions focus on club goods and individual benefits rather than more general societal-level security-related public goods. As regards transnational sites, a similarly gloomy picture emerges. If we take the most prominent case of the EU, with its history of attenuated forms of public or individual accountability (ironically, a product of the reluctance of states to cede political control over the traditionally state-sovereigntist functions of criminal justice to supranational institutions (Walker 2008)), there is a bias towards empowerment of professional transnational bureaucracies of crime control (such as Europol, Eurojust and various anti-terrorist groups) and their control-centred operational priorities.

We should not exaggerate the scale or intractability of these problems, and we should not ignore the opportunities for social democratic renewal which they bring in their wake. The size and influence of the commoditised private sphere of security, including whether there should be any sizeable private sphere at all, are political questions within the domain of the state, and so remain open to state clawback or (re)regulation. The influence of the supranational bureaucracy of crime control, too, is not set in stone. In the early days of EU security policy the familiar absence of organised voice on behalf of deviant groups as stakeholders was exacerbated by the remoteness of political voice in the EU and the lack of effective mechanisms for review and oversight by the Parliament or the Court of Justice. However, the situation in both respects has improved under the Treaty of Lisbon since 2009 and the subsequent Stockholm Programme with its emphasis on individual rights. The policy centrality and high profile of the new transnational Area of Freedom, Security and Justice over the past decade seems to have eclipsed early protestations that this domain could be retained in a 'grey zone' of semi-intergovernmentalism. Political control or influence over the criminal justice agenda at the European level remains attenuated, but in principle is no longer any more difficult than in any other supranational policy domain.

In the other area to which the central state may cede power, the municipal level, the traditions and prospects of social democratic thinking, potentially a counterweight to more conservative thinking at the centre, are somewhat stronger. There has been an unprecedented dialectic of divergence and convergence in local criminal justice in the UK and elsewhere, with the increasing diversification and specialisation of local 'policing' provision (general policing, traffic control, youth justice, community safety, environmental safety, housing control) leading to new forms of multi-agency coordination and new pressures for local accountability (Crawford 2008). The latest of these is the introduction from 2012 of a system of locally elected Police and Crime Commissioners in England and Wales (Muir and Loader 2011).

Beyond the problem of the dispersal of political authority, there is a deeper cultural one associated with eroding the authority of the institutional locale of the state. The nation-state is the paradigmatic historical site of social democratic mobilisation and implementation, and has become an intrinsic part of the social democratic vision. Social democracy is premised upon the viability of the state-based solidarity project. The associative bonds and integrated framework of social citizenship as a source of rights, responsibilities and societal status, which make it possible to imagine a strong programme of social (re) integration, presupposes a polity which not only retains regulatory sovereignty but also provides the primary focus of the political identity of its members. Where political identity is dispersed, it becomes harder to imagine what the solidaristic and reintegrative object of social democratic policy is. Which is the society of equals that the deviant is being asked to rejoin? What is the community of collective security to which we appeal in setting a criminal justice policy that supplies the bonds of solidarity against divisive and insecurity-breeding individual or group-based solutions?

There are two answers to this challenge. The first is not to exaggerate the scale of the problem. National communities may no longer be such dominant sites of political identity, but they remain the most significant. State citizenship for many people in many parts of the world remains the key organising political identity (Miller 2000). The second response is that the integrative goods we associate with an affirmative response to security needs, though often scaled at the level of the state, need not be confined to that level. The resilient centrality of states as integrative and reintegrative security communities does not mean that all other security relations within, between or across states need be non-integrative, or need be antagonistic towards state-level solidarities. In a porous world, our contexts of risk are scaled unevenly, as are our contexts of collective action generally. We are familiar with this at the sub-state, municipal level, where there are distinctive local security problems and needs and opportunities for building common security projects, and where there is a legible tradition of 'nesting' such projects within larger national security projects. At the other extreme, in areas such as nuclear risk, climate change and certain forms of organised crime or political terror, our relevant communities of risk are increasingly transnational or global in a manner that is unprecedented. With the assistance of the right kind of institutional machinery of political deliberation, it is still possible, if difficult, to envisage the development of an integrative sense of regional or global public goods in ways that recall the original social democratic vision of equal citizenship (Loader and Walker 2007: Ch. 9). Today, if we are to retain the social democratic project in crime and security, we have no choice but to reimagine that project as a dispersed rather than a nationally concentrated feature of our political existence.

# MULTILEVEL SOCIAL DEMOCRACY: CENTRALISATION AND DECENTRALISATION

Michael Keating

## Social democracy and the territorial state

Social democracy emerged within the nation-state at a time when states were consolidating institutionally and deepening their penetration of society. During the first half of the twentieth century, social democrats increasingly saw the state as the vehicle for realising their ambitions of social progress and popular control of the economy. Yet there are competing traditions within social democracy about the nature of the state, its unity and the degree of centralisation or decentralisation most compatible with social democratic aims. I am not concerned here with the debate between supporters of national vs international socialism, although the European question raises very important questions addressed in the contribution to this volume by Yves Mény. Nor do I address the important issue of whether the state should be the primary vehicle for change at all, as opposed to the industrial arena or civil society, an issue covered by Colin Crouch. My concern rather is with the territorial structure of the state itself.

The centralist vision of social democracy which characterised the twentieth century draws on various traditions. First is the patriotic left inherited from the French Revolution, for whom the unitary state is the basis for citizenship and equality, an attitude usually labelled, not entirely historically accurately, as 'Jacobin'. The entry of the masses into electoral politics from the late nineteenth century confirmed the importance of the nation-state as the centre for political struggle. As the unitary state became widely (but not universally) associated with liberation and progress, regions and localities were seen as bastions of reaction (especially in France). Second was the welfarist left which from the mid twentieth century saw the centralised state as the basis for social provision and redistribution. This was partly a practical matter, as the central state had the capacity to mobilise resources on a wide scale. Yet it also drew on ideas of the nation as a natural community of solidarity, so connecting to the patriotic left. Third was the economic left, especially from the 1930s, focused on nationalisation of industry and seizing the commanding heights of the economy, which was also seen to require centralisation, as were Keynesian economic management and economic and physical planning. Social democrats in poorer regions latched onto territorial redistribution to complement social equalisation. After the Second World War, trade unions were frequently drawn into corporatist intermediation or social dialogue with employers and the state, another force for centralisation, conducted as it was at the level of the nation-state.

Yet there are contrary traditions upon which social democrats were, and are, able to draw. Some varieties of socialism were strongly anti-statist, inclining to syndicalism or anarchism, and even outside these there was widespread suspicion of the state as the bastion of the established order and of its alliance with capitalism. In many countries, social democracy had both local and localist origins, viewing the central state with particular suspicion, especially in the face of anti-union legislation. Social struggles were often locally based and rooted in community as well as class resistance. Trade unions were also often local and regional, although gradually centralising in order to confront consolidated employers and the interventionist state. It was often at the municipal level that socialist and labour candidates were first successful, and municipal socialism thrived widely in the early twentieth century, building welfare from the bottom. There were alliances with forces of territorial dissent in peripheral regions and where there were nationality questions, social democrats needed to incorporate them into their appeals. So if regionalism or minority nationalism in France was often portrayed as conservative if not downright reactionary, such was not the case in Norway, some parts of Spain, or the United Kingdom. Even in countries with Jacobin traditions, like France or Italy, there were progressive strands of regionalism, while in Germany social democrats used local and intermediate institutions where they were available. Such opportunities were used to pursue progressive policies and municipal socialism. As social democratic parties became entrenched in local politics, the available resources, including housing, jobs and social welfare, were also used to establish systems of patronage and rooted party machines. Local patronage politics together with access to national resources proved a powerful combination, until municipal socialism was confronted with new social demands and social movements in the late twentieth century.

The high point of social democratic centralism was between the 1930s and the 1960s, with economic planning and social welfare the key considerations. From the late 1960s or early 1970s, however, the pendulum started to swing back. One reason was the experience of social democrats in opposition in countries like France and Italy, who were conducting a long 'march through the institutions', gaining power at local and regional level and using it as a stepping-stone to national office. In the process, they developed local instruments, and underwent something of an ideological shift, drawing on their earlier traditions to ease and legitimise the change. Social democrats had invested heavily in a mode of territorial management based upon diversionary regional policy and planning, or 'spatial Keynesianism', as a way of reconciling their national and local/ regional imperatives. The collapse of spatial Keynesianism under the pressure of global integration, the European single market and policy failures led to a rethinking of development strategies and the adoption of the emerging theories of endogenous or 'bottom-up' development (discussed below). Labour movements and their political allies were also drawn into local struggles over plant closures and coalitions of territorial defence in the face of the investment strategies of multinational enterprises.

At the same time, social democratic parties have faced the challenge of new social movements, including environmentalist campaigns, which are often locally based and locally oriented. Urban conflicts have focused on public services, housing, population displacement and the privatisation of public space in the process of urban renewal. These have created new political cleavages that correspond at best imperfectly with the class cleavages of industrial society as manifested in the workplace. The politics of regionalism and minority nationalism has in many (but by no means all) cases turned to the left and, more generally, social democratic parties have had to compete with territorial parties targeting their core constituency. This is true in the United Kingdom, Spain and, to a degree, Germany, where the *Links Partei* has served in many ways as a party of territorial defence. In Italy and Belgium, territorial and communitarian parties of the right have also made inroads into the working-class vote. In the realm of culture, neo-traditionalism has in some places been associated with the conservative right, as in the Alpine regions (Caramani and Mény 2005), but elsewhere it has come to be aligned with the radical and libertarian left, recapturing traditions of popular dissent.

Territory has also come to be used as a mobilising principle to defend community and the public sphere in the face of neo-liberalism. While in principle neo-liberalism might appear the natural ally of decentralisation, both suspicious of the central state, the opposite has tended to be true. The imposition of neo-liberalism has required a strong state apparatus and an attack (usually rather selective) on intermediary institutions. As the welfare state has been undermined at the state level (while surviving nevertheless), emphasis has shifted to local solidarity and the rediscovery and defence of community as an alternative basis for sharing.

Left-wing parties have found a variety of ideological rationales to incorporate a return to localism and regionalism. For a while, some radical intellectuals played with the idea of 'internal colonialism', a concept derived from Gramsci and redeployed by the Occitan activist Robert Lafont (1967).[1] Capitalism, in alliance with the state, was portrayed as subordinating not just social classes but also territories in a spatial division of labour. The theme was attractive during and immediately after the decolonisation of the European overseas empires, but the comparison lacked credibility and the idea faded. Social democrats also rediscovered and dusted down older traditions of municipal politics, peripheral dissent and region, citing distinguished forebears to give the claim legitimacy. For the most part, however, the embrace of decentralisation was not accompanied by the abandonment of the earlier centralist ideas and practices, leaving social democrats torn on the issue and often pursuing contradictory policies at the same time. The crisis of the national Keynesian model of economic management, the rescaling of welfare regimes, and the growing demands for recognition of national pluralism have all presented challenges to the twentieth-century model of centralised social democracy.

## Economic development

Social democratic parties often have their traditional support basis not just among deprived individuals but in regions suffering from under-development or deindustrialisation. During what is variously referred to as the *Trente Glorieuses* or the era of the Keynesian welfare state after the Second World War, social democratic parties embraced centralised economic policies but with a regional dimension. Regional policies were in principle centralised (even in Germany they came under the joint tasks framework), since only the centre had the capacity for spatial redistribution, but they needed to be delivered locally. Diversionary policies encouraged industry to relocate from congested areas into the development regions through tax incentives. These were accompanied by investment and infrastructure spending in needy regions and, increasingly, spatial planning in order to tie in economic development with urban growth and public service provision. This 'spatial Keynesianism' was sold as a non-zero-sum game since all regions could benefit: the needy regions would gain jobs and income; in the rich regions, congestion, infrastructure overload and inflationary pressures would be reduced; and the national economy would benefit from putting otherwise idle labour and other production factors to work. Over time, local and regional components of development policies were elaborated to mobilise what the French called the *forces vives*, dynamic and pro-development leaders challenging conservative and protectionist local elites. Often these took the form of neo-corporatist institutions bringing together the state, local government, business and labour, a formula that has in many cases persisted or been recreated.

This model entered into crisis with the oil shocks of the 1970s, when the donor regions experienced their own economic problems and the game could no longer be presented as non-zero-sum. There were criticisms of the effectiveness of some of the policies, especially where state-backed investments had not produced self-sustaining growth but only 'cathedrals in the desert'; the evidence is in practice very mixed. Under increased fiscal pressure, governments no longer had the resources to finance regional policies and the globalisation of capital made it less possible to lean on big firms or induce them to invest in development regions when they could leave the country altogether. From the 1980s, European competition rules strictly regulated the amount that could be given in state aid and banned cross-subsidisation of public utilities. The European Union's own regional development funds provide only a fraction of the amounts available under the old national programmes.

The institutionalisation of regional policy also created problems. Neo-corporatist forums were torn between the idea of applying national policy top-down, or bringing in a bottom-up perspective on development. Business and labour representatives were unclear of their role and there was no clear way of resolving differences other than by state diktat. At the urban level particularly, there were sharp tensions between exponents of a purely economic conception of development and those seeking a stronger social or environmental dimension.

From the 1960s there was a wave of reforms of local government systems, usually involving the creation of larger units and professionalisation of administration. Social democrats were caught in the middle. While social democratic governments were often committed to local government reform in the interests of welfare state expansion and urban renewal, there were tensions when modernising development policies and local government reform challenged forms of distributive politics. These included local welfare regimes based on housing and public services as well as patronage networks rooted in social democratic parties themselves.[2] More tensions arose when local social movements challenged the logic of property-based or business-driven development as in the case of the grand French development programmes piloted by DATAR in the 1960s and 1970s, or the English Urban Development Corporations in the 1980s. These localised movements called for a stronger social dimension to development policy challenging local social democratic parties who had often been insensitive to the question.

This coincided with a change in academic thinking about spatial development, with a move away from a top-down vision towards endogenous growth strategies. In the new way of thinking, territory itself, or rather factors inseparable from it, are the key drivers of growth (Scott 1998). Traditional locational factors such as proximity to raw materials, water transport or markets are less important, and even hard infrastructure is downplayed in favour of 'soft' factors including human capital, research and development capacity and essentially cultural factors including entrepreneurship and innovative ideas. Emphasis is placed on the social construction of particular places, with heavy reliance on the fashionable notion of social capital. Another element in this new thinking is the idea of local and regional production systems, based on complementary firms and sectors and strong spatial linkages (Crouch et al. 2001). In a further move, regions and localities are sometimes seen as competing with each other for capital, technology, skilled personnel and markets.

This new regionalist thinking provided powerful analytical tools but in some versions presents a simplification of a complex reality and encourages wishful thinking about the possibilities of resolving the perennial social democratic dilemmas. The concept of social capital has been stretched by Robert Putnam (1993) and his followers into a catch-all concept that facilitates both economic growth and social cohesion and can be found by shifting institutions and policy-making to the right spatial scales; this is what Lovering (1999) calls the 'vulgar' new regionalism. The concept of 'governance' has come to dominate the field, usually in a depoliticised way to suggest that regional and local policy-making is a matter of consensus and finding the optimum solution to shared problems. All of this bears a strong resemblance to 'Third Way' versions of social democracy, which dodge serious issues about the balance of power and the distribution of benefits.

Regions and cities are, compared with states (even in the European Single Market), open economies, unable to influence macro-economic conditions and faced with mobile capital which increasingly shops among locations for the best terms. The implications of this, however, are not at all obvious. Michael Porter (2001) and his followers have promoted the idea of regional competitiveness but then extended it to suggest that all regions can become more competitive. This is logically impossible. All regions can become more prosperous by a better division of labour based on *comparative* advantage, but *competitive* advantage is another matter since in a competition there are winners and losers. Competitive regionalism, on the contrary, may encourage a 'race to the bottom', competitively cutting taxes and social overheads to attract investment. This is Kenichi Ohmae's (1995) neo-liberal utopia, but a social democratic dystopia. The vulnerability of local and regional governments to the heavy-handed tactics of Ryanair, which regularly extracts subsidies as a condition of locating their operations, shows the dangers this poses. Such a race to the bottom will increase inter-regional inequality as the richest regions can most easily afford it, and the most competitive individuals and sectors will be able to gain rents from the threat to relocate.

The focus on competitive development also affects the balance of power within localities. As development is presented as a shared territorial interest, social democratic parties and trade unions have been drawn into productivist development coalitions with business and local governments, often formalised in development councils or agencies. This has often put them at odds with environmentalists, who in other respects are their natural allies and may be necessary to form a winning electoral platform. It also creates tensions with local social movements based on extending social provision or defending the social or public use of space. The fact is that any development strategy will create winners and losers, in either absolute or relative terms, and this is true both within and between cities and regions.

We should be wary, however, of deterministic theories like this, and evidence of a race to the bottom in Europe is limited. There may equally be a race to the top, as regions and cities compete to satisfy the demands of their citizens and expand social provision. A social democratic regionalism puts more emphasis on social inclusion and balanced development. At the same time, the idea that regions are in competition must be seen partly as a fact and partly an ideological construction, used to legitimate the idea of a shared territorial interest and close off internal debate in the face of a perceived need to compete. Competition serves here, as it does in other social and cultural spheres, to trump other considerations and impose a single policy imperative. This will depend on the continued existence, at national or European level, of rules to regulate spatial competition, and on the construction of politics within the regions and cities themselves. Decentralisation in itself guarantees neither the productivist utopia of the vulgar new regionalism, nor the social Darwinism of a race to the bottom. These remain matters of political contestation at all spatial levels.

## Social solidarity and welfare

In the course of the twentieth century, social democrats came to locate social solidarity above all at the level of the nation-state and it is here that welfare states have been constructed. There were a number of reasons for this choice, which no longer all point in the same direction. One is that the nation generates the affective identity that underpins and rationalises sharing and redistribution – the analogy of the family is often invoked. David Miller (1995) has provided an explicitly social democratic defence of the nation on just these grounds. A slightly different argument sees welfare as the third generation of citizen rights, following from civil and political rights, as elaborated by Marshall (1992), while citizenship is vested in the nation-state. A practical reason for centralisation is that the highest possible scale is desirable in order to engage in the broadest redistribution and harness most resources. In many cases, it was only the central state which had the means and capacity to extend welfare, especially where there was local conservative opposition. Social democrats have also sometimes argued that national-level solidarity is somehow more complete and even universal, despite the fact that the nation-state is itself a particularist territorial form. Public goods theorists have argued that, while allocative and development responsibilities can be assigned to local and regional levels, redistribution should be a state-level competence, so as to limit races to the bottom and mobilise resources over a larger area. Social democrats have generally accepted this to mean that at least cash transfers and social insurance should be state-wide.

The so-called Keynesian welfare state provided that the market and the area of social solidarity were coterminous, so allowing revenues to be captured for welfare and social compromises to be forged. Neither capital nor labour had an exit option and so were forced into social compromise within the state. Such social compromises could, moreover, be positive sum, with labour benefiting from higher employment and the 'social wage' while employers were assured of a healthy and educated workforce and social stability. Having gained a place within such state-level systems of intermediation, labour movements and parties then tended to defend them, fearing that a shift of venue could put this position at risk.

Spatial rescaling at the supranational, transnational and sub-state levels has brought these state-level bargains into question. There was always a certain tension between social democratic aspirations to cosmopolitanism and universal welfare and their commitment to what was in practice national welfare, if not welfare nationalism. Now the nation-state is increasingly called into question, its mystique and normative supremacy challenged by the rise of new forms of transnational order, notably in the form of European integration, and of sub-state nationalisms and regionalist movements. Nor are the practical arguments for centralisation so convincing. The largest scale of public policy is no longer the nation-state but the European Union, yet Europe lacks the affective solidarity found in the old nation-state. The scales of market regulation and social solidarity no longer necessarily coincide, so undermining national social compromises and encouraging 'partial exits' from national politics on the part of those able to do so (Bartolini 2005). Business, for example, can opt out of national social compromises by relocating or disinvesting.

Partial exit may also take the form of regions de-solidarising from their poorer co-nationals, claiming the needs of competitive regionalism. Evidence is available of a 'revolt of the rich' in wealthy regions including Bavaria, Flanders, Catalonia and Northern Italy. 'World cities' (Scott et al. 2001) appear increasingly linked into global economic circuits and less connected to their national hinterlands. City and regional governments are caught between an external environment that seems to dictate that economic competitiveness be the main criterion for public policy, and internal pressures from social movements protesting against the effects of this and calling for more solidarity. This would suggest that rescaling away from the nation-state necessarily both upwards to Europe and downwards to sub-state territories entails a threat to social solidarity, a grim lesson for social democrats. Seeking to reinvent the old integrated nation-state would, however, seem to be futile, except perhaps in the Nordic zone. Nor does Europe provide a compensating form of protection and solidarity. The institutional design of the EU, biased as it is to market competition, threatens to undermine national welfare states as discussed in the chapter in this volume by Yves Mény. Yet the weakening of a state-level social solidarity does not necessarily entail a loss of solidarity itself, as long as it can be reconstructed at new levels.

The first step is a critical deconstruction of the idea of the nation-state. For some political scientists and almost all scholars of international relations, the term refers to a sovereign unit in the international community, although in this case one might object that the prefix 'nation' is either redundant or should be replaced with something like 'sovereign'. In another sense, nation-state refers to a situation in which nation and state coincide. Yet we know that there are cases where they do not, or where there are multiple levels of national identity. The United Kingdom is a case in point. Segall (2007), for example, takes me to task for suggesting that social solidarity could be located at the 'sub-national'[3] level of Scotland rather than at the level of the (British) political community. Such critics assume that 'national' level and 'political community' must correspond to the state. In Scotland, the term 'national' commonly refers to the Scottish nation (sometimes, confusingly, to Britain, and occasionally to the United Kingdom) and the political community is being reconstituted at the Scottish level. The point is that in plurinational states, the terms 'nation' and 'political community' are disputed, as are the boundaries of belonging. A less prejudicial argument might therefore be that social solidarity is best located at that level where solidarity is strongest, which might be at the state or the sub-state level. In Scotland, the final push for the Home Rule movement after a hundred years of campaigning was the widespread feeling that a UK government, which never commanded even a plurality of support there, was undermining welfare provision and solidarity. Territory and a reshaped sense of Scottish identity were mobilised, in the context of weakened class identities, to resist this and gain a degree of autonomy. Surveys continue to show that most Scots would like the main welfare services to be organised on a Scottish basis while also showing that British-wide solidarity has not disappeared. Similar arguments have been made in Quebec (Noël 1999) and elsewhere (Béland and Lecours 2008). Just as states have used welfare provision to build national identity, citizenship and solidarity, so governments in devolved territories engaged in region-building or 'stateless nation-building' (Keating 1997) may do the same (McEwen 2006). Where regions and stateless nations have a strong sense of shared identity, this might replace state-level identity as the focus for solidarity. New forms of citizenship could emerge at new institutional levels. Cities can also become arenas for solidarity. It is true that larger units can mobilise greater resources for redistribution but we know that nation-states themselves are of widely different sizes and, if anything, it is the smaller ones that are more redistributive. They are also more generous providers of assistance to developing countries.

Another challenge is posed by the transformation of welfare itself away from the old emphasis on income support towards new social risks and linking to labour market policies as employment is seen as the key to social inclusion. Inequality is not to be measured purely by class but reflects new and more complex patterns of stratification, by employment status, neighbour-hood, gender and ethnicity. Welfare is both changing its scope to take in these challenges and spatially rescaling at the supranational and subnational levels (Ferrera 2006; Greer 2006). It is no longer the case (if it ever was) that redis-tribution can be identified solely with cash transfers. Almost any public policy can have a redistributive effect.

The way public services are financed and the conditions for receiving them have distributive implications. 'Third Way' advocates, including New Labour, have argued that the mode of delivery of services is irrelevant to the question of distribution and social solidarity, since they concern only the technical matter of efficiency. Competition and diversity, moreover, will help protect citizens from rent-seeking public providers (Le Grand 2003). Indeed, with semantic sleight-of-hand, New Labour exponents from the late 1990s started to speak of all public service providers (but never private ones) as 'producer interests'. Yet modes of provision are far from being mere technical matters. The conver-sion of citizens into consumers represents a major shift in social democratic thinking and different modes of provision do privilege some groups against others. They allow governments at different levels to frame social need differ-ently, to go for universalism or selectivity and to devise their own definitions of the deserving poor. Colin Crouch's chapter in this volume demonstrates the deep implications of all this. There is a strong territorial dimension as differ-ences in modes of public service delivery represent one of the most important forms of policy divergence at the emerging regional level in European states. The differences between England and Scotland are now as great as those normally found between different welfare states, and they promise to become greater. Scotland has free medical prescriptions; no university fees; a unified health service with no internal market and no private provision in the public sector; comprehensive education; and 'free' personal care for the elderly. Whether or not all of these are justifiable on redistributive grounds, they do represent a different and more traditional model of social democracy from that pursued by Labour in England.

Urban planning and economic development can impact unevenly on differ-ent sections of the population. Economic development is often postulated as a consensus policy from which everyone within the city or region will benefit, but any given policy will have a differential effect on different social groups and neighbourhoods. There are trade-offs to be made between economic development, social cohesion and environmental considerations. Economic development coalitions including trade unions and social democratic local governments have thus found themselves in conflict with social movements concerned with environmental, neighbourhood and social issues. The sub-state territory, whether stateless nation, region or city, is thus inescapably an arena for social contestation and compromise.

Of course, such a rescaling of welfare and the emergence of local welfare settlements means that individuals will be treated differently according to where they live within the state, as devolved governments make different policy choices. This is an anomaly and an injustice to those who see social citizenship as working only at the level of the whole state but not above or below it. Such a view, however, is difficult to sustain either on the grounds of normative universalism (which would point to global equity) or on the grounds of communitaristic solidarity (which could operate at various levels). It is another example of the statist blindness that still affects large areas of social science.

This still leaves the question of inter-territorial solidarity. Territorial equity is an inchoate concept, which has a complex relationship with individual-level equity (Heald 1983), but it has now been incorporated by the EU in the Lisbon Treaty in the form of 'territorial cohesion'. Social democrats, on the other hand, have tended to favour interpersonal equity as the criterion of justice. Clearly, taken to their logical extremes the two principles are incompatible, but social democracy has never been about achieving absolute equality on either dimension. There may be different policy lines in different places about the emphasis on equity and, particularly, how to define and achieve it.[4] There might be an emphasis on different target groups or on defining what used to be known as the 'deserving poor'. These are legitimate bases for differentiation in so far as they reflect local democratic decisions. They are to be distinguished from (although often confused with) the 'postcode lottery', which correctly refers to arbitrary difference in access to public services within centralised systems. Such differences may be compatible with overall solidarity if there is a system of equalisation to ensure that all regions have comparable revenue bases for the provision of public services. There also need to be systems of regulation such as do exist at state and European levels to restrain territorial fiscal competition and the race to the bottom.

## Political community

Social democrats in the early twentieth century were caught in the competing claims of cosmopolitan universalism, stateless nations and regions, and the consolidating nation-state. As the central empires collapsed into nation-states after the First World War, bringing down with them ideas of plurinational social democracy, it was the patriotic left that prevailed. Social democracy was tied to a conception of political community rooted in the unitary nation-state.[5] Self-determination and the creation of new political communities were regarded as progressive only in the context of colonial liberation. The twenty-first century, however, has seen the assertion of new claims for political community, both above and below the state. One is at the European level, a matter dealt with by Yves Mény in this volume. Another is represented by the revival of sub-state nationalism, and minority politics have posed challenges and raised competitors to social democracy in both Western and East Central Europe.

Minority nationalisms come in all ideological colours from extreme right to extreme left. Some are associated with racism and xenophobia or based on ascriptive forms of ethnic identity, forming part of the European populist right; examples are in the Vlaams Belang and the Lega Nord. Others, however, have presented themselves as civic and inclusive, appealing to all who reside in the relevant territory. In this they imitate the civic state nationalism that underpins the patriotic left itself. Indeed, sometimes they are social democratic, seeking to reconstitute a space of solidarity in the face of neo-liberal dominance at the state level; Scotland would be an example. They can also be strongly pro-European.

This multinational challenge should be distinguished from the multicultural challenge, which is about how different ways of life can be accommodated within a liberal and secular (or at least religiously neutral) state. Paradoxically, the more inclusive civic nationalisms may in some ways pose more of a challenge to state-wide understandings of political community since they are competing on the same normative ground, appealing to the same values, but are seeking to reconfigure the boundaries of political community, and with it social solidarity and recognition. Indeed, along with European integration, they are showing up the arbitrary nature of the nation-state level, previously unquestioned as the legitimate frame for social solidarity.

A second site of challenge to the statist view of political community is the city. This is the site of distinct social struggles, which do not always follow the class contours of state-wide contestation. It is a potential arena for social inclusion, solidarity and new understandings of citizenship. It is also the location of intercultural exchange and the reception of new immigrants. A conception of urban citizenship may be another way of asserting equality and negotiating the balance between unity and diversity. Proposals for giving non-citizens a local government franchise in some countries are evidence that local citizenship can be detached from the national frame. This terrain, however, has often been abandoned to social movements which are no longer part of the social democratic family, although, as Colin Crouch notes, they can potentially be important elements in the recreation of social democracy as practice.

Yet social democrats in many states have been drawn back into state nationalism on civic-republican or patriotic left lines as a way of asserting a common public space and common values. This is mostly a reaction to the multicultural challenge but also responds to citizen feelings of powerlessness in the face of globalisation and the lack of democracy within European institutions. The ideological tangles into which this can lead social democracy are exposed by the Labour Party's Britishness debate, in which Britishness was essentialised in all kinds of strange ways (Keating 2009b). It also promises yet more frustration since the centralised nation-state is no longer capable of meeting the new challenges of economic change and social cohesion.

## Multilevel social democracy

Social democracy has often been tied to the sovereign nation-state as the vehicle of change, but in many ways this is paradoxical, since social democrats did not invent the nation-state and early social democracy was often hostile to it. In some strands of social democracy there is the realisation that it would be futile to try and recreate the structures of the nation-state by reproducing them at the European level, or by breaking existing states up into separate entities. Accepting the deeper implications of divided and shared sovereignty, however, has been harder.

Social democratic parties have widely embraced the idea of decentralisa-tion as part of their ideological and policy portfolio. In government they have often been the ones to pursue decentralisation, although their zeal has tended to diminish with their years in office. Yet they retain strong centralist elements, presenting a constant tension in France, where decentralisation was launched by the Socialists in 1981 but progressed haltingly; and in Italy, where the main centre-left party proclaims federalism but mostly interprets it in a narrow, administrative way. In Germany, social democrats have faced both ways on federal reform, often depending on where they come from. The Labour Party in Britain launched devolution for Scotland and Wales and then, if Tony Blair is to be believed, regretted it; they were torn two ways on English regional reform. Spanish socialists are divided on the autonomy issue. There is a long way to go for social democrats to reconcile themselves to multilevel politics, institutions and policy.

They also have difficulty in accepting the idea of a balance of powers inher-ent in federal systems of government. This means that governments do not always get their own way and that policy often has to be negotiated across the territorial divide. This is an idea that social democrats have found it easy to accept when in national opposition but less easy to translate in government or to give a hard institutional expression. This extends also to policy divergence. There are differing models of social democracy and multiple ways of running public services.

Competitive regionalism does indeed pose a danger of a race to the bottom but there are equally possibilities of a race to the top, depending on how local and regional policy systems are constructed. The relationship between the market and society is mediated at multiple levels, not just that of the state. Since the 1990s, there has been a revival of social concertation in some European countries, as a way of facing global competition; Martin Rhodes (2001) has described this as 'competitive corporatism'. In the face of functional restructuring and political devolution, there is evidence that representative groups for capital, labour and social causes are also restructuring and engaging in policy-making at multiple levels (Keating and Wilson 2010). There is less evidence of social compromises being struck at the regional and local level, or of meso-level concertation. Business groups try to avoid entanglement in local and regional networks except in so far as they serve the development agenda. Trade unions are weakened everywhere and are still oriented primarily to the workplace and to national government. Partnership thus tends to be defined as public-private cooperation in development operations rather than broader forms of social compromise. The theme of inter-territorial competition is used to subordinate wider questions to a single economic imperative. Economic development itself is defined in rather narrow terms. If we see cities and regions as political arenas, however, such conceptions can be challenged and questions about the quality and distributive impact, as well as just the quantity of growth, can be raised. This requires that sub-state spaces be politicised, pointing to political decentralisation and not merely administrative de-concentration, special-purpose agencies or public-private partnerships; to local and regional government rather than business- or state-dominated 'governance' regimes.

Diversity can lead to innovation and, given the right conditions, policy learning and a race to the top. Minimum income policies ('the minimum income of insertion') in France and Spain were pioneered at local and regional level before spreading across the state as a whole. Scotland's system of paying for care for the elderly (misleadingly described as 'free') has posed a constant challenge in England. After years attempting to discredit the Scottish system (invariably described as 'unaffordable'), policy-makers in London had, by the 2010 election, come round to the view that something had to be done for England. This does not mean that policies can simply be borrowed or transposed wholesale. Rather, social democrats should learn to appreciate how policies can develop under local conditions and be applied appropriately.

There is an emerging territorial component to political and social citizenship which challenges state-bound conceptions of solidarity but which could equally provide new ways for social democracy to advance. Stateless nations, regions and cities are sites for social struggles and the redefinition of social relations, and provide the basis for renewed forms of solidarity which are not necessarily less broad or more exclusive than those at state level. In this way, the politics of solidarity and of community can be reclaimed from populist and right movements that have used them for their own purposes.

Some observers continue to argue that social democracy is incompatible with decentralisation, and that the unitary nation-state is its necessary vehicle (Walker 2002). Yet the strong and unitary nation-state represented a moment in history that has largely passed, if it ever really existed outside the Nordic area. Social democracy has always been a complex ideology and set of practices. Class politics is one reference point, but there have been multiple cleavages that it has also addressed. It has continually faced the challenge of reconciling ideas of civic, social and economic equality with the recognition of diversity. Social democracy was always about making compromises and trade-offs, notably between the market and politics, and seeking to make these serve positive-sum rather than negative outcomes. Social democrats face new dilemmas in the context of spatial rescaling, increasing social complexity and territorial assertion and there is no simple or definitive way of resolving them. The classic policy choices arise at all levels and cannot be subordinated to any determinist logic.

Social democracy has enlarged its vision to encompass various forms of social pluralism, taking on board feminism, multiculturalism and life-style choices to a greater or lesser extent in various countries. These can all be presented as aspects of liberation and self-determination not inconsistent with social democratic values, although questioning older understandings of civil equality. Similarly, social democracy is often renewing itself in distinct ways from the bottom, reconnecting with civil society and local struggles and social movements.

## Notes

1. It has become better known in the English-speaking world from the rather far-fetched formulation of Michael Hechter (1975).
2. In Britain, there was a lot of talk about improving the 'calibre' of local councillors and bringing back local business people as well as a great deal of managerialism.
3. To be absolutely clear, I should note that I did not use the term 'sub-national' in the article in question.
4. In passing, we should beware of the trap of saying that this is because local communities 'prefer' more or less equality. It will reflect the balance of electoral opinion and the institutional configuration of the region or city, which presents particular policy choices.
5. Even in federal Germany, social democrats have rather consistently favoured a unitary reading of the constitution.

# CONCLUSION

Michael Keating and David McCrone

> Two forms of social order died in our big Europe during the years after about 1980: the Communist system embedded in the fifty-year continental order of the Cold War, but also the regulated, social democratic welfare order developed in the nations of Western Europe after 1945. One of these deaths should gladden the soul. But the second should trouble it. (Ascherson 2012: 17)

Is social democracy dead? Or, rather, as Neal Ascherson formulates it, is 'the regulated, social democratic welfare order' dead? Readers will possibly have reached their own conclusion, as well as their assessment as to whether it is the more troubling death, if death it is. Our own view is that it is possibly more complicated than that, dependent, as it is, on what we mean by 'social democracy' and, crucially, the health or otherwise of its political carriers. History should make us wary of jumping to a conclusion. In this concluding chapter, we will focus on the following key issues: the extent to which social democracy is tied to the changing fortunes of eponymous political parties; what might account for the relative decline in party electoral fortunes; the extent to which social democracy is defined by its social programme, or whether it is more akin to a philosophy or ideology; and finally its prognosis in the post-2008 'crisis of capitalism'.

It is easy to fall into the trap of assuming that social democracy is time-bound, and in particular was inextricably linked to *Trente Glorieuses*. After all, with the exception of the Nordic countries – and even there it was not straightforward – social democratic parties were more out of government than in. Yet social democratic ideas on social welfare and management of the economy were pervasive, and widely shared by Christian democrats, conservatives and progressive liberals. These include state ownership; a commitment to the redistribution of income and wealth; social welfare and social security;

economic Keynesianism; labour and employment law; equality of educational opportunities; and, later on, multiculturalism and 'diversity'; gender equality; environmentalism. In the 1990s, on the other hand, social democratic parties were in power across much of Europe but social democratic ideas were in retreat. We therefore need to distinguish between the fate and the future of social democratic parties of the familiar type, and social democracy as a broader project.

There is no shortage of accounts seeking to explain the decline of social democratic parties (for example, Cronin et al. 2011; Meyer and Rutherford 2012). Most of these focus on 'supply side' factors such as that electorates no longer find such parties attractive. Thus, the changing shape of the class structure, and in particular the relative decline of an organised manual working class, might seem an obvious factor in eroding support for social democratic parties. The problem with that explanation is that there never was a strong and straightforward association between class and politics in most Western democracies. There were too many regional and cultural (notably religious) variations in play to make that possible. In any case, the heyday of *Trente Glorieuses* was one in which organised labour did not vote straightforwardly for the centre-left. Neither does the 'end of class' thesis square with rising levels of social inequalities in many Western democracies. Social class may have changed its shape but it has not disappeared. In any case, social democracy in practice was based on a variety of social forces, differing from one country to another.

The second, and related, explanation for social democratic electoral decline focuses on changing attitudes and values. The electorate has supposedly become less solidaristic, more individualistic and 'right-wing'. This is more easily asserted than proven. In the UK, for example, the success of Mrs Thatcher's Conservatives was in spite of, rather than because of, the steadfastly centrist, even social democratic, views of the electorate (Heath et al. 1994, 2001). Much more had to do with the perceived economic competence, or lack of it, of contending parties, and far less with supposed 'post-materialist values' (Inglehart 1990) generated among electorates.

Finally, there are explanations based in the hegemony of 'globalisation' and globalised markets, with their particular impacts on the role of the state (see, for example, Cronin et al. 2011: 7). Such explanations seem to us to explain too much as well as too little to account for the changing fortunes of Western European social democratic parties. Much depends on how individual states decide to address global issues, and the contrasts between 'Anglo-American' and continental European are too great to be explained by a single set of processes.

So there seems to us too much variation in the success and failure of social democratic parties in Western Europe to give credence to any straightforward explanation by 'supply side' factors. Nor can we claim that the demand for social democracy has disappeared, as seemed likely a few years ago, given the continued existence of social inequality and deprivation.

Perhaps social democracy should be seen as a philosophy rather than a set of parties, a narrative, a *projet* which sits comfortably and naturally on the centre-left. It does not cease to be 'social democratic' if certain elements are missing and can adapt over time. Pre-eminently, social democracy implies a commitment to social equality, or at least reducing inequalities of life chances; of opportunities rather than outcomes. Once more, flatter systems of social inequality as in the Nordic countries are a condition for, as well as a creation of, social democracy. The sentiment that one can be 'intensely relaxed about people getting filthy rich as long as they pay their taxes', as the New Labour politician Peter Mandelson commented in 1998, is not one which sits easily in a social democratic politics.[1]

Social democracy also rejects the idea that greater equality necessarily comes at the expense of economic performance or, indeed, that the economic and social spheres can so easily be distinguished. The chapters in this volume by Rhodes, Crouch, and Hilpert and Hickie show that social democracy is, and must be, both a social and an economic project, an idea that seems to have been lost some time in the 1990s. The commitment to social justice while improving life chances and economic performance in social democracies leads to an emphasis on the role of education and training, both instrumentally and as a feature of the good society. Western societies (most successfully in the Nordic countries and in Germany) can only hope to compete if they have well-educated and skilled labour forces. They will lose if they enter a race to the bottom. Universalism plays a role here, in binding everyone into the project and creating a virtuous circle of improved economic performance and social cohesion, as the chapters on the Nordic cases demonstrate.

Social democracy has historically assigned an important role to the state as an agent of social change. This need not, indeed does not, imply state ownership of the means of production so much as an interventionist role in managing capitalism, setting the ground rules, managing the framework. Social democratic belief in the benign potential of the state has too easily been caricatured as paternalistic, inefficient and expensive, but the disasters of unregulated markets in recent years, not to mention the growth of unaccountable corporate power (as noted by Crouch), now show the state in a better light and remind us of the need for proper regulation, the latter concern shared also by thoughtful conservatives and liberals.

One weakness in traditional social democracy has been the assumption that the state necessarily equals the 'nation-state'. As Keynesianism in one state becomes impossible, social democrats have looked to Europe for the creation of a regulated market, but, as Mény shows, the European Union we have contains a structural bias in favour of market competition and its expansion into areas formerly considered the realm of social policy. The entrenchment of monetarist doctrine in successive stability and fiscal pacts is exacerbating this problem, while European social democratic parties fail to come together to address it. The distancing of Nordic and British social democrats from the core European project merely weakens social democracy as a whole. Similarly, social democrats have yet to address the rescaling of public policy below the nation-state and the challenges of multiculturalism, as noted by Keating and by Meret and Siim. There is as yet little willingness to accept and develop difference and divergence across the state in benefits and life-style outcomes. Social democracy's struggles in dealing with 'multiculturalism' and diversity (see Meret and Siim) have allowed it sometimes to be outflanked by the extreme right in competing for working-class votes.

Of course, the state, at whatever level, is not and cannot be the only vehicle for social democracy. Growing an active and rich civil society between 'state' and 'market' is more likely to guarantee not only personal liberty but also social justice. A concern with the quality of life extends social democracy into the realm of environmental politics, and makes it a more congenial bedfellow for green politics and parties. Not for nothing is it more common to find electoral alliances, formal and informal, between social democrats (rather than centre-right parties) and greens. Social democracy is predicated on the idea of a public domain that is not reducible to the market or to the state and a broader public interest not reducible to the sum of individual interests. This takes us into Milner's concept of civic literacy, based on an understanding that our own interests are often also the common ones (which is not to deny that there are also differences of interest). Given the decline of political parties as vehicles for public education and mass mobilisation, it may be, as Crouch argues, that new social movements in civil society will play the larger role here.

What is the prognosis for social democracy in the second decade of the twenty-first century? Sassoon shows that economic crises in capitalism do not automatically work to the benefit of social democracy. Social democrats have had to make and seize opportunities, forging new policies to update their core values and forging social alliances, at one time with advanced liberals and later with greens, feminists, new leftists and territorial movements. Where, as in the UK, the electoral line was crossed such that social democracy gave way to social liberalism, the centre-left lost power. Where, as in the Nordic countries, social democrats tried to reconcile social justice, individual liberty and economic efficiency (Pierson 2001), they were much more electorally successful, if nowhere near the levels reached in the post-war period. What we have is a variety of social democratic models rather than a single one. As Alfred Pfaller pointed out, 'ultimately, it is social democracy that matters, not Social Democracy' (Pfaller 2009: 20).

The post-2008 crisis of capitalism, brought on by the banking crisis, provides the context and challenge for social democracy. What Colin Crouch has called 'the strange non-death of neoliberalism' (2011) signals that the return of social democracy is by no means certain. It remains to be seen how the reaction to 'austerity politics' in Western Europe will express itself, for shifts to the radical right or left are possible, as well as government from the centre. The challenge for social democracy is to be a key part of Europe's future rather than an episode of its history.

## Note

1. Out of office in 2012, Mandelson subsequently described his remarks as 'spontaneous and unthoughtful' (<http://www.guardian.co.uk/politics/2012/jan/26/mandelson-people-getting-filthy-rich> (last accessed 6 March 2013)), but the comment came to stand for New Labour's break with its social democratic past.

# BIBLIOGRAPHY

Abel, J., and R. R. Deitz (2009), *Do Colleges and Universities Increase their Region's Human Capital?*, New York: Federal Reserve Bank of New York.

Abendroth, W. (1972), *A Short History of the European Working Class*, London: New Left Books.

Åberg, R. (1989), 'Distributive mechanisms of the welfare state – a formal analysis and an empirical application', *European Sociological Review*, 5 (2), pp. 188–214.

Abraham, D. (1985), 'Labor's way: On the successes and limits of socialist parties in interwar and post-World War II Germany', *International Labor and Working-Class History*, 28, pp. 1–24.

Ackers, L. (2005), 'Moving people and knowledge: Scientific mobility in the European Union', *International Migration*, 43 (5), pp. 99–131.

Adema, W., P. Fron and M. Ladaique (2011), 'Is the European welfare state really more expensive? Indicators on social spending, 1980–2012', *OECD Social, Employment and Migration Working Papers 124*, Paris: OECD.

AFP/The Swedish Wire (2011), 'Sweden's economy "strong as Pippi Longstocking"', *The Swedish Wire*, 20 January 2011, <http://www.swedishwire.com/economy/8170-swedens-economy-strong-as-pippi-longstocking> (last accessed 11 March 2013).

Akkerman, T. (2012), 'Comparing radical right parties in government: Immigration and integration policies in nine countries (1996–2010)', *West European Politics*, 35 (3), pp. 511–29.

Alber, J. (2006), 'Das "europäische Sozialmodell" und die USA', *Leviathan – Berliner Zeitschrift für Sozialwissenschaft*, 2, pp. 207–40.

Albrekt Larsen, C. (2011), 'Ethnic heterogeneity and public support for welfare', *Scandinavian Political Studies*, 34 (4), pp. 332–53.

Albrekt Larsen, C., and E. Thomas Dejgaard (2012), 'The institutional logic of images of the poor and welfare recipients: A comparative study of British, Swedish and

Danish newspapers', *CCWS Working Papers 78*, Aalborg: Centre for Comparative Welfare Studies.

Andersen, J. G. (2004), 'Danmark: Fremskridtspartiet og Dansk Folkeparti', in J. Rydgren and A. Widfeldt (eds), *Från Le Pen till Pim Fortuyn – Populism och Parlamentarisk Högerextremism i Dagens Europa*, Malmo: Liber, pp. 147–70.

Andersen, J. G., and T. Bjørklund (2000), 'Radical right-wing populism in Scandinavia: From tax revolt to neo-liberalism', in P. Hainsworth (ed.), *The Politics of the Extreme Right: From the Margins to the Mainstream*, London: Pinter, pp. 193–223.

Anderson, C. J., and P. Beramendi (2012), 'Left parties, poor voters, and electoral participation in advanced industrial societies', *Comparative Political Studies*, 45 (6), pp. 714–46.

Andersson, J. (2009), *The Library and the Workshop: Social Democracy and Capitalism in an Age of Knowledge*, Stanford: Stanford University Press.

Arter, D., and A. Widfeldt (2010), 'What sort of semi-Presidentialism do Finns want? An intra-systemic comparative analysis', *West European Politics*, 33 (6), pp. 1,278–98.

Ascherson, N. (2012), 'Memories of Amikejo', *London Review of Books*, 34 (6), p. 17.

Azmanova, A. (2004), 'The mobilisation of the European left in the early 21st century', *Archives Européennes de Sociologie*, 45 (3), pp. 273–306.

Bairoch, P. (1993), *Economics and World History*, New York and London: Harvester.

Bairoch, P. (1997), *Victoires et déboires: histoire économique et sociale du monde du XVIe siècle à nos jours*, vol. 2, Paris: Gallimard Folio.

Balogh, E. S. (2012), 'The latest polls: Fidesz is losing but MSzP is not gaining', *Hungarian Spectrum*, 17 May 2012.

Balogová, B. (2010), 'Slovak parliament passes austerity budget', *Prague Post*, 15 December 2010.

Banting, K., R. Johnston, W. Kymlicka and S. Soroka (2006), 'Do multicultural policies erode the welfare state?', in K. Banting and W. Kymlicka (eds), *Multiculturalism and the Welfare State*, Oxford: Oxford University Press, pp. 49–91.

Banting, K., and W. Kymlicka (2006), 'Introduction', in K. Banting and W. Kymlicka (eds), *Multiculturalism and the Welfare State*, Oxford: Oxford University Press, pp. 1–45.

Barbier, J.-C. (2011), *SSGIs: A Cross-National Perspective and the French Case*, unpublished report, European Union FP7 Project GUSTO.

Barnard, C. (2010), 'Solidarity and the Commission's "Renewed Social Agenda"', in M. Ross and Y. Borgmann-Prebil (eds), *Promoting Solidarity in the European Union*, Oxford: Oxford University Press, pp. 73–106.

Barr, N. (1992), 'Economic theory and the welfare state: A survey and interpretation', *Journal of Economic Literature*, 30, pp. 741–803.

Barr, N. (2004), *The Economics of the Welfare State*, 4th edn, Oxford: Oxford University Press.

Bartolini, S. (2005), *Restructuring Europe*, Oxford: Oxford University Press.

Bauman, Z. (1982), *Memories of Class: The Pre-History and After-Life of Class*, London: Routledge & Kegan Paul.

Bayley, D. (1990), *Patterns of Policing: A Comparative International Analysis*, New Brunswick, NJ: Rutgers University Press.

Beck, U. (1992), *Risk Society: Towards a New Modernity*, London: Sage.

Béland, D., and A. Lecours (2008), *Nationalism and Social Policy: The Politics of Territorial Solidarity*, Oxford: Oxford University Press.

Bercovitz, J., and M. Feldman (2006), 'Entrepreneurial universities and technology transfer: A conceptual framework for understanding knowledge-based economic development', *Journal of Technology Transfer*, 31, pp. 175–88.

Bergh, A. (2006), 'Is the Swedish welfare state a free lunch?', *Economic Journal Watch*, 3 (2), pp. 210–35.

Bergh, A., and G. O. Erlingsson (2009), 'Liberalizing without retrenchment: Understanding the consensus on Swedish welfare state reforms', *Scandinavian Political Studies*, 32 (1), pp. 71–93.

Bergqvist, C., A. Borchorst, A.-D. Christensen, V. Ramstedt-Silén, N. C. Raaum and A. Styrkásdóttir (eds) (1999), *Equal Democracies? Gender and Politics in the Nordic Countries*, Oslo: Scandinavian University Press.

Bergström, O. (2009), *Anticipating and Managing Restructuring Sweden*, European Commission, Directorate-General for Employment, Social Affairs and Equal Opportunities.

Berman, S. (2006), *The Primacy of Politics: Social Democracy and the Making of Europe's Twentieth Century*, New York: Cambridge University Press.

Berry, C., and E. Glaeser (2005), 'The divergence of human capital levels across cities', *NBER Working Paper Series*, Cambridge: National Bureau of Economic Research.

Betz, H.-G. (1994), *Radical Right-Wing Populism in Western Europe*, Basingstoke: Palgrave Macmillan.

Betz, H.-G., and S. Meret (2012), 'Right-wing populist parties and the working class vote: What have you done for us lately?', in J. Rydgren (ed.), *Class Politics and the Radical Right*, London: Routledge, pp. 107–21.

Bigo, D. (2002), 'Security and immigration: Towards a critique of the governmentality of unease', *Alternatives*, 27, pp. 63–92.

Björklund, A. (ed.) (2005), *The Market Comes to Education in Sweden: An Evaluation of Sweden's Surprising School Reforms*, New York: Russell Sage Foundation.

Bjørklund, T. (2009), 'To mål på arbeiderklasse: Yrke og klassetilhørighet Norske velgere og partier fra 1965 til 2005', *Norsk Statsvitenskapelig Tidsskrift*, 1, pp. 5–30.

Bjørklund, T. (2011), 'The radical right in Norway: The development of the Progress Party', in N. Lagenbacher and B. Schellenberg (eds), *Is Europe on the 'Right' Path?*, Berlin: Friedrich Ebert Stiftung, pp. 271–94.

Blair, M. (2011), 'An economic perspective on the notion of "human capital"', in A. Burton-Jones and J.-C. Spender (eds), *The Oxford Handbook of Human Capital*, Oxford: Oxford University Press, pp. 49–70.

Blinkhorn, M. (ed.) (1990), *Fascists and Conservatives: The Radical Right and the Establishment in Twentieth Century Europe*, London: Unwin Hyman.

Block, F. (2011), 'Innovation and the invisible hand of government', in F. Block and M. Keller (eds), *State of Innovation: The U.S. Government's Role in Technology Development*, Boulder, CO: Paradigm, pp. 1–40.

Block, F., and M. Keller (2009), 'Where do innovations come from? Transformations in the US economy, 1970–2006', *Socio-Economic Review*, 7 (3), pp. 459–83.

Boeri, T. (2009), 'What happened to European unemployment?', *De Economist*, 157 (2), pp. 215–28.

Bonoli, G. (2007), 'Time matters: Postindustrialization, new social risks, and welfare state adaptation in advanced industrial democracies', *Comparative Political Studies*, 40 (5), pp. 495–520.

Bonoli, G. (2012), 'Active labour market policy and social investment: A changing relationship', in N. Morel, B. Palier and J. Palme (eds), *What Future for Social Investment?*, Stockholm: Institute for Futures Studies, pp. 181–204.

Booth, C. (1903), *Life and Labour of the People of London*, vol. 1, London: Macmillan.

Borchardt, K. (1991), *Perspectives on Modern German Economic History*, trans. P. Lambert, Cambridge: Cambridge University Press.

Borchorst, A., and B. Siim (2008), 'The women-friendly policies and state feminism', *Feminist Theory*, 9, pp. 185–207.

Borevi, K. (2010a), 'Dimensions of citizenship: European integration policies from a Scandinavian perspective', in P. S. Bengtsson and A.-H. Bay (eds), *Diversity, Inclusion and Citizenship in Scandinavia*, Newcastle: Cambridge Scholars Publishing, pp. 19–46.

Borevi, K. (2010b), 'Sverige: Mångkulturalismens fagskepp I Norden', in G. Brochmann and A. Hagelund (eds), *Velferdens grenser*, Oslo: Universitetsforlaget, pp. 41–130.

Bornschier, S. (2010), *Cleavage Politics and the Populist Right: The New Cultural Conflict in Western Europe*, Philadelphia: Temple University Press.

Bozóki, A., and J. T. Ishiyama (eds) (2002), *The Communist Successor Parties of Central and Eastern Europe*, Armonk, NY: M.E. Sharpe.

Bräutigam, D., O. H. Fjeldstad and M. Moore (2008), *Taxation and State-Building in Developing Countries: Capacity and Consent*, Cambridge: Cambridge University Press.

Breidahl, K. N. (2012), 'Når staten lærer: En historisk og komparativ analyse af statslig policy læring og betydningen heraf for udviklingen i den arbejdsmarkedsrettede del af indvandrerpolitikken i Sverige, Norge og Danmark fra 1970 til 2011', PhD dissertation, Institute of Political Science, Aalborg University.

Brochmann, G., and A. Hagelund (2010), *Velferdens grenser, Del 1: Velfærdsstat, Nasjon og Innvandring, og Del 5: En model med tre unntak?*, Oslo: Universitetsforlaget.

Brooks, D. (2005), 'Fear and rejection', *New York Times*, 2 June 2005.

Bryson, A., and J. Forth (2010), 'Trade union membership and influence 1999–2009', NIESR Discussion Paper 362.

Buckley, N., C. Bryant and K. Eddy (2011), 'Orban drags Hungary through rapid change', *Financial Times*, 7 February 2011.

Campbell, D. (2012), 'Interview – Gabriel Scally: A systematic destruction of civil society', *The Guardian*, 4 July 2012.

Cantillon, B. (2011), 'The paradox of the social investment state: Growth, employment and poverty in the Lisbon era', *Journal of European Social Policy*, 21 (5), pp. 432–49.

Caramani, D., and Y. Mény (eds) (2005), *Challenges to Consensual Politics: Democracy, Identity and Populist Protest in the Alpine Region*, Brussels: Presses interuniversitaires européennes/Peter Lang.

Ceka, B. (2012), 'The perils of political competition: Explaining participation and trust in political parties in Eastern Europe', *Comparative Political Studies*, <http://cps.sagepub.com/content/early/2012/11/22/0010414012463908.full> (last accessed 12 March 2013).

Clark, T. (2012), 'Poor policies that refuse to die', *The Guardian*, 18 April 2012.

Clarke, K. (2011), Speech to Prison Reform Trust, Annual General Meeting minutes 2011.

Cook, L. J., and M. A. Orenstein (1999), 'The return of the left and its impact on the welfare state in Russia, Poland, and Hungary', in L. J. Cook, M. A. Orenstein and M. Rueschemeyer (eds), *Left Parties and Social Policy in Postcommunist Europe*, Boulder, CO: Westview Press, pp. 47–108.

Crawford, A. (2008), 'Plural policing in the UK: Policing beyond the police', in T. Newburn (ed.), *Handbook of Policing*, 2nd edn, Cullompton: Willan, pp. 147–81.

Cronin, J., G. Ross and J. Schoch (eds) (2011), *What's Left of the Left: Democrats and Social Democrats in Challenging Times*, Durham, NC and London: Duke University Press.

Crosland, C. A. R. (1956), *The Future of Socialism*, London: Jonathan Cape.

Crouch, C. (1981), 'The place of public expenditure in socialist thought', in D. Lipsey and R. L. Leonard (eds), *The Socialist Agenda: Crosland's Legacy*, London: Jonathan Cape, pp. 156–85.

Crouch, C. (1999), 'Ottimisti e pessimisti nel dibattito del mercato di lavoro', *Stato e Mercato*, 2, pp. 243–8.

Crouch, C. (2011), *The Strange Non-Death of Neoliberalism*, Cambridge: Polity Press.

Crouch, C. (2013), 'Class relations and labour market reforms', in M. Keune and A. Serrano (eds), *Deconstructing Flexicurity: Alternative Perspectives*, London: Routledge.

Crouch, C., P. Le Galès, C. Trigilia and H. Voelzkow (2001), *Local Production Systems in Europe: Rise or Demise?*, Oxford: Oxford University Press.

Cruddas, J. (2009), *The Future of Social Democracy*, London: Compass.

Cunningham, W. (1891), 'Nationalism and cosmopolitanism in economics', *Journal of the Royal Statistical Society*, 54 (4), pp. 644–62.

Cuperus, R. (2010), 'No power, no morale? A Dutch commentary on the SPD blues', in J. N. Engels and G. Maaß (eds) *The View from Europe: Analysis of the Crisis of Social Democracy after the German Federal Elections*, Berlin: Friedrich Ebert Stiftung, pp. 19–25.

Dahlby, B. (2008), *The Marginal Cost of Public Funds: Theory and Applications*, Cambridge, MA: MIT Press.

Dahlström, C. (2004), 'Rhetoric, practice and the dynamics of institutional change: Immigrant policy in Sweden, 1964–2000', *Scandinavian Political Studies*, 27 (3), pp. 287–310.

Dalla Vecchia, G. (1898), 'The Revolt in Italy', *The Contemporary Review*, 74, pp. 113–20.

Dansk Folkepartis Folketingsgruppe (2001), *Danmarks fremtid – dit land, dit valg*, Copenhagen: Broløs Grafisk Form og Tryk ApS.

Deegan-Krause, K. (2010), '2010 Slovak parliamentary elections: Post-election report', *Pozor Blog*, 14 July 2010, <http://www.pozorblog.com/2010/07/2010-slovak-parliamentary-elections-post-election-report> (last accessed 12 March 2013).

Deegan-Krause, K., and T. Haughton (2009), 'Toward a more useful conceptualization of populism: Types and degrees of populist appeals in the case of Slovakia', *Politics & Policy*, 37 (4), pp. 821–41.

Deegan-Krause, K., and T. Haughton (2012), '2012 parliamentary elections in Slovakia: The building blocks of success', *Pozor Blog*, 14 March 2012, <http://www.pozor blog.com/2012/03/2012-parliamentary-elections-in-slovakia-the-building-blocs-of-success> (last accessed 12 March 2013).

Della Porta, D. (2003), *I new global*, Bologna: Il Mulino.

Della Porta, D., and H. Reiter (2003), *Polizia e protesta*, Bologna: Il Mulino.

De Los Reyes, P., I. Molina and D. Mulinari (2003), *Maktens olika förklädnadar: Kømn, klasse og etnicitet i det post-koloniale Sverige*, Stockholm: Atlas.

Derthick, M. (1979), *Making Policy for Social Security*, Washington, DC: The Brookings Institution.

De Witte, B. (2009), 'The rules of change in the European Union – the lost balance between rigidity and flexibility', in C. Moury and L. de Sousa (eds), *Institutional Challenges in Post-Constitutional Europe: Governing Change*, Abingdon: Routledge, pp. 33–42.

Dickinson, S., D. Thompson, M. Prabhakar, J. Hurstfield and C. Doel (2008), 'Migrant workers: Economic issues and opportunities', *Viewpoint Series*, 2, SQW Consulting.

Dilnot, A. (Chair) (2011), *Fairer Care Funding: The Report of the Commission on Funding of Care and Support*, London: Department of Health.

Dinesen, P. T. (2011a), 'When in Rome, do as the Romans do: An analysis of the acculturation of generalized trust of non-western immigrants in western Europe', dissertation, Aarhus University.

Dinesen, P. T. (2011b), 'Where you come from or where you live? Examining the cultural and institutional explanation of generalized trust using migration as a natural experiment', *European Sociological Review*, 6 (4), pp. 1–15.

Dorling, D. (2012), 'Fairness and the changing fortunes of people in Britain

1970–2012', Beveridge Memorial Lecture to the Royal Statistical Society, 27 June 2012.

Duggan, C. (2002), *Francesco Crispi: From Nation to Nationalism*, Oxford: Oxford University Press.

Dujisin, Z. (2010), 'Hungary: Austerity fatigue sends IMF home', Inter Press Service News Agency, 2 August 2010, <http://www.ipsnews.net/2010/08/hungary-auster ity-fatigue-sends-imf-home> (last accessed 12 March 2013).

Duncan, F. (2006), 'A decade of Christian Democratic decline: The dilemmas of the CDU, ÖVP and CDA in the 1990s', *Government and Opposition*, 41 (4), pp. 469–90.

Eaves, E. (2006), 'The "let us eat cake" generation', *Foreign Policy*, online special, 4 April 2006, <http://www.foreignpolicy.com/articles/2006/04/03/the_lsquolet_us_ eat_cake_generation> (last accessed 15 March 2013).

*Economist, The* (2001), 'Is government disappearing?', *The Economist*, 19 September 2001.

Edwards, C., and V. de Rugy (2002), 'International tax competition', in J. Gwartney and R. Lawson, *Economic Freedom around the World: Annual Report 2002*, Vancouver: Fraser Institute, pp. 43–58.

Elchardus, M., and B. Spruyt (2012), 'The contemporary contradictions of egalitarianism: An empirical analysis of the relationship between the old and new left/right alignments', *European Political Science Review*, 4 (2), pp. 217–39.

Emerek, R., and M. Bak Jørgensen (2009), *Network on Socio-Economic Experts in the Non-Discrimination Field, Country Report 1: Denmark*, unpublished.

Emmenegger, P. (2010), 'The long road to flexicurity: The development of job security regulations in Denmark and Sweden', *Scandinavian Political Studies*, 33 (3), pp. 271–94.

Esping-Andersen, G. (1990), *The Three Worlds of Welfare Capitalism*, Princeton: Princeton University Press.

Esping-Andersen, G. (ed.) (1996), *Welfare States in Transition: National Adaptations in Global Economies*, London: Sage.

Esping-Andersen, G. (1999a), *Social Foundations of Postindustrial Economies*, Oxford: Oxford University Press.

Esping-Andersen, G. (1999b), 'Serve la deregolazione del mercato del lavoro?', *Stato e Mercato*, 2, pp. 185–212.

Esping-Andersen, G., with D. Gallie, A. Hemerijck and J. Myles (2002), *Why We Need a New Welfare State*, Oxford: Oxford University Press.

European Commission (2006), *Communication on A Citizens' Agenda: Delivering Results for Europe*, Brussels: COM.

European Commission (2007), *Opportunities, Access and Solidarity: Towards a New Social Vision for 21st Century Europe*, Brussels: COM.

European Union (2007), *Treaty of Lisbon*, Brussels: COM.

Evans, G., and S. Whitefield (1993), 'Identifying the bases of party competition in Eastern Europe', *British Journal of Political Science*, 23, pp. 521–48.

Fagan, C., J. O'Reilly and B. Halpin (2005), 'Job opportunities for whom? Labour market dynamics and service sector employment growth in Germany and Britain', *Wissenschaftszentrum Berlin für Sozialforschung (WZB) Discussion Paper*, SP 2005–110.

Fernandes, S., and E. Rubio (2012), *Solidarité dans la zone euro: Combien, pourquoi, jusqu'à quand?*, Paris: Notre Europe.

Fernández-Macías, E. (2012), 'Job polarization in Europe? Changes in the employment structure and job quality, 1995–2007', *Work and Occupations*, 39 (2), pp. 157–82.

Ferrera, M. (2006), *The New Boundaries of Welfare*, Oxford: Oxford University Press.

Ferrera, M. (2009), 'The JCMS annual lecture: National welfare states and European integration: In search of a "virtuous nesting"', *Journal of Common Market Studies*, 47 (2), pp. 219–33.

Fiscal Affairs Department (2011), *The Challenge of Public Pension Reform in Advanced and Emerging Economies*, Washington, DC: International Monetary Fund.

Florida, R. (2002), 'The Economic Geography of Talent', *Annals of the Association of American Geographers*, 92 (4), pp. 743–55.

Flynn, R. (1988), 'Political acquiescence, privatisation and residualisation in British housing policy', *Journal of Social Policy*, 17 (3), pp. 289–312.

Fontaine, A. (1981), *Un seul lit pour deux rêves: Histoire de la 'détente', 1962–1981*, Paris: Fayard.

Fourastié, J. (1979), *Les Trente Glorieuses, ou la révolution invisible de 1946 à 1975*, Paris: Fayard.

Franco, A. M., and D. Filson (2000), 'Knowledge diffusion through employee mobility', *Research Department Report 272*, Minneapolis: Federal Reserve Bank of Minneapolis.

Freedland, M. (2001), 'The marketization of public services', in C. Crouch, K. Eder and D. Tambini (eds), *Citizenship, Markets, and the State*, Oxford: Clarendon Press, pp. 90–110.

Freeman, G. P. (1986), 'Migration and the political economy of the welfare state', *Annals of the American Academy of Political and Social Science*, 485, pp. 51–63.

Freeman, G. P. (2009), 'Immigration, diversity, and welfare chauvinism', *The Forum*, 7 (3), pp. 1–16.

Friedman, T. L. (1999), *The Lexus and the Olive Tree*, New York: Farrar, Straus & Giroux.

Gamble, A. (1988), *The Free Economy and the Strong State: The Politics of Thatcherism*, Basingstoke: Palgrave Macmillan.

Ganev, V. (2007), *Preying on the State: The Transformation of Bulgaria after 1989*, Ithaca, NY: Cornell University Press.

Garland, D. (1985), *Punishment and Welfare: A History of Penal Strategies*, Aldershot: Gower.

Garland, D. (2001), *The Culture of Control*, Oxford: Oxford University Press.

Gawande, A. (2009), 'The cost conundrum', *The New Yorker*, 1 June 2009.

Genschel, P. (2004), 'Globalization and the welfare state: A retrospective', *Journal of European Public Policy*, 11 (4), pp. 613–36.

Giddens, A. (1998), *The Third Way: The Renewal of Social Democracy*, Cambridge: Polity.

Giffin, F. C. (1975), 'The "First Russian Labor Code": The law of June 3, 1886', *Russian History*, 2 (1), pp. 83–100.

Gildea, R. (1987), *Barricades and Borders: Europe 1800–1914*, Oxford: Oxford University Press.

Glassner, V., and M. Keune (2010), 'Collective bargaining responses to the economic crisis in Europe', *ETUI Policy Brief*, Brussels: European Trade Union Institute.

Greer, S. (ed.) (2006), *Territory, Democracy and Justice: Regionalism and Federalism in Western Democracies*, London: Palgrave Macmillan.

Grigorescu, A. (2006), 'The corruption eruption in East Central Europe: The increased salience of corruption and the role of intergovernmental organizations', *East European Politics and Societies*, 20 (3), pp. 516–49.

Grönlund, K., and H. Milner (2006), 'The determinants of political knowledge in comparative perspective', *Scandinavian Political Studies*, 29 (4), pp. 386–406.

Grzymała-Busse, A. (1998), 'Reform efforts in the Czech and Slovak Communist Parties and their successors, 1988–1993', *East European Politics and Societies*, 12 (3), pp. 442–71.

Grzymała-Busse, A. (2002), *Redeeming the Communist Past*, Cambridge: Cambridge University Press.

Gualmini, E., and M. Rhodes (2011), 'Welfare states in trouble: Policy reform in a period of crisis', in E. Jones, M. Rhodes, P. Heywood and U. Sedelmeier (eds), *Developments in European Politics 2*, Basingstoke: Palgrave Macmillan, pp. 173–97.

Gullestad, M. (2006), *Plausible Prejudice: Everyday Practices and Social Images of Nation, Culture and Race*, Oslo: Universitetsforlaget.

Habermas, J., C. P. Cronin and P. De Greiff (2000), *The Inclusion of the Other: Studies in Political Theory*, Cambridge, MA: MIT Press.

Hacker, J. (2006), *The Great Risk Shift*, New York: Oxford University Press.

Hall, P. A., and M. Lamont (eds) (2009), *Successful Societies: How Institutions and Culture Affect Health*, New York: Cambridge University Press.

Hall, P. A., and D. Soskice (eds) (2001), *Varieties of Capitalism*, Oxford: Oxford University Press.

Hall, S., C. Critcher, T. Jefferson, J. Clarke and B. Roberts (1978), *Policing the Crisis*, London: MacMillan.

Hanley, S. (2004), 'Getting the right right: Redefining the centre-right in post-Communist Europe', *Journal of Communist Studies and Transition Politics*, 20 (3), pp. 9–27.

Hanley, S. (2007), *The New Right in the New Europe: Czech Transformation and Right-Wing Politics, 1989–2006*, New York: Routledge.

Hanley, S. (2010), 'Czech Republic: What the elections mean', *Dr Sean's Diary*, 2 June

2010, <http://drseansdiary.wordpress.com/2010/06/02/czech-republic-what-the-elections-mean> (last accessed 12 March 2013).

Hansard (1944), *House of Commons, vol 396: cols 207–322*, 19 January 1944.

Harsh, D. (1993), *German Social Democracy and the Rise of Nazism*, Chapel Hill: University of North Carolina Press.

Hattersley, R., and K. Hickson (2011), 'In praise of social democracy', *The Political Quarterly*, 83 (1), pp. 5–12.

Haughton, T., T. Novotna and K. Deegan-Krause (2010), 'The 2010 Czech and Slovak parliamentary elections: Red cards to the winners', *West European Politics*, 34 (2), pp. 394–402.

Häusermann, S. (2010a), 'Party political implications of economic dualism and immigration', paper for the workshop 'Economic Integration and Political Fragmentation? Parties, Interest Groups and Democratic Capitalism in Eastern and Western Europe', Florence, European University Institute, 11–12 June 2010.

Häusermann, S. (2010b), *The Politics of Welfare State Reform in Continental Europe: Modernization in Hard Times*, Cambridge and New York: Cambridge University Press.

Heald, D. A. (1983), *Public Expenditure: Its Defence and Reform*, Oxford: Martin Robertson.

Heald, D. A. (2012), 'Why is transparency about public expenditure so elusive?', *International Review of Administrative Sciences*, 78 (1), pp. 30–49.

Heald, D. A., and G. Georgiou (2011), 'The macro-fiscal role of the U.K. Whole of Government Account', *Abacus*, 47 (4), pp. 446–76.

Heath, A. F., R. M. Jowell and J. K. Curtice, with B. Taylor (eds) (1994), *Labour's Last Chance? The 1992 Election and Beyond*, Aldershot: Dartmouth.

Heath, A. F., R. M. Jowell and J. K. Curtice (2001), *The Rise of New Labour: Party Policies and Voter Choices*, Oxford: Oxford University Press.

Hechter, M. (1975), *Internal Colonialism: The Celtic Fringe in British National Development, 1536–1966*, London: Routledge & Kegan Paul.

Hedetoft, U., B. Petersson and L. Sturfelt (2006), *Invandrare och integration i Danmark och Sverige*, Centrum For Danmarksstudier, Gothenburg and Stockholm: Lunds University/Makadam.

Hellman, J. S. (1998), 'Winners take all: The politics of partial reform in postcommunist transitions', *World Politics*, 50 (2), pp. 203–34.

Hellström, A. (2010), 'Det nya Folkhemspartiet', *Fronesis*, 34, pp. 110–24.

Hellström, A., and T. Nilsson (2010), '"We are the good guys": Ideological positioning of the nationalist party Sverigedemokraterna in contemporary Swedish politics', *Ethnicities*, 10 (1), pp. 55–76.

Hellström, A., T. Nilsson and P. Stoltz (2012), 'Nationalism vs. nationalism: The challenge of the Sweden Democrats in the Swedish public debate', *Government and Opposition*, 47 (2), pp. 186–205.

Hemerijck, A., M. Keune and M. Rhodes (2006), 'European welfare states: Diversity, challenges and reforms', in E. Jones, P. Heywood, M. Rhodes and E. Sedelmeier (eds), *Developments in European Politics*, Basingstoke: Palgrave Macmillan, pp. 259–79.

Henjak, A. (2010), 'Political cleavages and socio-economic context: How welfare regimes and historical divisions shape political cleavages', *West European Politics*, 33 (3), pp. 474–504.

Hernes, H. M. (1987), *Welfare State and Women Power*, Oslo: Norwegian University Press.

Herzog, H. W., A. Schlottmann and D. Johnson (1986), 'High-technology jobs and worker mobility', *Journal of Regional Science*, 26 (3), pp. 445–59.

Hills, J. (Chair) (2010), *An Anatomy of Economic Inequality in the UK: Report of the National Equality Panel*, London: Government Equalities Office and Centre for Analysis of Social Exclusion.

Hilpert, U. (1991), *State Policies and Techno-Industrial Innovation*, London: Routledge.

Hilpert, U. (1992), *Archipelago Europe: Islands of Innovation*, Fast Programme DG XII, Commission of the European Communities, Brussels.

Hilpert, U. (ed.) (2003), *Regionalisation of Globalised Innovation: Locations for Advanced Industrial Development and Disparities in Participation*, London: Routledge.

Hilpert, U. (2005), 'Innovation und Beschäftigung', research report prepared for the Hans Böckler Foundation, Jena.

Hilpert, U. (2006), 'Knowledge in the region: Development based on tradition, culture and change', *European Planning Studies*, 14 (5), pp. 581–99.

Hilpert, U., and H. Lawton Smith (2012), *Networking Regionalized Innovative Labour Markets*, London: Routledge.

Hilpert, U., and A. Nagler (2011), 'Divergent patterns of metropolitan economies: Does advanced manufacturing matter?', paper presented at the Regional Studies Winter Conference, London, 25 November 2011.

Hinnfors, J., A. Spehar and G. Bucken-Knapp (2012), 'The missing factor: Why social democracy can lead to restrictive immigration policy', *Journal of European Public Policy*, 19 (4), pp. 585–603.

Hinrichs, K., and M. Jessoula (2012), *Labour Market Flexibility and Pension Reforms: Flexible Today, Secure Tomorrow?*, Basingstoke: Palgrave Macmillan.

Hirsch, F. (1977), *Social Limits to Growth*, London: Routledge & Kegan Paul.

Hodgson, J. H. (1967), *Communism in Finland: A History and Interpretation*, Princeton: Princeton University Press.

Höpner, M. (2008), 'Usurpation statt Delegation: Wie der EuGH die Binnenmarktintegration radikalisiert und warum er politischer Kontrolle bedarf', MPIfG Discussion Paper 08/12, Cologne: Max Planck Institute for the Study of Societies.

Howard, C. (2007), *The Welfare State Nobody Knows*, Princeton: Princeton University Press.

Huberman, M. (2004), 'Working hours of the world unite? New international evidence of worktime, 1870–1913', *The Journal of Economic History*, 64 (4), pp. 964–1,001.

Husak, D. (2008), *Overcriminalization*, Oxford: Oxford University Press.

Huysmans, J. (2006), *The Politics of Insecurity: Fear, Migration and Asylum in the EU*, London: Routledge.

Inglehart, R. (1990), *Culture Shift in Advanced Industrial Society*, Princeton: Princeton University Press.

Inglehart, R. (1997), *Modernization and Postmodernization: Cultural, Economic and Political Change in 43 Societies*, Princeton: Princeton University Press.

Irwin, D. A. (2011), *Peddling Protectionism: Smoot-Hawley and the Great Depression*, Princeton: Princeton University Press.

Ishiyama, J. T. (1997), 'The sickle or the rose? Previous regime type and the evolution of ex-Communist parties', *Comparative Political Studies*, 30, pp. 299–334.

Iversen, T. (1999), *Contested Economic Institutions: The Politics of Macroeconomics and Wage Bargaining in Advanced Democracies*, Cambridge: Cambridge University Press.

Iversen, T., and D. Soskice (2009), 'Dualism and political coalitions: Inclusionary versus exclusionary reforms in an age of rising inequality', paper prepared for presentation at the Annual Meeting of the American Political Science Association, Toronto, 3–6 September 2009.

Iversen, T., and J. D. Stephens (2008), 'Partisan politics, the welfare state, and three worlds of human capital formation', *Comparative Political Studies*, 41 (4–5), pp. 600–37.

Iversen, T., and A. Wren (1998), 'Equality, employment, and budgetary restraint: The trilemma of the service economy', *World Politics*, 50 (4), pp. 507–46.

Jakszentis, A., and U. Hilpert (2007), *Wie spezifisch sind die Entwicklungen in Ostdeutschland? Angleichung der industriellen Modernisierungsprozesse in Ost- und Westdeutschland am Beispiel von Jena und Göttingen, Rostock und Kiel, Chemnitz und Braunschweig*, Berlin: Otto Brenner Foundation.

Jochem, S. (2012), 'The politics of crisis management in egalitarian capitalism', paper presented at the workshop on 'Varieties of Capitalism and Varieties of Response to the European Employment Crisis', University of Denver, 1–2 June 2012.

Jones, T., and T. Newburn (1998), *Private Security and Public Policing*, Oxford: Oxford University Press.

Jønsson, H. V., and K. Petersen (2010), 'Danmark: den nationale velfærdsstat møder verden', in G. Brochmann and A. Hagelund (eds), *Velferdens grenser*, Oslo: Universitetsforlaget, pp. 131–210.

Kahanec, M., and K. F. Zimmerman (2011), *Ethnic Diversity in European Labor Markets: Challenges and Solutions*, London: Edward Elgar.

Kaldor, M. (2006), *New and Old Wars*, 2nd edn, Cambridge: Polity.

Kay, J. A. (2010), 'A good economist knows the true value of the arts', *Financial Times*, 11 August 2010.

Kearns, A., and J. Bannister (2009), 'Conceptualising tolerance: Paradoxes of tolerance and intolerance in contemporary Britain', *Italian Journal of Sociology of Education*, 2, pp. 125–47.

Keating, M. (1997), 'Stateless nation-building: Quebec, Catalonia and Scotland in the changing state system', *Nations and Nationalism*, 3 (4), pp. 689–717.

Keating, M. (1998), *The New Regionalism in Western Europe: Territorial Restructuring and Political Change*, Cheltenham: Edward Elgar.

Keating, M. (2009a), *The Independence of Scotland: Self-Government and the Shifting Politics of Union*, Oxford: Oxford University Press.

Keating, M. (2009b), 'Social citizenship, solidarity and welfare in regionalized and plurinational states', *Citizenship Studies*, 13 (5), pp. 501–13.

Keating, M., and A. Wilson (2010), 'Territorial policy communities', conference on 'Towards a Regional Political Science', University of Edinburgh.

Keman, H. (2010), 'Third ways and social democracy: The right way to go?', *British Journal of Political Science*, 41, pp. 671–80.

Kershaw, C., S. Nicholas and A. Walker (2008), *Crime in England and Wales in 2007/08: Findings from the British Crime Survey and Police Recorded Crime*, Home Office Statistical Bulletin 07/08, London: Home Office.

Kestilä, E., and P. Söderlund (2007), 'Local determinants of radical right-wing voting: The case of the Norwegian Progress Party', *West European Politics*, 30 (3), pp. 549–72.

Khadria, B. (2001), 'Shifting paradigms of globalization: The twenty-first century transition toward generics in skilled migration from India', *International Migration*, 39 (5), pp. 45–71.

Kindleberger, C. P. (2000), *Manias, Panics and Crashes: A History of Financial Crisis*, 4th edn, London: Palgrave Macmillan.

Kirby, D. G. (1979), *Finland in the Twentieth Century*, London: C. Hurst & Co.

Kitschelt, H. (1992), 'The formation of party systems in East Central Europe', *Politics and Society*, 20, pp. 7–50.

Kitschelt, H. (1994), *The Transformation of European Social Democracy*, Cambridge: Cambridge University Press.

Kitschelt, H. (1999), 'European social democracy between political economy and electoral competition', in H. Kitschelt, P. Lange, G. Marks and J. D. Stephens (eds), *Continuity and Change in Contemporary Capitalism*, Cambridge: Cambridge University Press, pp. 317–45.

Kitschelt, H. (2004), *Diversification and Reconfiguration of Party Systems in Postindustrial Democracies*, Digital Library: Friedrich Ebert Foundation.

Kitschelt, H., and A. J. McGann (1995), *The Radical Right in Western Europe: A Comparative Analysis*, Ann Arbor: University of Michigan Press.

Kjellberg, A. (2009), 'The Swedish model of industrial relations: Self-regulation and combined centralisation-decentralisation', in C. Phelan (ed.), *Trade Unionism Since 1945: Towards a Global History*, Oxford: Peter Lang, pp. 155–97.

Klitgaard, M. B. (2007), 'Why are they doing it? Social democracy and market-oriented welfare state reforms', *West European Politics*, 30 (1), pp. 172–94.

246 ] *The crisis of social democracy in Europe*

Koopmans, R., and P. Statham (2000), *Challenging Immigration and Ethnic Relations Politics: Comparative European Perspectives*, Oxford: Oxford University Press.

Kopecký, P., and C. Mudde (2002), 'The two sides of euroscepticism: Party positions on European integration in East Central Europe', *European Union Politics*, 3 (3), pp. 297–326.

Korpi, W. (1983), *The Democratic Class Struggle*, London: Routledge & Kegan Paul.

Korpi, W., and J. Palme (1998), 'The paradox of redistribution and strategies of equality: Welfare state institutions, inequality, and poverty in the Western countries', *American Sociological Review*, 63 (5), pp. 661–87.

Korthouwer, G. (2010), 'Party politics as we knew it? Failure to dominate government, intraparty dynamics and welfare reforms in continental Europe', dissertation, University of Amsterdam.

Kosiara-Pedersen, K. (2012), 'The 2011 Danish Parliamentary election: A very new government', *West European Politics*, 35 (2), pp. 415–24.

Kraus, P. (2011), 'The politics of complex diversity: A European perspective', *Ethnicities*, 12 (1), pp. 3–25.

Kriesi, H., E. Grande, R. Lachat, M. Dolezal, S. Bornschier and T. Frey (2008), *West European Politics in the Age of Globalization*, New York: Cambridge University Press.

Kumlin, S., and B. Rothstein (2010), 'Questioning the new liberal dilemma: Immigrants, social networks and institutional fairness', *Comparative Politics*, 41 (1), pp. 63–87.

Lacey, N. (2008), *The Prisoners' Dilemma*, Cambridge: Cambridge University Press.

Lafont, R. (1967), *La Révolution régionaliste*, Paris: Gallimard.

Lamping, W. (2010), 'Mission impossible? Limits and perils of institutionalizing post-national social policy', *Promoting Solidarity in the European Union*, 1 (9), pp. 46–73.

Lansley, S. (2011), *The Cost of Inequality: Three Decades of the Super-Rich and the Economy*, London: Gibson Square.

Lawton Smith, H., and R. Waters (2005), 'Employment mobility in high-technology agglomerations: The cases of Oxfordshire and Cambridgeshire', *Area*, 37 (2), pp. 189–98.

Layard, R. (1989), *Lessons from the Great Depression*, Cambridge, MA and London: MIT Press.

Leconte, C. (2010), *Understanding Euroscepticism*, Basingstoke: Palgrave Macmillan.

Lee, S. J. (1987), *The European Dictatorships 1918–1945*, London: Routledge.

Le Grand, J. (2003), *Motivation, Agency and Public Policy: Of Knights and Knaves, Pawns and Queens*, Oxford: Oxford University Press.

Leo XIII, Pope (1891), *De Rerum Novarum*, Vatican.

Liberal Democratic Party (2010), *Liberal Democrat Manifesto 2010*, London.

Lidtke, V. L. (1966), *The Outlawed Party: Social Democracy in Germany 1878–1890*, Princeton: Princeton University Press.

Lindbeck, A., P. Molander, T. Persson, O. Petersson, A. Sandmo, B. Swedenborg and

N. Thygesen (1994), *Turning Sweden Around*, Cambridge, MA and London: MIT Press.

Lindbom, A. (2008), 'The Swedish Conservative Party and the welfare state: Institutional change and adapting preferences', *Government and Opposition*, 43 (4), pp. 539–60.

Lindert, P. H. (2004), *Growing Public: Social Spending and Economic Growth Since the Eighteenth Century*, Cambridge: Cambridge University Press.

Lindvall, J. (2012), 'The electoral consequences of two great crises', paper presented at the 19th International Conference of Europeanists, Boston, 22–4 March 2012.

Lipset, S. M., and S. Rokkan (1967), *Party Systems and Voter Alignments: Cross-National Perspectives*, New York: Collier and Macmillan.

Loader, I., and R. Sparks (2012), 'Beyond lamentation: Reinventing a social democratic politics of crime and justice', in T. Newburn and J. Peay (eds), *Policing: Politics, Culture and Control*, Oxford: Hart Publishing, pp. 11–41.

Loader, I., and N. Walker (2007), *Civilizing Security*, Cambridge: Cambridge University Press.

Lombardo, E., P. Meier and M. Verloo (eds) (2009), *The Discursive Politics of Gender Equality*, London: Routledge.

Lööw, H. (2011), 'The extreme right in Sweden: Growing slowly', in N. Lagenbacher and B. Schellenberg (eds), *Is Europe on the 'Right' Path?*, Berlin: Friedrich Ebert Stiftung, pp. 253–69.

Lovering, J. (1999), 'Theory led by policy: The inadequacies of the "New Regionalism"', *International Journal of Urban and Regional Research*, 23 (2), pp. 379–90.

McCrone, D., and M. Keating (2007), 'Social democracy in Scotland', in M. Keating (ed.), *Scottish Social Democracy: Progressive Ideas for Public Policy*, Brussels: PIE/Peter Lang, pp. 17–38.

McEwen, N. (2006), *Nationalism and the State: Welfare and Identity in Scotland and Quebec*, Brussels: PIE/Peter Lang.

Maddison, A. (1982), *Phases of Capitalist Development*, Oxford and New York: Oxford University Press.

Maddison, A. (2007), *Contours of the World Economy*, Oxford: Oxford University Press.

Madeley, J. (2002), 'The Swedish model is dead! Long live the Swedish model!', *West European Politics*, 26 (2), pp. 165–73.

Madsen, P. K. (2007), 'Flexicurity: A new perspective on labour markets and welfare states in Europe', *Tilburg Law Review*, 14 (1–2), pp. 57–79.

Maduro, M. P. (1998), *We the Court: The European Court of Justice and the European Economic Constitution: A Critical Reading of Article 30 of the EC Treaty*, Oxford: Hart Publishing.

Mahroum, S. (1999), 'Global magnets: Science and technology disciplines and departments in the United Kingdom', *Minerva*, 37, pp. 379–90.

Mahroum, S. (2000), 'Scientific mobility, an agent of scientific expansion and institutional empowerment', *Science Communication*, 21, pp. 367–78.

Mair, P. (2003), 'Political parties and democracy: What sort of future?', *Central European Political Science Review*, 4 (13), pp. 6–20.

Majone, G. (2009), *Europe as the Would-Be World Power: The EU at Fifty*, New York: Cambridge University Press.

Malecki, E. J. (1989), 'What about people in high technology? Some research and policy considerations', *Growth and Change*, 20, pp. 67–78.

Malik, S. (2012), 'Peter Mandelson gets nervous about people getting "filthy rich"', *The Guardian*, 26 January 2012.

Marenin, O. (1982), 'Parking tickets and class repression: The concept of policing in critical theories of criminal justice', *Contemporary Crises*, 6, pp. 241–66.

Marginson, S. (2006), 'Dynamics of national and global competition in higher education', *Higher Education*, 52, pp. 1–39.

Marier, P. (2010), 'Improving Canada's retirement saving, lessons from abroad, ideas from home', *IRPP 9*, Montreal: IRPP.

Marks, G., L. Hooghe, M. Nelson and E. Edwards (2006), 'Party competition and European integration in East and West: Different structure, same causality', *Comparative Political Studies*, 39 (2), pp. 155–75.

Marquand, D. (2004), *Decline of the Public*, Cambridge: Polity.

Marshall, T. H. [1950] (1992), 'Citizenship and Social Class', in T. H. Marshall and T. Bottomore (eds), *Citizenship and Social Class*, London: Pluto, pp. 31–51.

Martín-Artiles, A., G. Meardi, O. Molina and A. Van den Berg (2012), *Uncertainty and Migration*, unpublished report, European Union FP7 Project GUSTO.

Materska-Sosnowska, A. (2010), 'The crisis of social democracy in Poland: A new start for the left?', *Internationale Politik und Gesellschaft*, 4, pp. 207–22.

Mazzucato, M. (2011), *The Entrepreneurial State*, London: Demos.

Melby, K., A.-B. Ravn and C. Carlsson-Wetterberg (eds) (2008), *Gender Equality as a Perspective on Welfare: The Limits of Political Ambition*, Bristol: Policy Press.

Mény, Y. (1987), *The Politics of Steel: Western Europe and the Steel Industry in the Crisis Years*, Berlin and New York: Walter De Gruyter Inc.

Mény, Y. (2003), 'De la démocratie en Europe: Old concepts and new challenges', *Journal of Common Market Studies*, 41 (1), pp. 1–13.

Mény, Y. (2007), *An Institutional Triangle with Only Two Poles? Challenge Europe. Europe@50: Back to the Future*, Brussels: European Policy Centre.

Mény, Y., and Y. Surel (2002), *Democracy and the Populist Challenge*, Basingstoke: Palgrave Macmillan.

Meret, S. (2010), *The Danish People's Party, the Italian Northern League and the Austrian Freedom Party in a Comparative Perspective: Party Ideology and Electoral Support*, SPIRIT PhD Series, Aalborg University.

Meret, S., and B. Siim (2013), 'Gender, populism and politics of belonging', in M. Mokre and B. Siim (eds), *Negotiating Gender and Diversity in an Emerging European Public Sphere*, Basingstoke: Palgrave Macmillan, pp. 78–96.

Meyer, H., and J. Rutherford (eds) (2012), *The Future of European Social Democracy: Building the Good Society*, London: Palgrave Macmillan.

Miles, D. (2012), 'Winding and unwinding extraordinary monetary policy', RBS Scottish Economic Society Annual Lecture, Edinburgh, 11 September 2012.

Miller, D. (1995), *On Nationality*, Oxford: Clarendon Press.

Miller, D. (2000), *Citizenship and National Identity*, Oxford: Oxford University Press.

Milner, H. (1989), *Sweden: Social Democracy in Practice*, Oxford: Oxford University Press.

Milner, H. (1994), *Social Democracy and Rational Choice: The Scandinavian Experience and Beyond*, London: Routledge.

Milner, H. (2002), *Civic Literacy: How Informed Citizens Make Democracy Work*, Hanover, NH: University Press of New England.

Milner, H. (2010), *The Internet Generation: Engaged Citizens or Political Dropouts*, Hanover, NH: University Press of New England.

Mirrlees, J. (Chair) (2011), *Mirrlees Review: Reforming the Tax System for the 21st Century: Tax by Design*, London: Institute for Fiscal Affairs.

Mitchell, B. R. (1978), 'Statistical Appendix', in C. Cipolla (ed.), *The Fontana Economic History of Europe: Contemporary Economies, Part 2*, Glasgow: Fontana/Collins, pp. 687–94.

Moene, K.-O., and M. Wallerstein (2001), 'Targeting and political support for welfare spending', *Economics of Governance*, 2 (1), pp. 3–24.

Morel, N., B. Palier and J. Palme (2012), *Towards a Social Investment Welfare State?*, Bristol: Policy Press.

Moschonas, G. (2011), 'Historical decline or change of scale? The electoral dynamics of European social democratic parties, 1950–2009', in J. Cronin, G. Ross and J. Schoch (eds), *What's Left of the Left: Democrats and Social Democrats in Challenging Times*, Durham, NC and London: Duke University Press, pp. 50–85.

Mowbray, R. (2012), 'Letter – Labour's fiscal policies caused more damage than the banks', *The Herald,* 4 July 2012.

MTI (2011), 'Tarki poll finds support for gov't on downward slide, but still well over opposition', 24 February 2011, <http://www.politics.hu/20110224/tarki-poll-finds-support-for-govt-on-downward-slide-but-still-well-over-opposition> (last accessed 12 March 2013).

Mudde, C. (2007), *Populist Radical Right Parties in Europe*, Cambridge: Cambridge University Press.

Muir, R., and I. Loader (2011), *Progressive Police and Crime Commissioners: An Opportunity for the Centre-Left*, IPPR briefing.

Mulinari, D., S. Keskinen, S. Irni and S. Tuori (2009), 'Introduction', in S. Keskinen, S. Tuori, S. Irni and D. Mulinari (eds), *Complying with Colonialism: Gender, Race and Ethnicity in the Nordic Region*, Farnham: Ashgate, pp. 1–16.

Musgrave, R. A. (1959), *The Theory of Public Finance*, New York: McGraw-Hill.

Naurin, E. (2011), *Election Promises, Party Behaviour and Voter Perceptions*, Basingstoke: Palgrave Macmillan.

Newburn, T. (2001), 'The commodification of policing: Security networks in the late modern city', *Urban Studies*, 38, pp. 829–48.

*Newsnight* (2005), BBC television programme, 21 April 2005.

Nicolaïdis, K., and J. Viehoff (2012), 'The choice for sustainable solidarity in post-crisis Europe', in G. Bajnai, T. Fischer, S. Hare, S. Hoffmann, K. Nicolaïdis, V. Rossi, J. Viehoff and A. Watt, *Solidarity: For Sale? The Social Dimension of the New European Economic Governance: Europe in Dialogue*, Gütersloh: Bertelsmann Stiftung, pp. 23–45.

Noël, A. (1999), 'Is decentralization conservative?', in R. Young (ed.), *Stretching the Federation: The Art of the State in Canada*, Kingston, ON: Institute of Intergovernmental Relations, Queen's University, pp. 195–218.

Nohlen, D., and P. Stöver (eds) (2010), *Elections in Europe: A Data Handbook*, Baden-Baden: Nomos Verlagsgesellschaft.

Nordström, N. (2010), 'The failure of Sweden's Red-Green alliance', *Policy Network*, 21 October 2010, <http://www.policy-network.net/pno_detail.aspx?ID=3906&tit le=The+failure+of+Sweden%e2%80%99s+Red-Green+alliance> (last accessed 11 March 2013).

North, D. C., J. J. Wallis and B. R. Weingast (2009), *Violence and Social Orders: A Conceptual Framework for Interpreting Recorded Human History*, Cambridge: Cambridge University Press.

Ochel, W. (2008), 'The political economy of two-tier reforms of employment pro-tection in Europe', *CESifo Working Paper Series No. 2461*, <http://ssrn.com/abstract=1303387> (last accessed 6 March 2013).

OECD (2011), *Divided We Stand: Why Inequality Keeps Rising*, Paris: OECD.

Offe, C. (1999), 'Il reddito di cittadinanza: Una strategia inevitabile per controllare la disoccupazione', *Stato e Mercato*, 2, pp. 213–42.

Ohmae, K. (1995), *The End of the Nation State: The Rise of Regional Economies*, New York: Free Press.

Orenstein, M. A. (1998), 'A genealogy of Communist successor parties in East Central Europe and the determinants of their success', *East European Politics and Societies*, 12 (3), pp. 472–99.

Orenstein, M. A. (2011), 'The political economy of financial crisis in Central and Eastern Europe', paper presented at the European Union Studies Association Conference, Boston, March 2011; forthcoming in V. Schmidt and M. Thatcher (eds), *Resilient Liberalism: European Political Economies through Boom and Bust*, Cambridge: Cambridge University Press.

Oscarsson, H. (2007), 'A matter of fact? Knowledge effects on the vote in Swedish general elections,1985–2002', *Scandinavian Political Studies*, 30 (3), pp. 301–20.

Oscarsson, H., and S. Holmberg (2011), *Swedish Voting Behavior*, Gothenburg: The Swedish Election Studies Program.

Østerud, Ø. (2005), 'Introduction: The peculiarities of Norway', *West European Politics*, 28 (4), pp. 705–20.

Park, A., E. Clery, J. Curtice, M. Phillips and D. Utting (2012), *British Social Attitudes 29: 2012 Edition*, London: NatCen Social Research.

Paterson, W. E., and A. H. Thomas (eds) (1986), *The Future of Social Democracy*, Oxford: Clarendon Press.

Pelinka, A. (2008), 'Austria's democratic wound', *Open Democracy*, 2 October 2008, <http://www.opendemocracy.net/article/austria-s-democratic-wound> (last accessed 11 March 2013).

Pfaller, A. (2009), *European Social Democracy: In Need of Renewal*, Berlin: Friedrich Ebert Stiftung.

Picot, G. (2012), *Politics of Segmentation: Party Competition and Social Protection in Europe*, London and New York: Routledge.

Pierson, C. (2001), *Hard Choices: Social Democracy in the Twenty-First Century*, Oxford: Blackwell.

Pierson, P. (1998), 'Irresistible forces, immovable objects: Post-industrial welfare states confront permanent austerity', *Journal of European Public Policy*, 5 (4), pp. 539–60.

Plunkett, J. (2011), *Growth without Gain? The Faltering Living Standards of People on Low-to-Middle Incomes*, London: Resolution Foundation.

Polasky, J. (1992), 'A revolution for socialist reforms: The Belgian general strike for universal suffrage', *Journal of Contemporary History*, 27 (3), pp. 449–66.

Pontusson, J. (1995), 'Explaining the decline of European social democracy', *World Politics*, 47 (4), pp. 495–533.

Pontusson, J. (2011), 'Once again a model: Nordic social democracy in a globalized world', in J. Cronin, G. Ross and J. Schoch (eds), *What's Left of the Left: Democrats and Social Democrats in Challenging Times*, Durham, NC, and London: Duke University Press, pp. 89–115.

Pontusson, J., and D. Rueda (2010), 'The politics of inequality: Voter mobilization and left parties in advanced industrial states', *Comparative Political Studies*, 43 (6), pp. 675–705.

Pop-Eleches, G. (2010), 'Throwing out the bums: Protest voting and unorthodox parties after Communism', *World Politics*, 62 (2), pp. 221–60.

Porter, M. (2001), 'Regions and the new economics of competition', in A. J. Scott (ed.), *Global City Regions: Trends, Theory, Policy*, Oxford: Oxford University Press, pp. 139–57.

Portes, J. (2012), 'Back to the G20 future on growth', *Public Finance*, 4 July 2012, <http://opinion.publicfinance.co.uk/2012/07/back-to-the-g20-future-on-growth/> (last accessed 11 March 2013).

Power, D., and M. Lundmark (2004), 'Working through knowledge pools: Labour market dynamics, the transference of knowledge and ideas, and industrial clusters', *Urban Studies*, 41 (5–6), pp. 1,025–44.

Puissant, J. (1988), '1886, la contre-réforme sociale?', in P. Van Der Vorst (ed.), *Cent ans de droit social belge*, Brussels: Bruylant, p. 93.

Putnam, R. (1993), *Making Democracy Work: Civic Traditions in Modern Italy*, Princeton: Princeton University Press.

Rahkonen, J. (2011), 'Perussuomalaisten ruumiinavaus: Onko työväen protestipuolueen kannatus saavuttanut vielä ylärajaansa?', *Yhteiskuntapolitiikka*, 76 (4), pp. 425–35.

Raunio, T., and M. Wiberg (2008), 'The Eduskunta and the parliamentarisation of Finnish politics: Formally stronger, politically still weak?', *West European Politics*, 31 (3), pp. 581–99.

Reepalu, I., and G. Rosberg (2010), 'From smokestack city to environmental leader', *Inroads*, 27, pp. 82–93.

Reeskens, T., and W. van Oorschot (2012), 'Disentangling the "New Liberal Dilemma": On the relation between general welfare redistribution preferences and welfare chauvinism', *International Journal of Comparative Sociology*, 53 (2), pp. 120–39.

Regets, M. C. (2007), 'Research issues in the international migration of highly skilled workers: A perspective with data from the United States', SRS 07–203, Arlington, VA: Division of Science Resources Statistics, National Science Foundation.

Reiner, R. (2000), *The Politics of the Police*, 3rd edn, Brighton: Harvester.

Reiner, R. (2010), 'Citizenship, crime, criminalization: Marshalling a social democratic perspective', *New Criminal Law Review*, 13, pp. 241–61.

Rhodes, M. (2001), 'The political economy of social pacts: "Competitive corporatism" and European welfare reform', in P. Pierson (ed.), *The New Politics of the Welfare State*, Oxford: Oxford University Press, pp. 165–94.

Rhodes, M., and Y. Mény (1998), *The Future of European Welfare: A New Social Contract?*, Basingstoke: Palgrave Macmillan.

Roberts, A. (2008), 'Hyperaccountability: Economic voting in Central and Eastern Europe', *Electoral Studies*, 27, pp. 533–46.

Rodrik, D. (1998), 'Why do more open economies have bigger governments?', *Journal of Political Economy*, 106 (5), pp. 997–1,032.

Rohrschneider, R., and S. Whitefield (2005), 'Responsible party government? Party stances on European integration in postcommunist Eastern Europe', presented at the American Political Science Association, Washington, DC, 31 August–4 September 2005.

Rothstein, B. (1998), *Just Institutions Matter: The Moral and Political Logic of the Universal Welfare State*, Cambridge: Cambridge University Press.

Rothstein, B., and E. M. Uslaner (2005), 'All for all: Equality, corruption and social trust', *World Politics*, 58 (3), pp. 41–73.

Rueda, D. (2005), 'Insider-outsider politics in industrialized democracies: The challenge to social democratic parties', *American Political Science Review*, 99 (1), pp. 61–74.

Rydgren, J. (ed.) (2012a), *Class Politics and the Radical Right*, London: Routledge.

Rydgren, J. (ed.) (2012b), *Right Wing Populism and the Working Class*, London: Routledge.

Sassoon, D. (2010), *One Hundred Years of Socialism*, 2nd edn, London: I. B. Tauris.

Saul, S. B. (1969), *The Myth of the Great Depression 1873–1896*, London: Macmillan.

Schäfer, A. (2010), 'Consequences of social inequality for democracy in Western Europe', *Zeitschrift für Vergleichende Politikwissenschaft*, 4 (1), pp. 131–56.

Scharpf, F. W. (1988), 'The joint-decision trap: Lessons from German federalism and European integration', *Public Administration*, 66 (3), pp. 239–78.

Scharpf, F. W. (1996), 'Negative and positive integration in the political economy of European welfare states', in G. Marks, F. W. Scharpf, P. C. Schmitter and W. Streeck (eds), *Governance in the European Union*, London: Sage, pp. 15–39.

Scharpf, F. W. (1997), 'Economic integration, democracy and the welfare state', *Journal of European Public Policy*, 4 (1), pp. 18–36.

Scharpf, F. W. (1999), *Governing in Europe*, Oxford: Oxford University Press.

Scharpf, F. W. (2001), 'Notes towards a theory of multilevel governing in Europe', *Scandinavian Political Studies*, 24 (1), pp. 1–26.

Scharpf, F. W. (2009), *The Double Asymmetry of European Integration, Or: Why the EU Cannot Be a Social Market Economy*, MPIfG Working Paper 09/12, Cologne: Max Planck Institute for the Study of Societies.

Scharpf, F. W. (2010), *Community and Autonomy: Institutions, Policies and Legitimacy in Multilevel Europe*, Frankfurt: Campus Verlag.

Schiller, B. (1975), 'Years of crisis, 1906–1914', in S. Koblik (ed.), *Sweden's Development from Poverty to Affluence*, Minneapolis: University of Minnesota Press, pp. 197–228.

Schmid, G. (2006), 'Social risk management through transitional labor markets', *Socio-Economic Review*, 4 (1), pp. 1–33.

Schmid, G. (2008), *Full Employment in Europe: Managing Labour Market Transitions and Risks*, Cheltenham: Edward Elgar.

Schuknecht, L., and V. Tanzi (2000), *Public Spending in the 20th Century: A Global Perspective*, Cambridge: Cambridge University Press.

Schulz, W., J. Ainley, J. Fraillon, D. Kerr and B. Losito (2010), *Initial Findings from the IEA International Civic and Citizenship Education Study*, Amsterdam: IEA.

Schwab, K. (2011), *Competitiveness Report 2011–2012*, Geneva: World Economic Forum.

Schwander, H., and S. Häusermann (2011), 'Explaining welfare preferences in dualized societies', paper presented at the Oxford/Sciences Po joint doctoral seminar 'The Dynamics of Politics and Inequalities', Paris, 25–6 May 2011.

Schwartz, H. (2010), 'Small states in the rear-view mirror: Legitimacy in the management of economy and society', *European Political Science*, 9 (3), pp. 365–74.

Scott, A. J. (1998), *Regions and the World Economy: The Coming Shape of Global Production, Competition, and Political Order*, Oxford: Oxford University Press.

Scott, A. J., J. Agnew, E. Soja and M. Storper (2001), 'Global city-regions', in A. J. Scott (ed.), *Global City-Regions: Trends, Theory, Policy*, Oxford: Oxford University Press, pp. 11–33.

Segall, S. (2007), 'How devolution upsets distributive justice', *Journal of Moral Philosophy*, 4 (2), pp. 257–72.

Siim, B. (2007), 'The challenge of recognizing diversity from the perspective of gender equality: Dilemmas in Danish citizenship', *Critical Review of International Social and Political Philosophy*, 10 (4), pp. 491–512.

Siim, B., and A. Borchorst (2010), 'The multicultural challenge to the Danish welfare state: Social politics, equality and regulating families', in J. Fink and Å. Lundqvist (eds), *Changing Relations of Welfare: Families, Gender and Migration in Britain and Scandinavia*, Aldershot: Ashgate, pp. 133–54.

Siim, B., and H. Skjeie (2008), 'Tracks, intersections and dead ends: Multicultural challenges to state feminism in Denmark and Norway', *Ethnicities*, 8 (3), pp. 322–44.

Šimecka, M. M. (2012a), 'Slovakia for Sale', *Project Forum: Salon*, 20 February 2012.

Šimecka, M. M. (2012b), 'Arrival of the Left', *Project Forum: Salon*, 4 June 2012.

Simon, J. (2007), *Governing through Crime*, Oxford: Oxford University Press.

Simonen, J., and P. McCann (2008), 'Firm innovation: The influence of R&D cooperation and the geography of human capital inputs', *Journal of Urban Economics*, 64 (1), pp. 146–54.

Singh, V., and C. Briem (2012), 'Metropolitan area migration patterns of the scientific and engineering workforce within the United States', in U. Hilpert and H. Lawton Smith (eds), *Networking Regionalized Innovative Labour Markets*, London: Routledge, pp. 78–95.

Sinn, H.-W. (1994), *A Theory of the Welfare State*, Cambridge: National Bureau of Economic Research.

Sirovátka, T. (2011), *SSGIs in the Czech Republic*, unpublished report, European Union FP7 Project GUSTO.

Sol, C. C. A. M., and M. R. Van der Vos (2011), *SGEI: The Casus of Social Housing in the Netherlands*, unpublished report, European Union FP7 Project GUSTO.

Spendzharova, A., and M. A. Vachudova (2012), 'Catching up? Consolidating liberal democracy in Bulgaria and Romania after EU accession', *West European Politics*, 35 (1), pp. 39–58.

Stanley, B. (2012), 'Bitter friendship: Palikot, Miller and the Polish left', *Polish Party Politics*, 2 May 2012, <http://polishpartypolitics.com/2012/05/02/bitter-friendship-palikot-miller-and-the-polish-left-weekly-update-02-05-2012> (last accessed 13 March 2013).

Statistics Sweden (2011), 'A more equal election turnout', press release, 14 April 2011, <http://www.scb.se/Pages/PressRelease____311614.aspx> (last accessed 11 March 2013).

Steinmo, S. (1993), *Taxation and Democracy: Swedish, British and American Approaches to Financing the Modern State*, New Haven: Yale University Press.

Steinmo, S. (2010), *The Evolution of Modern States: Sweden, Japan and the United States*, New York: Cambridge University Press.

Stephens, P. (2012), 'Europe says goodbye to solidarity', *Financial Times*, 23 February 2012.

Stone Sweet, A. (2004), *The Judicial Construction of Europe*, Oxford: Oxford University Press.

Streeck, W. (2009), *Re-Forming Capitalism: Institutional Change in the German Political Economy*, Oxford: Oxford University Press.

Sundberg, J. (2008), 'Finland', *European Journal of Political Research*, 47 (7–8), pp. 969–75.

Svallfors, S. (2011), 'A bedrock of support? Trends in welfare state attitudes in Sweden, 1981–2010', *Social Policy & Administration*, 45 (7), pp. 806–25.

Swaan, A. de (1994), 'Perspectives for transnational social policy in Europe: Social transfers from West to East', in A. de Swaan (ed.), *Social Policy Beyond Borders: The Social Question in Transnational Perspective*, Amsterdam: Amsterdam University Press, pp. 101–13.

Swank, D., and H.-G. Betz (2003), 'Globalization, the welfare state and right-wing populism in Western Europe', *Socio-Economic Review*, 1, pp. 215–45.

Swedish National Agency for Education (2010), *Facts and Figures 2009: Pre-School Activities, School-Age Childcare, Schools and Adult Education in Sweden*, Government of Sweden.

Szczerbiak, A. (2007), 'Social Poland defeats liberal Poland? The September–October 2005 Polish parliamentary and presidential elections', *Journal of Communist Studies and Transition Politics*, 23 (2), pp. 203–32.

Taggart, P., and A. Szczerbiak (2004), 'Contemporary Euroscepticism in the systems of the European Union candidate states of Central and Eastern Europe', *European Journal of Political Research*, 43, pp. 1–27.

Tanzi, V. (2001), 'Globalization, technological developments, and the work of fiscal termites', *Brooklyn Journal of International Law*, 26 (4), pp. 1,261–84.

Taylor-Gooby, P. (ed.) (2004), *New Risks, New Welfare: The Transformation of the European Welfare State*, Oxford: Oxford University Press.

Taylor-Gooby, P. (2012), *A Left Trilemma: Progressive Public Policy in the Age of Austerity*, London: Policy Network.

Teece, D. (2011), 'Human capital, capabilities, and the firm: Numerati, literati, and entrepreneurs in the twenty-first century enterprise', in A. Burton-Jones and J.-C. Spender (eds), *The Oxford Handbook of Human Capital*, Oxford: Oxford University Press, pp. 527–62.

Temin, P. (1989), *Lessons from the Great Depression*, Cambridge, MA and London: MIT Press.

Tilly, N. (2008), 'Modern approaches to policing: Community, problem-oriented and intelligence-led', in T. Newburn (ed.), *Handbook of Policing*, 2nd edn, Cullompton: Willan, pp. 373–403.

Tobin, J. (1970), 'On limiting the domain of inequality', *Journal of Law and Economics*, 13 (2), pp. 263–78.

Treasury (2012), *Public Expenditure: Statistical Analyses 2012*, Cm 8376, London: Stationery Office.

Trippl, M. (2012), 'Star scientists, islands of innovation and internationally networked labour markets', in U. Hilpert and H. Lawton Smith (eds), *Networking Regionalized Innovative Labour Markets*, London: Routledge, pp. 58–77.

Trippl, M. (2013), 'Islands of innovation as magnetic centres of star scientists?

Empirical evidence on spatial concentration and mobility patterns', *Regional Studies*, 47 (2), pp. 229–44.

Tritter, J. (2011), 'Trouble in paradise: The erosion of the Nordic welfare state', paper for conference on 'Beyond the Public Realm?', University of Warwick Business School, Coventry, November 2011.

Tylecote, A. (1991), *The Long Wave in the World Economy*, London: Routledge.

Tylecote, A. (2006), 'Twin innovation systems and intermediate technology: History and prospect for China', *Innovation Management, Policy and Practice*, 8 (1–2), pp. 62–83.

U.S. Census Bureau (2012), *U.S. Trade in Goods and Services – Balance of Payments (BOP) Basis*, Washington, DC: U.S. Census Bureau.

Vachudova, M. A. (2005), *Europe Undivided: Democracy, Leverage and Integration after Communism*, Oxford: Oxford University Press.

Vachudova, M. A. (2008), 'Tempered by the EU? Political parties and party systems before and after accession', *Journal of European Public Policy*, 15 (6), pp. 861–79.

Vachudova, M. A., and L. Hooghe (2009), 'Postcommunist politics in a magnetic field: How transition and EU accession structure party competition on European integration', *Comparative European Politics*, 7 (2), pp. 179–212.

Vandenbroucke, F., and K. Vleminckx (2011), 'Disappointing poverty trends: Is the social investment state to blame?', *Journal of European Social Policy*, 21 (5), pp. 450–71.

Van der Brug, W., and J. Van Spanje (2009), 'Immigration, Europe and the "new" cultural dimension', *European Journal of Political Research*, 48, pp. 309–34.

Van Duijn, J. J. (1983), *The Long Wave in Economic Life*, London: Allen and Unwin.

Van Kersbergen, K. (2003), 'The politics and political economy of social democracy', *Acta Politica*, 38, pp. 255–71.

Van Kersbergen, K., and A. Hemerijck (2012), 'Two decades of change in Europe: The emergence of the social investment state', *Journal of Social Policy*, 41, pp. 475–92.

Van Vliet, O., and H. Nijboer (2012), 'Flexicurity in the European Union: Flexibility for outsiders, security for insiders', Department of Economics Research Memorandum, February 2012, Leiden University.

Vauchez, A. (2008), '"Integration-through-law": Contribution to a socio-history of EU political common sense', *EUI Working Papers RSCAS 2008/10*, San Domenico di Fiesole: European University Institute.

Visser, J. (2012), 'The rise and fall of industrial unionism', *Transfer: European Review of Labour and Research*, 18 (2), pp. 129–41.

Walker, D. (2002), *In Praise of Centralism*, London: Catalyst Forum.

Walker, N. (2008), 'The pattern of transnational policing', in T. Newburn (ed.), *Handbook of Policing*, 2nd edn, Cullompton: Willan, pp. 119–46.

Whipp, L. (2012), 'In the picture: Romney's 47%', *Financial Times*, 18 September 2012.

Wilkinson, R., and K. Pickett (2009), *The Spirit Level: Why Equality Is Better for Everyone*, London: Allen Lane.

Williams, A. M., V. Baláž and C. Wallace (2004), 'International labour mobility and uneven regional development in Europe: Human capital, knowledge and entrepreneurship', *European Urban and Regional Studies*, 11, pp. 27–46.

Wodak, R., B. Mral and M. Koshrav Nik (forthcoming), *Right-Wing Populism in Europe: Politics and Discourse*, London: Bloomsbury.

World Economic Forum (2010), *Global Competitiveness Report 2010–2011*, Geneva: World Economic Forum.

Yergin, D. (2008), *The Prize: The Epic Quest for Oil, Money, and Power*, New York: Simon & Schuster.

Zakaria, F. (2012), 'Incarceration nation', *CNN*, 30 March 2012.

Zedner, L. (2009), *Security*, London: Routledge.

Zoltan, D. (2010), 'Austerity fatigue sends IMF home', *Inter Press Service*, 2 August 2010.

# INDEX